14.95

D1381456

Roy Fuller

NEW AND COLLECTED POEMS
1934–84

*London Magazine Editions
also publish the following
by Roy Fuller:*

AUTOBIOGRAPHY
Souvenirs
Vamp Till Ready
Home and Dry

POETRY
The Reign of Sparrows

ROY FULLER

New and Collected Poems

1934–84

SECKER & WARBURG
LONDON
in association with
LONDON MAGAZINE EDITIONS

First published in England 1985 by
Martin Secker & Warburg Limited
54 Poland Street, London W1V 3DF
in association with
London Magazine Editions

British Library Cataloguing in Publication Data

Fuller, Roy
New and collected poems, 1934–84.
I.   Title
821'.912   PR6011.U55

ISBN   0–436–16790–5

Typeset by Inforum Ltd, Portsmouth
Printed in Great Britain by
Redwood Burn Ltd, Trowbridge, Wiltshire

TO KATE

CONTENTS

[vii]

[x]

PART ONE

From

Poems

(1939) and other sources

THE CHANNEL

In a normal rainfall the channel was adequate,
But all that summer, under dripping trees,
I waited watching pyrotechnics on macadam.
The bosom of the wounded land was swollen
And gaped revealing the red clay.
Subterranean courses percolated, causing
Litigation among former neighbours.
In the roaring gutters the leaves became sodden
Like bread in a sink, and exercised, perhaps, control.
From the ground coiled unknown roots,
Fantastic and demanding sustenance.
The whole territory was darkened under veils.
Along lines of communication to my room
The crystal beads ran fast and runnelled
From porcelain pots, boring the noisy gravel.
Under hot sheets I listened
Hoping yet not hoping the channel was adequate,
And in the black morning after brief slumber,
Waking startled to the sound of it and a thundery sky.

THE RUMOUR

The murdered man was rumoured up again.
One saw him drinking, and another
Bending to kiss an unsuspecting child.
Reports at once denied by wife and mother.

But still his famous figure had been seen.
The ports were watched and locals boarded.
Only the exhumation clearly showed
The man there, lying with the rumour, murdered.

LEGENDS

The swan that ploughs the lucid lake
With crooked wings and feathers like
Stiff paper, gives the perfect lie
To legends where the prince lived happily.

In the enchanted palace, walls
Are thick to stopper dying wails.
The waters cough against the stone,
And rock the waxy feathers' scarlet stain.

The priest is telling history;
Bringing the uncle, peasants row:
Someone might take a loaf to them:
The former heroine has pricked her thumb.

The history, the lake, the sampler
Portrayed the usual scene much simpler.
The blood ran, bird sang, without force:
The infant cupid had a florid face.

BIRTHDAY POEM

Offspring of promise, the farmer's fantasy
Of tithe commuted to a raspberry,
You are born to walk these hills, mere lingering frowns
Of an old volcanic wrath, your soul to glide
Over anachronistic villages.

Today the hunt has smoked our cigarettes;
The rector painfully came afterwards:
Hacking along the turnpike, he was thrown
Through the nonfeasance of the RDC.

Tomorrow we shall drive along the bypass,
By blooms of nurserymen like spindles massed
Idle in Oldham factories, through the downs,
To that alluvial valley where your fathers
Are crouched among their flints and animals.

Your life is all arranged, the entail waits,
The droppings fertilize the future ploughlands;
And to great doubt you also are the heir –
Whether they find the level you make cultured.

THE VISITS

In the morning I visited her again, she lay
O horror! bloodless and the curtain flapping;
While over the violet sky I thought a bat
Flew blindly like a bit of black crêpe paper.

I would not have believed it, but the second
Weekday on the emaciated visage,
With two blank eyeholes for the unseeing eyes,
Rested a little mask of black crêpe paper.

FUTURE FOSSILS

Our doom a commonplace of history –
The creeping icecap's hunger, plenty's cancers;
Implements lost or broken before the fire
Blackens the soil and scabs a finished epoch.
The seeds of the wild strawberry will show
Among bare ribs, the summer death ordained
By declaration of demented leaders.

But yet on many nights by foothills where
The sky's slack velvet curtain's blown away,
The future fossils walk with prickling skin
To sense their progeny at the start of eras.
Such haunting times, the recompense for failure,
Are evidenced by marks of black and red
That flesh the fragments of extinct hyenas.

THE JOURNEY

Torrid blossoms of snow lay on the trees,
  Rooks courted in the hollow,
The light came like a mirror's flash
  From even ploughed and fallow.

He'd travelled all day to reach that place,
  The house of local stone
Below the line of conifers
  That shadowed it like a spine.

As he reached the gate the sun went down,
  The frost came with a crackle
And bound the snow on the trees' windward side
  And the path as hard as metal.

On the gate-posts he saw a carven shield,
  On each gate the same symbol,
A shield with a carven deathshead in stone.
  His feet began to stumble.

'I am like a man in an ancient ballad
  Drawn to the strangest doom.
Oh what will happen to me that thought
  To live gently from the womb?'

A tree grew in the chimney there
  Like a flower in a madman's hat,
And the door for a handle grew a hand
  And an open mouth for a latch.

'Come in, come in, you honest stranger.'
  'I fear you and I fear – '
'Come in and dry your sodden shoes
  Before our faggot fire.'

He's passed the door and in the long hall
  And no fire can he see.
He's up the stairs and in the bedchamber
  And no need of fire has he.

For he's wrestling with the hardest sinews of all,
  With strength the most insane,
And he's tangled himself in the long curtains
  That bear the deathshead sign.

In his cracking brain, his tortured thews,
  A little world is burning:
The snow, the treading rooks, the plan
  Of a last mistaken journey.

CENTAURS

The folded land a horse could stamp through
Raised the centaur with lighter hoof.
The glossy vandyke wake of plough

And painted crops were saved: the truth
Is that the centaur did not eat.
The country never set a roof

Amongst its smoky trees; the sweet
Stables of the centaur lay
Quite open to their augean fate.

What of the land's economy,
Its plans to keep alive the beast,
Whose muscular beauty, white and ghostly,

Stood still against the darker boast?
Being half man it would not draw
The plough or bear the summer harvest:

The other half refused the straw
Shelter, and the elements
Commenced to operate the law.

Clouds covered like a scab the blenched,
Raw sky, and from its arching hangar
Slipped bolts that tore the earth to fragments,

Splashing amongst the seething danger
Below the cardboard base the centaur
Had pawed with merely human anger.

END OF A CITY

Birds in the pattern of a constellation,
Blank pale blue sky, white walls of a citadel,
Silence of country without inhabitants.
The shining aqueducts, elaborate drains,
Puffed fountains, cleanse a sheeted culture
Where the greatest movement is the soft
Wear of stone by water that leaves no trace
Of green, coming from static glaciers.

By night in the city, stars like heraldic birds,
The square, the plinth with the sacred articles,
The statue of the shade of Spartacus,
No change appears, the cooling is unheard
Of monuments of easy living in
The dark air. But the crack is widening
Between the sun and moon, the rest and flow,
The vomitorium and immense sewers.

See how the separate layers come to life.
The sloping theatre rolls down its bodies
To mingle with the last act's tragedy
Upon the stage; from tarnished bed both king
And mistress tumble; pens fall from the hands
Of nerveless bureaucrats; and, rubbing sockets
Of eyeless skulls, the naked slaves awake,
Who face another epoch of draining work.

Within the temple sits the noble JA,
Bearded with seaweed and his elephant's legs
Crossed in the droppings. The lamp has long gone out,
The offerings are mouldy and the priests
Dust in the chancel. This was he who ordered
For his tremendous dropsy the sanitation,
But whose emissaries sent timely hence
Brought no green leaf to soothe his helplessness.

[8]

This day is surely lucky for the city.
The last trumpet blown with leaking cheeks
Rouses the oldest tenants from their sleep.
They are the ancestors whose tombs were levelled
At the last cataclysm, but they come
Like grass between the stones, though grass like hair,
And growing goatishly along the sewers,
Over the stage, the temple and on JA.

TO M. S., KILLED IN SPAIN

Great cities where disaster fell
In one small night on every house and man,
Knew how to tell the fable from the flesh:
One crying O, his mouth a marble fountain;
Her thigh bones in immortal larva
At compass points, the west and east of love.

Necks bent to look for the seditious geese,
Or over blocks, gazing into freedom;
Heads all alike, short noses, brows
Folded above, the skin a leather brown;
Wrists thick, the finger pads worn down
Building oppression's towering stone.

Now uncovered is the hero,
A tablet marks him where his life leaked out
Through grimy wounds and vapoured into air.
A rusty socket shows where in the night
He crammed his torch and kept by flame at bay
Dark, prowling wolves of thought that frightened him.

The poor outlasted rope and crucifix,
We break the bones that blenched through mastic gold;
And excavate our story, give a twist
To former endings in deliberate metre,
Whose subtle beat our fathers could not count,
Having their agile thumbs too far from fingers.

[9]

I fear the plucking hand
That from our equal season
Sent you to war with wrong
But left me suavely wound
In the cocoon of reason
That preluded your wings.

As the more supple fin
Found use in crawling, so
Some new and rapid nerve
Brought close your flesh to brain,
Transformed utopia
To death for human love.

And my existence must
Finish through your trauma
The speechless brute divorce
Of heart from sculptured bust:
Turn after five acts' drama
A placid crumpled face.

I see my friend rising from the tomb,
His simple head swathed in a turban of white cloth.
The vault is spotted with a brownish moss,
One corner broken, fallen to the floor,
Whereon I read SPAIN as he advances like
An invalid, changed terribly with pain.

A quiet room holds him, half-raised from the bed,
Eyes big and bright, a waxwork, and the blood
Of waxworks running down his cheek. Two candles
Rock their light. The bed is moving, tilting,
And slips him rigidly to take a new position,
The elbow sharp, the skin a yellow leaf.

The third time he stands against a summer country,
The chestnuts almost black in thunderous air,
The silver green of willow lining dykes
Choked with flesh. He moves along the furrows
With labourer's fingers, spreading death against
The imperishable elements of earth.

What is the meaning of these images?
The wish to leave all natural objects richer,
To quicken the chemistry of earth, to be
Immortal in our children. Such desires
Are bodies in a pit, the rotting and bloody
Backwash of a tidal pestilence.

> The scalpel in my back
> That broke my uneasy dream
> Has extended in a scythe,
> Is passing through the quick,
> Forcing like strychnine
> My body to its curve.

> The future is not waking,
> Nor the name and number
> Of distorted figures, and knowledge
> Of pain. It is the breaking
> Before we slumber
> Of the shaping image.

> So from the nightmare, from
> The death, the war of ghosts,
> Those chosen to go unharmed
> May join the tall city, the swan
> Of changing thoughts
> Set sailing by the doomed.

BALLAD OF THE LAST HEIR

Lord Ashby the eldest son came down
  And sprawled beside the shallow lake;
He saw the acres of his reversion
  In planes about, immaculate.

No blade had wrinkled the green parkland
  And grazing only were the hunters
With yellow bilious eyeballs, threshing
  Tails, a black company of haunters.

[11]

'These lands are bound to my ancient father
   And I am the next to inherit them.
The hunt will ride over his deathbed –
   And over my own in a little time.

'To the vault in the nave of that grey church
   With the names carved there that are my own,
To the yew trees out of tenant and serf
   In the graveyard growing heavy and green
I am bound like a falling stone to earth.

'My face has a history but no future,
   The dead compiled the chivalrous usage,
Raping for ever love and ambition,
   And only time rots their marble visage.

'The heirlooms are clasped by a savage law
   On the body of any that I may love;
The sombre settings and florid gems
   Will spoil young flesh with stain and groove.

'No wanton girl like a slender fish
   Will slip from my bed with a harlot's mime:
I am empty of lust, a grotesque form
   Evolved by a clumsy inbred line.'

Ashby rose up and saw the sun
   Between the trees and the grey church tower
Like a gout of blood on an egg-blue skin,
   An image of internecine war.

He left the lake on his sinister hand,
   Treading a path between the yews:
A bird flew swiftly under the branches
   And down the dark glade beyond his view.

He pressed on the wormy door and drew
   The dusty scarlet cloth aside
And entered the spacious gloom of the church
   With a gleam on brass and flowers relieved.

The sanitary neatness of Bedlam was there,
   A dry spare skull with the brains all gone:
The arches frugally preserved
   Against a greater, a final ruin.

Ashby confronted the fatuous altar,
  The plain high windows of dove-grey light:
The strength of his empty face was the eyes
  Like those a sculptor dared not sight.

But quickly against the reredos,
  Flooding its ghostly alabaster,
A magnesium bud of flaming fiercely
  Showed his pupils who was master.

A cord of terror combed his scalp.
  The symbol snaked and burned dull red
And faded in the theatrical glare
Of pouring light, where dust and where
  The explosion's smoke crepitated and coiled.

Then in the glow stood a solid figure
  With clothes stained red as though in wine,
And from the forehead, like pallid fungus,
Two horns grew in the shape of fingers.
  The ported appendage was silky and fine.

'I know you, Ashby, I know your sorrow.'
  Ashby had gone had he but dared.
The lips of the apparition smiled
  And shaped like butter the separate words.

'Throw off your fear and tradition, Ashby.
  A man should often welcome the devil.'
'Frankly I fear you,' Lord Ashby replied,
  'And tradition tells me you are evil.'

'Your tradition is dead, I'll give you a better.
  The gold of your settings will run in its flame,
The dross be purged from your mouldering gems
  And the land reveal a more fertile loam.

'Your riches are static, I'll make them flow.'
  'What good will avail, my heart's the hurt?'
'It lies in stiff unyielding cerements
  And must be freed if it must beat.'

[13]

'But what would you want of me in exchange?'
  'And what would you give me?' the devil said.
'I'll give you a share of the new-minted wealth.'
  'Then sign the bond in your own fine blood.'

'You'll control the way my bread is got.'
  'Cake,' said the devil, his eyes aslant.
'And that you'll determine my way of life
  Is patent from your own argument.'

'O specious youth to apply the standards
  Of hoary winter to your new Spring.
Under my rule my laws are good;
  The argument shows that morals are shifting.'

The trees brushed against the arching windows,
  A thin wind jangled a ghost of bells.
The devil gathered his hired red robes.
'This place is haunted.' He twitched the lobes
  Of his pointed ears. 'Grasp my shoulders well.

'I'll show you the forge for your raw rich lumber,
  The boundless realm of our company;
Strange food to stop your foolish mouth
  And passion to fill your questioning eye.'

Then Ashby hung on the devil's shoulders:
  He smelt the heat of the body's rages,
The dust from the woollen scarlet cloak,
  An odour of shoddy provincial stages.

Then he saw the altar far beneath
  And soon the grey church tower, the trees,
The toy horses and the pleasure grounds,
  Until the half-light smeared these views.

The devil turned his animal head
  And spoke with the cold diluted air.
'The winking limits of aerodrome
The dark north prick like a waking dream
  With wings you will inherit there.

'And to the south the esplanade
  Of the sweet immoral watering place,
A glittering snake coiled round the bight,
Promises a press of thighs in moonlight,
  A bright moist path to Dian's grace.'

They flew until Lord Ashby could see
  The yellow slots of factory windows,
And they rested upon a grey slag heap
  To see the town's industrial wonders.

The gas lit streets were laid with cobbles,
  Their people a pale diminutive race.
'These are the craftsmen of your metal.'
  'I fear the bitter collective face.'

'They are the genii of the ring,
  They are phantoms with only strength to slave.'
'I have no confidence in oppression
  And strength is a menace without their love.

'If our kingdom should rest on these Nibelungs
  I think our reign is brief indeed.'
'You will not again view this crude country,
  Its vapours require a healthier breed.

'I'll save your aristocratic frame
  From the shocks of such elemental scenes.
Your function is not to produce but dispose:
  You should not be hampered by questions of means.'

Then Ashby's uneasy flesh was borne
  Across one squalid eaten face
Of the serf-made pyramid of power.
  He turned his eyes from the smoky place.

The glow of the forge fell back in the dark,
  The high-pitched rattle of spindles ceased,
The slow death in the oppressive house
  Tinctured the final narrow street.

In the velvet of the upper air,
  Curving a planetary path,
The devil, his arm supporting Ashby,
  Attempted to soothe the startled youth.

'Your home is a palace of many rooms,
  Its porcelain walls trap cool white air,
In shapely pots are luxuriant posies,
Tongued orchids and soft ceruminous roses,
  And waxen ivy wreaths the stair.

'You mount to the roof with an airman's eye
  Of the sunlit landscape, flat as paving,
And in the middle distance find
The necessary objects waving
  Tendrils of parasites under sand.

'The sphinx as lover with flawless breasts,
  The broken lintels of exchanges,
A novel machine in idleness,
Arranged in isolation replace
  Rough nature's wasteful wearing hinges.

'Breaking the quivering horizon stands,
  In lovely visual form, the trust
Of death, a marble skyscraper,
  Lonely devourer of the rest.'

The devil produced from his narrow bosom
  A parchment and a pointed reed.
'You sign and touch this seal and say
  "I deliver this my act and deed".'

The devil's gesture had swift effect.
  'You've taken me from my own country,
From the dusty cherry and phallic chestnut
  That in spring would have delighted me.

'You've saved me from the dreaded symbols:
  The flattened rabbit in the road,
The yellow winds in the cutting fall,
  Blunt proper knives for scraping scab.

[16]

'You promised me freedom where I had none.
   Let me return to the entailed land.'
Lord Ashby's words were hurried and shrill.
'For I will not live in your insane hell.'
   Some white showed on the other's hand.

They were falling with the falling sky
   And the globe's gear began to engage with them.
The devil said 'You damned aristo,
   Mine was a decent charity home.

'The last of your race in a tottering house,
   The door grown over with lurid weeds,
Whom do you think would succeed to the corpse,
   The broken stones and moss-blanked words?

'If you want the truth, you are useless, a ghost.'
   'And what are you but a superstition?'
'Die!' screamed the devil. 'I'll steal your world.'
   'Then inherit,' said Ashby, 'a realm of attrition.'

The devil loosed his supporting arm
   And the boy whirled down from the dark domain
Like a parachute after the turning earth,
A fluttering convulsive effort at birth:
   But below were scattered his bright remains.

THE PURE POET

He spoke of poetry: his lips had shrunk
To lines across the gums: he also stank.
He said that since the Greeks few had the gifts,
That syphilis and lice were perquisites.
He brought a charnel breath and spotted cloths,
The swansdown shroud was fluttered when he coughed
His postulate of the sufficient word.
I felt viridian when he launched on blood,
Perceived the surgery behind the trance,
That his long travels in pursuit of tense
Were clearly all compelled by social syntax;

[17]

And but for his unpleasant human antics
I could have pitied him for being dead.
Still he sat on and told me how he made
His money, villa, servants, the model globe,
His regular habits and the seven-faced cube.
Further I could not follow him among
The obscure allusions to important dung,
Nor as at length he tried a final scare
And vanished through the non-existent door.

FOLLOWER'S SONG

Oh to be simple and give the salute,
To be hopeful and happy,
For life to be sucked through the root
And the branches sappy.

Oh to be mad with marching and May,
To be bold, to be brutish,
To dream in the night and by day
To delight in duties.

And oh for the pointing finger to cube
To a gun and the feeling
Inside to come out of the tube
And kill with its healing;

The earth to be gone with its grave and the sky
With its season: forever
To shake in God's voice and to lie
Next his iron and leather.

AUGUST 1938

Mapping this bay and charting
The water's ribby base
By individual smarting
And walks in shifting sand,
We note the official place;
Dover with pursed-up lips
Behind the purple land
Blowing her little ships
To danger, large and bland:

Aeroplanes softly landing
Beyond the willowed marsh:
The phallic lighthouse standing
Aloof with rolling eye
From shingle flat and harsh:
And sequinned on the coast
Beneath the usual sky
The pleasure towns where most
Have come to live or die.

Far off the quinsied Brenner,
The open hungry jaw
Of Breslau and Vienna
Through day-old papers join
The mood of tooth and claw
To useless coastal road,
The excursion to Boulogne
And valedictory ode,
The hairy untanned groin.

Oh never is forever
Over this curving ground
When both the dull and clever
Leave for their town of graves,
And on the dissolving mound
By snowy seabirds signed
'Through all routes quit these waves,'
Lonely among his kind
The local spirit raves.

AFTER THE HOLIDAY

After the holiday the daws begin
To bore their holes of sound;
And on the lawn
The first brown crumbs of leaf.
I, looking through my snapshot album, find
The last a fatal X-ray negative.

FRAGMENTS

I

Blocking the light, he ran down steps of air
　　Between sloping walls of dazzling concrete, and
　　Through upright iron windows saw the bare
Executive gestures of the newly dead;
　　And in the chambers furniture of death,
　　Death petrified, imprinted pale as lead
Upon the glass behind the twisted fern;
　　And ledgers of enormous debt, with thumbs
　　Half peeled between the pages, marking the turn. . .

II

From windows of concrete trusts the clerks
Look over streams that cut the throats
Of cities, over roofs of works
Thrown back like stairs of insane sets.
Ropes, cranes, a new geometry
Propound each day, and invisible boats
Moan through the mist their dwindling freights.
But what else can they do but cry?

III

Over a mass of masonry the light,
Fan-wise and blue, suffused with chalk, descends
Into the dark and deathly living things
Which are piled up and poised upon the ground.
And there, between them and the final wall,
That alley of life, its sutured stone,
Is cut about with shadows, like a key.

Regard those arching ribs, the flesh pulled tight,
With stiff brocades pleated beneath, the ends
Tucked in the severed belly. Through the wings,
Folded above the cellular and round
Congruent breasts, the marked lights fall
On an open book, and words are shown:
Reactionary and barbarous monarchy.

In the black foreground on the extreme right,
Wreathed in tough sprigs of lilac, ruffed, depends
The head. This has a history of kings
Flooding the separate teeth, the oyster drowned
In pink. White worms with eyes for faces crawl
To the edge, and wave across the bone
Which, at the skull, splits to admit a tree.

Then, all that was a mystery to the sight
Turns the unwished-for, usual. . .

AFTER THE SPANISH CIVIL WAR

The common news tells me
How I shall live:
There are no other values.
In central Spain I lie,
Fed by what earth can give
Through an iron mesh.

The roads are blown to air;
Tracks drawn to wire with the chill
Of this snowy winter.
Along the air and wire
The news comes, even evil,
Fainter and fainter.

Though events stop happening,
There remain the forces:
The wrestlers immense outside,
Oiled and immobile; wrong
Red between love and faces
In broken shade.

THE CITIES

The crumbled rock of London is dripping under
Clouds of mechanical rain, and towns remoter
Lie frozen round their rivers and the thunder:
For these new decades open of disaster,
The poet dead by green enormous sculpture,
Roads sanded for expressionless invaders
And empty as flame the heavens for the vulture.
Here walk with open lips the pale persuaders
Of doom, over the concrete near the river,
Shadowed by trusts on whose retreating faces
The glassy light and crimson vapours quiver.
This town is full of ghosts: successive bases,
Lost to the living, send their last battalion.
There is no face tonight that is not alien.

THRILLER-WRITER

Conceiving X, the villain, trapped at night,
He went back to the necessary surprise,
Where Hawkshaw himself confessed, a daring ruse.
To make the thing mysterious and right
He set down incidents that gave to X
A charming manner and an honest face,
To Hawkshaw the ill-will of the police,
Beginning with the sun, the blood, the axe.

The plot entirely dovetailed in his mind,
He wrote the opening part about the weather
And showed the disposition of the weapon;
But, smoothing his hair, some crimson smeared his hand –
Hawkshaw, he saw, was dead, was X, was other,
And incidents were disinclined to happen.

FOR JULIAN SYMONS

Your face with its refulgent planes and sockets,
Your blue wild hair I see against the light
Of sunset, and, drawling vowels through the night
(Which like suburban trains, gold chains and lockets,
On London crawls), your voice announces: 'X
Intends to object. Aha! And Y will fight.
You must write a Kafka novel; you must *write*.
Christina was good, considering her sex.'

The hours revolve; soon the last train will slip
Away. Behind the vulcanite daffodil
You'll be a voice that makes impossible
Appointments – 'Meet me at five beneath the whip.'
Or only an image pressed between your verse,
Staining lost love, evenings that might be worse.

SESTINA

For A. Stanley Umpleby

It was the storm, the tree that had a face,
The moving cliff, the cold, the smoking mountain,
And the inevitable swaddling night;
And out of night the staring deathly moon,
The river of stars, which changed the mental demons
And gave them bodies and their ranging power.

And afterwards accretions to their power
Came from the puffy belly and livid face –
The dead, who were the image of the demons
That rode the storm and sat under the mountain.
The dead had countenances like the moon,
The living simulated death at night.

By sleep becoming like the dead at night
They saw at this time a peculiar power
Housed in invisible forces; and the moon
Was bayed to avert its full and maniac face,
An altar was erected on the mountain
And loved gods were evolved from hated demons.

By making gods they were not freed from demons:
Appearing among them out of general night,
Or falling from the country of the mountain,
Came giant men with an especial power,
With cunning mind and the ancestral face,
Who drove and ruled them like the pulling moon.

And some of them professed to read the moon
In all her postures, and to them the demons
Spoke the authoritative word: the face
Of living changed, and through the neutral night
The whips and voices of unquestioned power
Said: 'Save the kings, do not defile the mountain.'

But certain of the wretched dared the mountain
And saw the near dead surface of the moon;
And at that moment the oppressive power
Was broken of the kings and gods; the demons
Recoiled behind the truth-illumined night,
And from the obelisk took their fearful face.

Now, what is there to face upon the mountain,
To meet within the night, before the moon?
What demons are there still that these have power?

EASTER 1939

On Easter Monday at the fair
The axle of the roundabout
Revolved: it bore a group of shields
Painted with portraits of the great.

I watched as Kitchener KG
Came sailing round; French followed, then
Joffre, George Five and Jellicoe
Preceded Kitchener again.

The organ blew, drum tapped, the tune
That saw the Great Depression through.
With the dead monarch, and commanders,
Children rode; a ghostly crew.

TO MY BROTHER

A pistol is cocked and levelled in the room.
The running window opens to the sounds
Of hooters from the Thames at Greenwich, doom

Descends the chimney in the rustling grounds
Of soot. The Globe edition of Pope you gave me
Is open on the chair arm. There are bounds

To feeling in this suburb, but nothing can save me
Tonight from the scenic railway journey over
Europe to locate my future grave: the

Arming world rushes by me where you hover
Behind right shoulders on the German border,
Or at the *Terminus* removing a cover,

Taking perhaps your memories, like a warder,
The memories of our responsible youth,
To give the refugees a sense of order.

My real world also has a base of truth:
Soldiers with labial sores, a yellowish stone
Built round the common into cubes, uncouth

Reverberations from a breaking bone,
The fear of living in the body. Is it
Here we start or end? Tonight my own

Thoughts pay a merely temporary visit
To the state where objects have lost their power of motion,
Their laws which terrify and can elicit

A furious tale from casual emotion,
Where life with instruments surveys the maps
Of cut-out continent and plasticine ocean,

Far from the imminent and loud collapse
Of culture, prophesied by liberals,
Whose guilty ghosts can never say perhaps.

This kind of world Pope, with his quartz and shells,
Constructed in his azure Twickenham grotto,
Which in the daytime entertained the belles,

But glowed and writhed to form a personal motto
At night, with brute distraction in its lair;
The mirrors flattering as part of the plot: 'O

Alex, you are handsome; you have power
First to arrange a world and then to abstract
Its final communication; virtues shower

From the exercise of your genius; the pact
Of friendship is good and all your enemies only
In opposition to civilization act.'

When I am falsely elevated and lonely,
And the effort of making contact even with you
Is helped by distance, the life is finely

Shown which holds on contract, and the true
Perish in cities which revolve behind
Like dust.
           The window explodes, and now
The centre land mass breathes a tragic wind.

SEPTEMBER 1939

1

Nights soften as I walk over the common,
Though trees and grass come out a sharper green
In the last misty light. The yellow houses
On the still water are reversed and clean.
But the swan that curved in peace-time has departed.
Into the base of the penumbra lean
The shoulders of summer and our birds and flowers
Fly off to Cancer where shadows are unseen.

I imagine walking for ever in this air
With animals' ghosts and memories of love.
But silent also with the vibrant dove
Are nation after illusion-clutching nation.
And vanished in a day of proclamation,
A decade of profound and useless care.

And out of the excitement comes the blind
Feeling for men, a generalized compassion.
I see our culture's labyrinth and fashion,
The faltering old, the stupid and the kind,
And know it is the vulnerable haze
Of emotion set by us above the earth
Which makes the lampless night so dark, the birth
And death of time so rapid in these days.

Yes, here the invented clock of history
Passes some awful unfamiliar hour,
And all protection goes: the complex State,
That seems the origin of love and hate;
And then the body, with its manual power
To shield our eyes against the falling sky.

PART TWO

Mainly from
The Middle of a War
(1942) and
A Lost Season
(1944)

AUTUMN 1939

Cigar-coloured bracken, the gloom between the trees,
The straight wet by-pass through the shaven clover,
Smell of the war as if already these
   Were salient or cover.

The movements of people are directed by
The officious finger of the gun and their
Desires are sent like squadrons in the sky,
   Uniform and bare.

I see a boy through the reversing lens
Wearing a shirt the colour of his gums;
His face lolls on the iron garden fence
   Slobbering his thumbs.

I have no doubt that night is real which creeps
Over the concrete, that murder is fantasy,
That what should now inform the idiot sleeps
   Frozen and unfree.

THE BARBER

Reading the shorthand on a barber's sheet
In a warm and chromium basement in Cannon Street
I discovered again the message of the hour:
There is no place for pity without power.

The barber with a flat and scented hand
Moved the dummy's head in its collar band.
'What will you do with the discarded hair?'

The mirror showed a John the Baptist's face,
Detached and side-ways. 'Can you tell me how,'
It said, 'I may recover grace?

'Make me a merchant, make me a manager.'
His scissors mournfully declined the task.
'Will you do nothing that I ask?'

'It is no use,' he said, 'I cannot speak
To you as one in a similar position.
For me you are the stern employer,
Of wealth the accumulator.
I must ignore your singular disposition.'

He brushed my shoulders and under his practised touch
I knew his words were only a deceit.
'You spoke to me according to the rules
Laid down for dealing with madmen and with fools.'

'I do my best,' he said, 'my best is sufficient.
If I have offended it is because
I never formulate the ideal action
Which depends on observation.'

'And do you never observe and never feel
Regret at the destruction of wealth by war?
Do you never sharpen your razor on your heel
And draw it across selected throats?'

He smiled and turned away to the row of coats.
'This is your mackintosh,' he said, 'you had no hat.
Turn left for the station and remember the barber.
There is just time enough for that.'

THE PHONEY WAR

Sitting at home and reading Julien Benda;
Evening descending in successive gauzes –
Pantomime transformation scene reversed;
A point releasing Haydn from a groove
In waves alternately severe and tender:

A curious way to spend a night of war!

Though more and more clearly I see my bona-fides.
Under the growing pressure of the mould
I'm now compact, one of the very small
And disillusioned poets of the era;
Soothsayers who lived on into the Ides.

So action or avowal would be pretence.
Not that I now may draw back from the edge –
The threat of being pushed into real life
(Or realer death) – or even want to. Nor
Deny the times' need for handbooks of defiance.

Is it a lack or growth, this emollient lotion
Of words that keeps me sitting through the dusk,
To find in the martins' squeaking something sure
But vague to praise? This Frenchman says that war
Intensifies the craving for emotion.

He may be right. My own, however, shows
As an increasing fondness for Henry James;
And, if I crave at all, I crave that blight
Shall crumple less millions than thought possible,
And that on those I love shall fall few blows.

A curious war to bequeath me such a night!

FIRST WINTER OF WAR

There is a hard thin gun on Clapham Common,
Deserted yachts in the mud at Greenwich,
In a hospital at Ealing notices
Which read WOMEN GASSED and WOMEN NOT GASSED.

The last trains go earlier, stations are like aquaria,
The mauve-lit carriages are full of lust.
I see my friends seldom, they move in nearby
Areas where no one speaks the truth.

It is dark at four and on the peopled streets,
The ornamental banks and turreted offices,
The moon pours a deathly and powdered grey:
The city noises come out of a desert.

It is dark at twelve: I walk down the up escalator
And see that hooded figure before me
Ascending motionless upon a certain step.
As I try to pass, it will stab me with a year.

WAR POET

Swift had pains in his head.
Johnson dying in bed
Tapped the dropsy himself.
Blake saw a flea and an elf.
Tennyson could hear the shriek
Of a bat. Pope was a freak.
Emily Dickinson stayed
Indoors for a decade.
Water inflated the belly
Of Hart Crane, and of Shelley.
Coleridge was a dope.
Southwell died on a rope.
Byron had a round white foot.
Smart and Cowper were put
Away. Lawrence was a fidget.
Keats was almost a midget.

Donne, alive in his shroud,
Shakespeare, in the coil of a cloud,
Saw death very well as he
Came crab-wise, dark and massy.
I envy not only their talents
And fertile lack of balance
But the appearance of choice
In their sad and fatal voice.

BATTERSEA: AFTER DUNKIRK, JUNE 3,1940

Smoke corrugated on the steel-blue sky
From the red funnels of the power-station
Is blanched as the shocking bandages one sees
On soldiers in the halted train. Patience!
Still there is nothing definite to say –
Or do, except to watch disintegration,
The rightness of the previous diagnosis,
And guard oneself from pity and isolation.

The generator's titanic vessel floats
Beside the Thames; and smoke continues to pour.
Khaki and white move on as though to hide
In summer. What can keep the autumn fates
From breaking the perfect sky and sending power
For slaves to set against the pyramid?

SUMMER 1940

I

Charing Cross: where trains depart for the bombardment
And the leave-taking is particularly ardent;
The obelisk in the court-yard is streaming with lime,
The doves are crying in the dusk, and Time

Says: *I am money, I am all these people,*
The quality in light which changes to purple
When goods have been left with the owner of the mill
And the authority is his to sell.

I wipe my fingers on the hurrying faces,
And implant the wish to be in different places.
I am Too Late, I am the trees which grow
In everyone and blossom pale and grey.

II

The edges of the country are fraying with
Too much use; the ports are visited by wrath
In the shapes of the metal diver and the dart
With screaming feathers and explosive heart.

And the ships are guilty of a desire to return
To land, to three mile pits and the moulding urn.
England no longer is shaped like a begging dog,
Its shape is the shape of a state in the central bog,

With frontiers which change at the yawn of a tired ruler;
At last the push of time has reached it; realer
Today than for centuries, England is on the map
As a place where something occurs, as a spring-board or trap.

Oh what is to happen? Does that depend on Time
Alone? Will change of country eventually come
As slow erosion by the wind of mountains,
And of love as the green-slimed Cupid of the fountain?

Only people and not places are able to resist
Time for a space, to race their daily ghost
In the projectile of violent change: the power
Is in the people to pool their collective hours,

And reply to Time: *You are not all the people,*
You are the weak man underneath the steeple,
You are the exploiter and appropriator,
The hurt philosopher who murmurs Later,

You are all those who assisted death, who weighted
The curve with war and a system of hatred.
You are condemned as a reward or lash,
As an explosion, as a fear or wish.

III

Will you depart now? Will you become a place?
There is really no penalty, there may be peace.
Will you add yourself in the calculation of
The perimeter, the coast-line lost to love?

The third voice says this; it is almost our own.
The voice of pigeons as they drop from stone,
From the cornices of banks, the premises
Of rings and trusts, from all betrayed promises;

The voice of wings attractive to the cripple,
The soothing voice of tobacco-pipe and nipple,
Of introvert ambition which Icarus heard,
The voice of the weeping and isolated bird.

FIRST AIR-RAIDS

Not the moon's light –
Theatrical mauve,
Antiquing the city –
Nor winging danger
Nor guns in the grove,
Strange in the night,
Add beauty to anger;

But my undismayed
Pouring of love
In the crouching city
While things more certain
Than Hamlet's glove
Round reckless blade
Strike through the curtain.

Only when that dies
In sewers and streets
Will guns in the city
Fade with history;
Since love completes
Fear and it cries
For what can't be.

LONDON AIR-RAID, 1940

An ambulance bell rings in the dark among
The rasp of guns, and abstract wrong is brought
Straight to my riveted thought.

Tonight humanity is trapped in evil
Pervasive as plague or devil; hopelessly wages
With pain, like the Middle Ages.

My reading and the alimentary city
Freeze: crouching fear and licking pity's all
Of the handed animal.

TO MY WIFE

The loud mechanical voices of the sirens
Lure me from sleep and on the heath, like stars,
Moths fall into a mounting shaft of light.
Aircraft whirr over and then the night stays quiet;
The moon is peeled of cloud, its gold is changed
On stone for silver and the cap of sky
Glitters like quartz, impersonal and remote.
This surface is the same: the clock's bland face,
Its smiling moustaches, hide the spring, knotted
Like muscles, and the crouching jungle hammer.

The same but so different with you not here.
This evening when I turned from the clothes you left,
Empty and silk, the souls of swallows flickered
Against the glass of our house: I felt no better
Along the tree-massed alleys where I saw
The long pale legs on benches in the dark.
It was no vague nostalgia which I breathed
Between the purple colloids of the air:
My lust was as precise and fierce as that of
The wedge-headed jaguar or the travelling Flaubert.

But I only encountered the ghosts of the suburb,
Those ghosts you know and who are real and walk
And talk in the small public gardens, by the tawdry
Local monuments; the Witch and Big Head
And the others, fleeting and familiar as
Our memories and ambitions, and just as dead.
Being alone they stopped me; Big Head first.
Removing her unbelievable hat, she showed me
What before I had only conjectured, and she whispered:
O lucky you – you might have been born like this.

I knew it was true, but, hurrying on, the Witch
Lifted her cane and barred the way: she is
Lean and very dirty but hanging round
That skeleton are rags of flesh still handsome.
Moving her lips madly and in a foreign tone she said:
Oh do not hope, boy – you will come to this.
I ran, being certain that she had not erred,
Back to our room where now the only noise
Is the icy modulated voice of Mozart
And the false clock ticking on the mantelpiece.

Now in the bubble of London whose glass will soon
Smear into death, at the still-calm hour of four,
I see the shadows of our life, the Fates
We narrowly missed, our possible destiny.
I try to say that love is more solid than
Our bodies, but I only want you here.
*I know they created love and that the rest
Is ghosts; war murders love – I really say.*
But dare I write it to you who have said it
Always and have no consolation from the ghosts?

AUTUMN 1940

No longer can guns be cancelled by love,
Or by rich paintings in the galleries;
The music in the icy air cannot live,
The autumn has blown away the rose.

Can we be sorry that those explosions
Which occurring in Spain and China reached us as
The outer ring of yearning emotions,
Are here as rubble and fear, as metal and glass,

Are here in the streets, in the sewers full of people?
We see as inevitable and with relief
The smoke from shells like plump ghosts on the purple,
The bombers, black insect eggs, on the sky's broad leaf.

For these are outside the deathly self
Walking where leaves are spun across the lips
Bitten against tears which bridge no gulf,
Where swans on the flat full river are moving
                              like oared ships.

Death is solitary and creeps along the Thames
At seven, with mists and changing moons;
Death is in the music and the paintings, the dreams
Still amorous among the dispersing guns.

But where the many are there is no death,
Only a temporary expedient of sorrow
And destruction; today the caught-up breath –
The exhalation is promised for tomorrow.

And changed tomorrow is promised precisely by
The measure of the engendered hate, the hurt
Descended; the instinct and capacity
Of man for happiness, and that drowned art.

EPITAPH FOR JAMES JOYCE

January 13, 1941

Reader, do not stop to pity
This citizen without a city.
In the grave those eyes will get
No deeper darkness, and the heart
There enjoys perspectives that
Failed in his diurnal art.

SOLILOQUY IN AN AIR-RAID

The will dissolves, the heart becomes excited,
Skull suffers formication; moving words
Fortuitously issue from my hand.
The winter heavens, seen all day alone,
Assume the colour of aircraft over the phthisic
Guns.

But who shall I speak to with this poem?

Something was set between the words and the world
I watched today; perhaps the necrotomy
Of love or the spectre of pretence; a vagueness;
But murdering their commerce like a tariff.

Inside the poets the words are changed to desire,
And formulations of feeling are lost in action
Which hourly transmutes the basis of common speech.
Our dying is effected in the streets,
London an epicentrum; to the stench
And penny prostitution in the shelters
Dare not extend the hospital and bogus
Hands of propaganda.

Ordered this year:
A billion tons of broken glass and rubble,
Blockade of chaos, the other requisites
For the reduction of Europe to a rabble.
Who can observe this save as a frightened child
Or careful diarist? And who can speak
And still retain the tones of civilization?
The verse that was the speech of observation –
Jonson's cartoon of the infant bourgeoisie,
Shakespeare's immense assertion that man alone
Is almost the equal of his environment,
The Chinese wall of class round Pope, the Romantic
Denunciation of origin and mould –
Is sunk in the throat between the opposing voices:

I am the old life, which promises even less
In the future, and guarantees your loss.

[41]

And I the new, in which your function and
Your form will be dependent on my end.

Kerensky said of Lenin: *I must kindly*
Orientate him to what is going on.
Watching the images of fabulous girls
On cinema screens, the liberal emotion
Of the slightly inhuman poet wells up in me,
As irrelevant as Kerensky. It is goodbye
To the social life which permitted melancholy
And madness in the isolation of its writers,
To a struggle as inconclusive as the Hundred
Years' War. The air, as welcome as morphia,
This 'rich ambiguous aesthetic air'
Which now I breathe, is an effective diet
Only for actors: in the lonely box
The author mumbles to himself, the play
Unfolds spontaneous as the human wish,
As autumn dancing, vermilion on rocks.

EPITAPH ON A BOMBING VICTIM

Reader, could his limbs be found
Here would lie a common man:
History inflicts no wound
But explodes what it began,
And with its enormous lust
For division splits the dust.
Do not ask his nation; that
Was History's confederate.

ABC OF A NAVAL TRAINEE

A is the anger we hide with some danger,
Keeping it down like the thirteenth beer.
B is the boredom we feel in this bedlam.
C is the cautious and supervised cheer.

D is the tea dope and E English duping,
Too feeble for folly, too strong for revolt.
F is the adjective near every object,
The chief of desires for both genius and dolt.

G is the gun which can kill at, say, Greenwich
If fired at St Martin's, and H is our hate
Non-existent behind it wherever we wind it.
I is the image of common man's fate.

J is the Joan or the Jill or Joanna,
Appearing in dreams as a just-missed train.
K is the kindness like Christmas tree candles,
Unexpected and grateful as poppies in grain.

L is the lung or the limb which in languor
Rests after work and will soon be exposed
To M which is murder, a world rather madder,
Where what we pretend now's as real as your nose.

N is the nightingale's song that we're noting
When the sky is a lucid darkening silk,
When the guns are at rest and the heart is a cancer
And our mouths make O at the moon of milk.

Then we remember, no longer a number,
We think of our duties as poets and men:
Beyond us lie Paris, Quebec, Rome, where diaries
Of millions record the same troubles and pain.

S is the silence for brooding on violence.
T is the toughness imparted to all.
U is the unit that never will clown it
Again as the lonely, the shy or the tall.

V is the vastness: as actor and witness
We double our role and stammer at first.
W is war to start off the quarries –
Our everyday hunger and every night thirst.

X is the kiss or the unknown, the fissure
In misery stretching far back to the ape.
Y is the yearning for Eden returning;
Our ending, our Z and our only escape.

THE GROWTH OF CRIME

A sailor walks along the street,
His cap a halo on his head:
Out of a squalid window gleam
Curved surfaces of skin and red
Paint that profligate women use
And the brass knobs of a bed.

'Sailor, come in,' a soft voice calls.
Behind the house the night comes on
And each cloud on the blenching sky
Darkens and feels for the other one,
And down the road the docks grow dark;
The unmuffled noises of day are gone.

Bounding the town is the acid sea
Which nibbles the plates of the plying ships;
They fall down hills of black-green glass,
Are suspended on summits curled like whips,
And from rigging and gun, like a leaky house,
From body and clothing the grey sea drips.

'Come in, come in.' The voice is plucking
Softly the horizontal air.
The searchlights start to stain the night,
A trembling hum is everywhere.
He imagines the sea a film of blood,
Lopped bodies the shadows on the stair.

And through the walls the whispering
Of lovers, the crying, the old, the bored,
Comes like a touch to his ears. 'The rope
Keeps breaking.' 'I hate to be adored.'
'Give me death but take this pain.'
'Can we afford it? Can we afford?'

He climbs and enters the rose-lit room:
She smiles at him and does not move.
He sits beside her and sees the smile:
He looks at his hand in the shape of a dove,
His breathing trunk, his alien limbs.
And hides in her, crying: 'My love, my love.'

The images of waking brush
Like branches his suddenly staring eyes.
The room is dark, the processions go
Of distorted passion, haunting lies,
From window to bed, and make the world
Fearful as origin and as size.

And sleeping still beside him is
The woman: in her sleeping mask
The worm of his confessions grows.
What has he told her? What did he ask?
This sordid boneless oyster flesh
Is one of his symbols; the cave, the flask.

Some secret lives behind the brambles,
The wine brims up and can be spilled.
Madness and hatred grow in a night:
Strumpets are lonely and can be killed:
Nothing reminds him of day and its reason,
The logic of night, the violence that's willed.

Instead the voices in each ear
Are saying what he has never dared:
'Within its herded operatives
War swells and petrifies the bared
Egotistical and violent soul:
Fear and horror cannot be shared.

Each one has only his little world
Of sensuousness and memory,
And endeavours with the ghastly shell,
The savage skin, the cruel eye,
To save it: in that animal's
Rank den and bed of love it dies.'

He stops his ears; he moves the blind:
The common objects of the room
Glow like the rows of watching faces
In a theatre's powdered violet gloom;
The woman's shape beneath the sheets
Is a gross and convoluted bloom.

The empty bottles point their fingers,
The idiot clothes lie on the floor:
The time is the endless hinge of night,
The opening, slow and living door:
He puts his face near hers as though
To see the grinning yellow core.

She mutters: 'Here in my breast; I have had it
Ever' and 'Oh, horrible!' she cries.
Then from her sleep she moves into
The inch between, as wide as skies.
And he upon their opening sees
Death half an hour behind her eyes.

THE BAY

The semi-circular and lunar bay
Where tumbling, grey stones meet untidily
The grey volcanic waves: no man, no tree,
Breaks the cold greenness of the bitten lea –
This scene the orator of memory
Already knew: forbore till now to say.

But on the hill the gun's black twig, the moan
Of the convoy home from seas instinct with steel,
The hidden spies, the bomber's slanting keel
As slowly it takes the wind – all these remain
Unwished, undreamed, unknown. They are the days,
The escaping seconds, terrible and real,
Through which I live; which memory will seal
To keep and smear for ever future bays.

DEFENDING THE HARBOUR

We form a company to help defend
The harbour. Close against the quay a landed
Monster of a trawler huddles, grey, with sides
Flaking, and aft a grey untidy gun.
Mist shines the cobbles, dulls our waiting boots.

A climbing street links sea and town: we watch
Its pathetic burden of human purpose. All
The faces in my section are thumbed and known
As a pack of cards, and all the characters
Group and speak like a bad familiar play.

And nothing happens but the passage of time,
The monotonous wave on which we are borne and hope
Will never break. But we suspect already
The constant ache as something malignant and
Descry unspeakable deeps in the boring sand.

And on the quay, in our imagination,
The grass of starvation sprouts between the stones,
And ruins are implicit in every structure.
Gently we probe the kind and comic faces
For the strength of heroes and for martyrs' bones.

AUTUMN 1941

The objects are disposed: the sky is suitable.
Where the coast curves the waves' blown smoke
Blurs with the city's and the pencilled ships
Lumber like toys. The searchers for coal and driftwood
Bend; and the beach is littered with stones and leaves,
Antlers of seaweed, round gulls, to the belt
Of sand, like macadam, watered by the sea.

Well then? It is here one asks the question.
Here, under such a sky, with just that menace of purple,
One confronts the varieties of death and of people
With a certain sense of their inadequacy;
And the grandeur of historical conceptions,
The wheeling empires, appearance of lusty classes,
The alimentary organizations, the clever
Extrications from doom, seize the imagination
As though these forms, as gods, existed cruel,
Aloof, but eventually for our salvation.
And, like the shapes themselves of nature or
The inexorable patterns of nightmare, days
And the sequence of days pull our untidy acts
Into the formidable expression of time and destiny.

[47]

The tumbling ocean humps itself to Europe –
There the machines, the armies and the skies,
The stains of movement and the burning regions,
Have all the echoes of a myth and in
My blood reside inhuman power and guilt,
Whose fathers made both myth and progeny.

How will this end? The answer is not in doubt;
For the mood at last plunges to earth like a shot airman:
The only truth is the truth of graves and mirrors.
And people walk about with death inside them
Beseeching the poets to make it real. The sea,
The desolate sea, divides; the heavens are
Perpetual; and the city with its million
Falls to its knees in the sand. O heroes, comrades,
The world is no vision and is devoid of ghosts.

ROYAL NAVAL AIR STATION

The piano, hollow and sentimental, plays,
And outside, falling in a moonlit haze,
The rain is endless as the empty days.

Here in the mess, on beds, on benches, fall
The blue serge limbs in shapes fantastical:
The photographs of girls are on the wall.

And the songs of the minute walk into our ears;
Behind the easy words are difficult tears:
The pain which stabs is dragged out over years.

A ghost has made uneasy every bed.
You are not you without me and *The dead
Only are pleased to be alone* it said.

And hearing it silently the living cry
To be again themselves, or sleeping try
To dream it is impossible to die.

SATURDAY NIGHT IN A SAILORS' HOME

A honeycomb of cabins, boxes, cells,
To which each man retires alone.
A snatch of singing, like a groan,
Broken off quickly. Sour, damp smells.

The cell is never dark. There are
The drummings of fluid on enamel.
Behind the separating panel
The anxious voices speak in prayer:

I wish I could be sick and *Please
Shake me at five: God, what an hour
To wake!* The drugs have lost their power:
Still crawling in the naked light
Are the obscene realities.
The coughing goes on all the night.

THE END OF A LEAVE

Out of the damp black light,
The noise of locomotives,
A thousand whispering –
Sharp-nailed, sinewed, slight,
I meet that alien thing
Your hand, with all its motives.

Far from the roof of night
And iron these encounter;
In the gigantic hall
As the severing light
Menaces – human, small,
These hands exchange their counters.

Suddenly our relation
Is terrifyingly simple
Against our wretched times,
Like a hand which mimes
Love in this anguished station
Against a whole world's pull.

[49]

THE MIDDLE OF A WAR

My photograph already looks historic.
The promising youthful face, the matelot's collar,
Say 'This one is remembered for a lyric.
His place and period – nothing could be duller.'

Its position is already indicated –
The son or brother in the album; pained
The expression and the garments dated,
His fate so obviously preordained.

The original turns away: as horrible thoughts,
Loud fluttering aircraft slope above his head
At dusk. The ridiculous empires break like biscuits.
Ah, life has been abandoned by the boats –
Only the trodden island and the dead
Remain, and the once inestimable caskets.

WAITING TO BE DRAFTED

It might be any evening of spring;
The air is level, twilight in a moment
Will walk behind us and his shadow
    Fall cold across our day.

The usual trees surround an empty field
And evergreens and gravel frame the house;
Primroses lie like tickets on the ground;
    The mauve island floats on grey.

My senses are too sharp for what the mind
Presents them. In this common scene reside
Small elements with power to agitate
    And move me like a play.

I have watched a young stray dog with an affection
Of the eyes, and seen it peer from the encrusted
Lids, like a man, before it ran towards me,
    Unreasonably gay.

And watched it gnawing at a scrap of leather
In its hunger, and afterwards lying down,
Its ineffectual paws against its cracks
    Of eyes, as though to pray.

Pity and love one instant and the next
Disgust, and constantly the sense of time
Retreating, leaving events like traps: I feel
    This always, most today.

My comrades are in the house, their bodies are
At the mercy of time, their minds are nothing but
                              yearning.
From windows where they lie, as from quiet water,
    The light is taken away.

YMCA WRITING ROOM

A map of the world is on the wall: its lying
Order and compression shadow these bent heads.
Here we try to preserve communications;
The map mocks us with its dangerous blues and reds.

Today my friends were drafted; they are about
To be exploded, to be scattered over
That coloured square which in reality
Is a series of scenes, is boredom, cover,

Nostalgia, labour, death. They will explore
Minutely particular deserts, seas and reefs,
Invest a thousand backcloths with their moods,
And all will carry, like a cancer, grief.

In England at this moment the skies contain
Ellipses of birds within their infinite planes,
At night the ragged patterns of the stars;
And distant trees are like the branching veins

[51]

Of an anatomical chart: as menacing
As pistols the levelled twigs present their buds.
They have exchanged for this illusion of danger
The ordeal of walking in the sacred wood.

The season cannot warm them nor art console.
These words are false as the returning Spring
From which this March history has made subtraction:
The spirit has gone and left the marble thing.

ANOTHER WAR

Pity, repulsion, love and anger,
The vivid allegorical
Reality of gun and hangar,
Sense of the planet's imminent fall:

Our fathers felt these things before
In another half-forgotten war.

And our emotions are caught part
From them; their weaponed world it is
They should have left to the abyss
Or made an image of their heart.

ILLNESS OF LOVE

Love, the invaders of your mortal shape,
The thought of those marauders, chill me so
That now, as you lie helpless and asleep,
Only my fear is real and ghostly go
The bed, the chair, the clothes and all the rest
Of this particular moment of our story –
The slender guns, the nervous purple coast,
The time of war which is the time of history.

When I imagine I could lose to death
Those scraps of life I shored against my weakness,
The balancing of self upon events
Becomes irrelevant art, a waste of breath;
That weakness nothing when through fearful darkness,
Apish, its frame as though through jungle pants.

SPRING 1942

Once as we were sitting by
The falling sun, the thickening air,
The chaplain came against the sky
And quietly took a vacant chair.

And under the tobacco smoke:
'Freedom,' he said, and 'Good' and 'Duty'.
We stared as though a savage spoke.
The scene took on a singular beauty.

And we made no reply to that
Obscure, remote communication,
But only looked out where the flat
Meadow dissolved in vegetation.

And thought: O sick, insatiable
And constant lust; O death, our future;
O revolution in the whole
Of human use of man and nature!

HARBOUR FERRY

The oldest and simplest thoughts
Rise with the antique moon:
How she enamels men
And artillery under her sphere,
Eyelids and hair and throats
Rigid in love and war;
How this has happened before.

And how the lonely man
Raises his head and shudders
With a brilliant sense of the madness,
The age and shape of his planet,
Wherever his human hand,
Whatever his set of tenets,
The long and crucial minute.

Tonight the moon has risen
Over a quiet harbour,
Through twisted iron and labour,
Lighting the half-drowned ships.
Oh surely the fatal chasm
Is closer, the furious steps
Swifter? The silver drips

From the angle of the wake:
The moon is flooding the faces.
The moment is over: the forces
Controlling lion nature
Look out of the eyes and speak:
Can you believe in a future
Left only to rock and creature?

GOOD-BYE FOR A LONG TIME

A furnished room beyond the stinging of
The sea, reached by a gravel road in which
Puddles of rain stare up with clouded eyes:

The photographs of other lives than ours;
The scattered evidence of your so brief
Possession; daffodils fading in a vase.

Our kisses here as they have always been,
Half sensual, half sacred, bringing like
A scent our years together, crowds of ghosts.

And then among the thousand thoughts of parting
The kisses grow perfunctory; the years
Are waved away by your retreating arm.

[54]

And now I am alone. I am once more
The far-off boy without a memory,
Wandering with an empty deadened self.

Suddenly under my feet there is the small
Body of a bird, startling against the gravel.
I see its tight shut eye, a trace of moisture,

And, ruffling its gentle breast the wind, its beak
Sharpened by death: and I am yours again,
Hurt beyond hurting, never to forget.

TROOPSHIP

Now the fish fly, the multiple skies display
Still more astounding patterns, the colours are
More brilliant than fluid paint, the grey more grey.

At dawn I saw a solitary star
Making a wake across the broken sea,
Against the heavens swayed a sable spar.

The hissing of the deep is silence, the
Only noise is our memories.

       O far
From our desires, at every sweaty port,
Between the gem-hung velvet of the waves,
Our sires and grandsires in their green flesh start,
Bend skinny elbows, warn: 'We have no graves.
We passed this way, with good defended ill.
Our virtue perished, evil is prince there still.'

THE DREAM

I dreamed of my child's face, all bloody.
Waking, I heard
The tortured creak of wood, the whistling
Like some night-haunting, death-presaging bird.

O terrifying life that might
Do hurt to him
And sets me helpless on this ship,
Hub of the whirling ocean's constant rim.

And worse: allows the happy past
To hide in that distorting mind
Where sleep alone
Can make it realer than the world-blown wind.

IN AFRICA

Parabolas of grief, the hills are never
Hills and the plains,
Where through the torrid air the lions shiver,
No longer plains.

Just as the lives of lions now are made
Shabby with rifles,
This great geography shrinks into sad
And personal trifles.

For those who are in love and are exiled
Can never discover
How to be happy: looking upon the wild
They see for ever

The cultivated acre of their pain;
The clouds like dreams,
Involved, improbable; the endless plain
Precisely as it seems.

THE PHOTOGRAPHS

The faces in the obscene photographs
Gaze out with no expression: they are like
The dead, who always look as though surprised
In a most intimate attitude. The man
And woman in the photograph have faces
Of corpses; their positions are of love –
Which we have taken. I remember how
Once, coming from the waves, I found you chill
Beneath the *maillot* in a sun-warmed house;
And on such memories are now imposed
The phantasies engendered by these two.

Evening: the rows of anxious aircraft wait,
Speckled with tiny brown and crimson birds;
The plain extends to an escarpment lit
Softly as by a steady candle flame;
And then there is the great curve of the earth
And, after, you, whom two seas and a war
Divide.
            The dust blows up. As long as those
Photographs poison my imagination
I shall not dare to catch my countenance
In any mirror; for it seems to me
Our faces, bodies – both of us – are dead.

THE GREEN HILLS OF AFRICA

The green, humped, wrinkled hills: with such a look
Of age (or youth) as to erect the hair.
They crouch above the ports or on the plain,
Beneath the matchless skies; are like a strange
Girl's shoulders suddenly against your hands.
What covers them so softly, vividly?
They break at the sea in a cliff, a mouth of red:
Upon the plain are unapproachable,
Furrowed and huge, dramatically lit.

And yet one cannot be surprised at what
The hills contain. The girls run up the slope,
Their oiled and shaven heads like caramels.
Behind, the village, with its corrugated
Iron, the wicked habit of the store.
The villagers cough, the sacking blows from the naked
Skin of a child, a white scum on his lips.
The youths come down in feathers from the peak.
And over all a massive frescoed sky.

The poisoner proceeds by tiny doses,
The victim weaker and weaker but uncomplaining.
Soon they will only dance for money, will
Discover more and more things can be sold.
What gods did you expect to find here, with
What healing powers? What subtle ways of life?
No, there is nothing but the forms and colours,
And the emotion brought from a world already
Dying of what starts to infect the hills.

[57]

THE GIRAFFES

I think before they saw me the giraffes
Were watching me. Over the golden grass,
The bush and ragged open tree of thorn,
From a grotesque height, under their lightish horns,
Their eyes were fixed on mine as I approached them.
The hills behind descended steeply: iron-
Coloured outcroppings of rock half-covered by
Dull green and sepia vegetation, dry
And sunlit: and above, the piercing blue
Where clouds like islands lay or like swans flew.

Seen from those hills the scrubby plain is like
A large-scale map whose features have a look
Half menacing, half familiar, and across
Its brightness arms of shadow ceaselessly
Revolve. Like small forked twigs or insects move
Giraffes, upon the great map where they live.

When I went nearer, their long bovine tails
Flicked loosely, and deliberately they turned,
An undulation of dappled grey and brown,
And stood in profile with those curious planes
Of neck and sloping haunches. Just as when,
Quite motionless, they watched I never thought
Them moved by fear, a wish to be a tree,
So as they put more ground between us I
Saw evidence that these were animals
With no desire for intercourse, or no
Capacity.
           Above the falling sun,
Like visible winds the clouds are streaked and spun,
And cold and dark now bring the image of
Those creatures walking without pain or love.

THE PLAINS

The only blossoms of the plains are black
And rubbery, the spiked spheres of the thorn,
And stuffed with ants. It is before the rains:

[58]

The stream is parched to pools, occasional
And green, where tortoise flop; the birds are songless;
Towers of whirling dust glide past like ghosts.
But in the brilliant sun, against the sky,
The river course is vivid and the grass
Flaxen: the strong striped haunches of the zebra,
The white fawn black, like flags, of the gazelles,
Move as emotions or as kindly actions.
The world is nothing but a fairy tale
Where everything is beautiful and good.

At night the stars were faint, the plateau chill;
The great herds gathered, were invisible,
And coughed and made inarticulate noises
Of fear and yearning: sounds of their many hooves
Came thudding quietly. The headlights caught
Eyes and the pallid racing forms. I thought
Of nothing but the word *humanity*:
And I was there outside the square of warmth,
In darkness, in the crowds and padding, crying.
Suddenly the creamy shafts of light
Revealed the lion. Slowly it swung its great
Maned head, then – loose, suède, yellow – loped away.
O purposeful and unapproachable!
Then later his repugnant hangers-on:
A pair of squint hyenas limping past.
This awful ceremony of the doomed, unknown
And innocent victim has its replicas
Embedded in our memories and in
Our history. The archetypal myths
Stirred in my mind.

                    The next day, over all,
The sun was flooding and the sky rose tall.
Where rock had weathered through the soil I saw
A jackal running, barking, turning his head.
Four vultures sat upon the rock and pecked,
And when I neared them flew away on wings
Like hair. They left a purple scrap of skin.
Have I discovered all the plains can show?
The animals gallop, spring, are beautiful,
And at the end of every day is night.

[59]

ASKARI'S SONG

At dusk when the sky is pale,
Across a three-years' journey
I can see the far white hill
Which in my land is like a
Conscience or maker.

At dusk when cattle cross
The red dust of the roadway,
I smell the sweetish grass,
Half animal, half flowers,
Which also is ours.

At dusk the roads along
The separating plains are
So sad with our deep song
I could expect the mountain
To drift like a fountain,

And, conquering time, our tribe
Out of the dust to meet us
Come happy, free, alive,
Bringing the snow-capped boulder
Over their shoulder.

THE WHITE CONSCRIPT AND
THE BLACK CONSCRIPT

I do not understand
Your language, nor you mine.
If we communicate
It is hardly the word that matters or the sign,
But what I can divine.

Are they in London white
Or black? How do you know,
Not speaking my tongue, the names
Of our tribes? It could be as easily a blow
As a match you give me now.

Under this moon which the curdled
Clouds permit often to shine
I can see more than your round cap,
Your tallness, great eyes and your aquiline
Nose, and the skin, light, fine.

The British must be wicked:
They fight. I have been brought
From our wide pastures, from
The formal rules of conduct I was taught;
Like a beast I have been caught.

If only I could tell you
That in my country there
Are millions as poor as you
And almost as unfree: if I could share
Our burdens of despair!

For I who seem so rich,
So free, so happy, am
Like you the most despised.
And I would not have had you come
As I most loath have come.

Among our tribe, like yours,
There are some bad, some good –
That is all I am able to say:
Because you would not believe me if I could
Tell you it is for you, the oppressed, the good
Only desire to die.

CONVICTS WORKING ON THE
AERODROME

Curls powdered with chalk like a black Roman bust,
This prisoner, convicted of a lust
For maize, is whipped to building a great shed
For bombers; and bears the earth upon his head.

THE TRIBES

I think of the tribes: the women prized for fatness,
Immovable, and by a sympathetic
   Magic sustaining the herds,
   On whose strange humps sit birds;

And those with long dung-stiffened capes of hair,
And those that ceremonially eat their dead;
   The ornamental gashes
   Festered and raised with ashes;

The captured and dishonoured king compelled
To straddle a vertical and sharpened stake,
   Until, his legs hauled at,
   The point burst from his throat;

And all the prohibitions and the cheapness
Of life so hardly got, where it is death
   Even to touch the palace
   And poison expresses malice.

Now in the white men's towns the tribes are gathered
Among the corrugated iron and
   The refuse bins where rats
   Dispute with them for scraps.

Truly, civilization is for them
The most elemental struggle for bread and love;
   For all the tabus have gone,
   It is man against man alone.

On waste plots and in the decrepit shanties
They begin to discover the individual,
   And, with the sense in time
   Of Adam, perpetrate crime.

The most horrible things you can imagine are
Happening in the towns and the most senseless:
   There are no kings or poison,
   Are laws but no more reason.

TEBA

He fled. The long deserted street,
Moonlit, the moon so mauve, so near,
The sound of his naked throbbing feet,
And, looking back, the body's clear
And indestructible shape of fear –
Now these are memories and dreams:
Again life is nearly as it seems.

Across the plains, the mountain, white
At dawn, the country's ghostly fold,
Rose up, he knew, from distant bright
Forests of home. He turned: the cold
Downs fell to grasses parched and gold,
Thorn trees and fissures, slim dun birds,
Vast startled wheeling racing herds.

These plains are endless: as the day
Deepened the mountain faded and
The corrugated air drew clay-
Hued whirls of dust across the bland
Sky; the skin stiffened on his hand.
He tracked a half-dry stream until
Exhaustion overcame his will.

A nightmare clawed his sleep: he was
Before remote pale men. 'Confess!'
'I am not guilty of this thing because
Kwa bade me – if a man possess
A shamba he may ask, no less,
His friend to dig it.' This he knew
Was folly. The judges said: 'Untrue.'

A lizard flaming from the sun
Flickered across his skin: his eyes
Opened: the lizard seemed his sin.
The dreams and the realities
Fused in his heart-proceeding sighs:
'I am that Teba who has killed
And who cannot kill the pursuing world.'

But in the fluid air of dusk,
Beyond the purpling plains there gleamed
Once more that summit, like a tusk.
So every dawn and evening seemed
To promise he should be redeemed,
Changing the world's for the tribe's rebuke,
The cold for the fond regretful look –

Until the heavens, huge and light,
At last were filled by mountain. He
Was home: his sable skin scratched white
And red was stretched above the valley,
The coins of thatch, the childhood tree,
The half-bared rocks the shade of sand
Where nightly oblique hyenas stand.

Still as though frozen by its wizard,
The village lay, while over it
And him the shadow that a buzzard
Throws ominously slowly beat.
Now it is not his pursuers sit
Upon him but the crushing weight
Of the intolerable too-late.

And some strange commerce starts between
The making and the man, the lack
Within, the rich without; the green
Mutation and the later black.
At length he saw upon the track,
Puffed in the windless air like fumes
Of acid, white and belligerent plumes –

A warrior that the chief had sent,
The many's message to the one,
So feminine and insolent
In look, his voice so deep in tone,
Whose trappings wakened Teba's own
Archaic past, the ritual
In which he once had played a role.

The warrior's words fell like a net:
Beneath the ochre Teba saw
The features that a boy might get.
The paint said: 'Teba, I am law.
I am the chief's voice and I know
You have committed murder which
Cannot be hidden in a ditch.'

Whispered the face behind the paint:
'My friend, I know you. We live by
A creeping shade which here is faint
But which eventually will dye
All with the blackness of a lie.
The plumes are shabby, the paint no longer
Impresses, our arms will not kill danger.'

But the official mask still said:
'Death, Teba, has no longer reasons;
For with the white king I have made
A treaty, and through all the seasons
Of man and nature death holds feasance
Only to death, and we have lost
The mastery of that which is last.

'Further, I have agreed to give
Some warriors for the white man's war –
Gave you who have no right to live.
Such warriors I sent to shore
That opening and fearful door
That lets destructive spectres in,
Efficient and barbarian.

'I cannot judge you, Teba, only
Command. You must return to death.'
The warrior went down: the lonely
Forest expired its evening breath
As Teba took the other path,
And night extended rapidly
From roots and vermin to the sky.

Having no other link but languor
With this familiar, poignant place,
He lay between the two worlds' danger
And slept. And woke to find a face,
Vivid and weird, against the lace
Of green upon the cobalt's fleeced
Horizon: saw it was the priest.

His features were of crumpled paper,
The pupils of the eyes were running
Into the whites. A ritual caper
Rattled the bangles, and the cunning
Mouth said: 'It is no use shunning
The world of men or trying to hide
From what is certainly inside.'

Cried Teba: 'But I am condemned!'
'Your body,' said the priest, 'may be
In peril of extinction, hemmed
By warring temporal powers, but we
Are not concerned with that. The free
Part of you that remains is ours,
Which needs our bandages and flowers.

'There is no remedy for that
Ulcer of guilt except the old
Ceremonies of our race, the great
Purification of the bold.'
Said Teba: 'I have learned to hold
Life dear from those who thought me black
And cheap. I cannot give it back.'

The priest crouched on his withered hams,
Removed his cap of horns, and said:
'Useless to go on with the forms
When what inside them is quite dead;
But even the very old crave bread,
And I must try to justify
My powers to society.

'Teba, no doubt I do forget
How to make rain. And you may think
My dress ridiculous. And yet
I brought you once across the brink
Of youth, and when your parents shrink
From things which round the dying press
It is to me they will confess.'

Sleepy, he mumbled: 'The result
Is certain, and the white man's coming
Perhaps was good: now we get salt.'
In a high voice he started humming,
His head swayed to phantasmal drumming;
And from him Teba crept as one
Who finds his father merely man.

He saw, across the river's steep
Channel, the cattle and the crop
And, as he had imagined – deep
Breasts tolling as she hacked the slope
Of rusty earth, her gleaming rope
Of back curved gently down – his wife,
And all the darkness of his life.

He hurried past his moving heart
To where the sidling river fell,
And thrust the tall green weeds apart
And sank in misery, with all
The nameless and impossible
Desires of those who prowl the grove,
In whose tongue is no word for love.

And through his fingers saw the clear
Water beside the dove-smooth stone;
Dragonflies, colourless with sheer
Speed, rest on grasses and regain
The chemical brilliance of a stain;
Green hands of cactus, arteries –
Unearthed by water – of the trees.

His spirit then leaped out to face
Victim and warrior, priest and wife,
The whole procession of his race,
And in that moment knew the knife
Descending on their ancient life,
That must make, of necessity,
An end, could start their history;

And summoned up his people, saw
How they converse and always gaze
At the angle of the speaking jaw
And never at each other's eyes;
And how the young men go their ways
Hand clasping hand; and how the old
Retain the innocence of the wild:

Saw the huge eyes of youth with that
Which in their glistening whites is like
Another iris probing at
The unseen with an eager look:
And arms escaping in a lake
From stuff, like softest leather, bright
With innumerable points of light.

Teba withdrew his hands: the sun
Gilded his view. And down the rocks
And on the flower-blue sky moved men
That made his world a closing box.
The guns clicked and the word that knocks
Against the heart. But Teba, fuller
Than fear, was filled with rising colour.

AUTUMN 1942

Season of rains: the horizon like an illness
Daily retreating and advancing: men
Swarming on aircraft: things that leave their den
And prowl the suburbs: cries in the starlit stillness.

Into the times' confusion such sharp captions
Are swiftly cut, as symbols give themselves
To poets, though the convenient nymphs and elves
They know fall sadly short of their conceptions.

[68]

I see giraffes that lope, half snake, half steed,
A slowed-up film; the soft bright zebra race,
Unreal as rocking horses; and the face –
A solemn mandarin's – of the wildebeest.

And sometimes in the mess the men and their
Pathetic personal trash become detached
From what they move on; and my days are patched
With newspapers about the siege-like war.

Should I be asked to speak the truth, these are
What I should try to explain, and leave unsaid
Our legacy of failure from the dead,
The silent fate of our provincial star.

But what can be explained? The animals
Are what you make of them, are words, are visions,
And they for us are moving in dimensions
Impertinent to use or watch at all.

And of the men there's nothing to be said:
Only events, with which they wrestle, can
Transfigure them or make them other than
Things to be loved or hated and soon dead.

It is the news at which I hesitate,
That glares authentically between the bars
Of style and lies, and holds enough of fears
And history, and is not too remote.

And tells me that the age is thus: chokes back
My private suffering, the ghosts of nature
And of the mind: it says the human features
Are mutilated, have a dreadful lack.

It half convinces me that some great faculty,
Like hands, has been eternally lost and all
Our virtues now are the high and horrible
Ones of a streaming wound which heals in evil.

SADNESS, THEORY, GLASS

My poignant coffee does not last the twilight.
Gazing across the wide street through the central
Island of palms, I see the tight silk sky
As green as caterpillars, fretted by
The silhouettes of banks and consulates.
Cast up by war upon this neutral shore
I feel I should deliver a summing-up
Of all the passion, boredom, history,
Of all the suddenly important lives;
A rounded statement like Cézanne's of apples.
I wish I were as sure as he appears,
And wonder if the awful gaps in feeling,
Defects of seeing and experience,
Will vanish retrospectively, and this
Slight poetry, like a convex mirror, hold
A cosmos, Lilliputian but exact.

I see the future like a theory –
The proof of pamphlets, as ordained erectness
After an age of stooping, or the knowledge
Of murderous glaciers in a million years.
The future is tomorrow, but today
I fold my blanket and that moment is
Immense: I walk across the airfield and
The aircraft, like stuffed birds, are there for ever,
Horrible to the touch. The present is
A lucid but distorting medium,
As though the cunning of perspective had
Been lost by nature and all was flat and wild
And terribly more truthful. Only the past
Is real, because it stays as sadness, like
Old age remembering sexually its youth.
There is no luxury of sentiment –
Simply regret, as those regret in bedlams
Their last concession to their mania.

But we shall reach at last the day of death
Or hear guns die seditiously to silence.
There is a time when on reality
The vision fits, and sadness, theory, glass,
Fuse, and the mass directs its destiny.

The integration is the action, I
Can only scribble on the margin: here
We saw strange southern stars revolve above
The struck ship swaying from the pointed convoy;
Here kitted-up for sun, here snow; and strangely
Realized here that out of all the world
Only one other in our life would know us.

WHAT IS TERRIBLE

Life at last I know is terrible:
The innocent scene, the innocent walls and light
And hills for me are like the cavities
Of surgery or dreams. The visible might
Vanish, for all it reassures, in white.

This apprehension has come slowly to me,
Like symptoms and bulletins of sickness. I
Must first be moved across two oceans, then
Bored, systematically and sickeningly,
In a place where war is news. And constantly

I must be threatened with what is certainly worse:
Peril and death, but no less boring. And
What else? Besides my fear, my misspent time,
My love, hurt and postponed, there is the hand
Moving the empty glove; the bland

Aspect of nothing disguised as something; that
Part of living incommunicable,
For which we try to find vague adequate
Images, and which, after all,
Is quite surprisingly communicable.

Because in the clear hard light of war the ghosts
Are seen to be suspended by wires, and in
The old house the attic is empty: and the furious
Inner existence of objects and even
Ourselves is largely a myth: and for the sin

To blame our fathers, to attribute vengeance
To the pursuing chorus, and to live
In a good and tenuous world of private values,
Is simply to lie when only truth can give
Continuation in time to bread and love.

For what is terrible is the obvious
Organization of life: the oiled black gun,
And what it cost, the destruction of Europe by
Its councils; the unending justification
Of that which cannot be justified, what is done.

The year, the month, the day, the minute, at war
Is terrible and my participation
And that of all the world is terrible.
My living now must bear the laceration
Of the herd, and always will. What's done

To me is done to many. I can see
No ghosts, but only the fearful actual
Lives of my comrades. If the empty whitish
Horror is ever to be flushed and real,
It must be for them and changed by them all.

A WRY SMILE

The mess is all asleep, my candle burns.
I hear the rain sharp on the iron roof
And dully on the broad leaves by the window.
Already someone moans, another turns
And, clear and startling, cries 'Tell me the truth.'

The candle throws my shadow on the wall
And gilds my books: tonight I'd like to bring
The poets from their safe and paper beds,
Show them my comrades and the silver pall
Over the airfield, ask them what they'd sing.

Not one of them has had to bear such shame,
Been tortured so constantly by government,
Has had to draw his life out when the age
Made happiness a revolution, fame
Exile, and death the whimsy of a sergeant.

But without envy I remember them,
And without pity look at my condition:
I give myself a wry smile in the mirror
– The poets get a quizzical ahem.
They reflect time, I am the very ticking:

No longer divided – the unhappy echo
Of a great fault in civilization; inadequate,
Perhaps, and sad, but strictly conscious no one
Anywhere can move, nothing occur,
Outside my perfect knowledge or my fate.

SHORE LEAVE LORRY

The gigantic mass, the hard material,
That entering our atmosphere is all
Consumed in an instant in a golden tail,
Is not more alien, nor the moon more pale:
The darkness, countries wide, where muscled beasts
Cannot link fold on fold of mountains, least
Mysterious: the stars are not so still.
Compared with what? In low gear up the hill
The lorry takes its load of strange wan faces,
Which gaze where the loping lion has his bases,
Like busts. Over half the sky a meteor falls;
The gears grind; somewhere a suffering creature calls.

UPON A REVOLUTIONARY KILLED
IN THE WAR

One who would not escape
If he could, the boredom and danger;
A theory had visible shape
In his life. No delight or anger
Lightened his course, and all
The things that could occurred.
Actions can only kill:
Let his epitaph be a word.

[73]

SPRING 1943

I

The skies contain still groves of silver clouds,
The land is low and level, and the buzzards
Rise from a dead and stiff hyena. Hazards
Of war and seas divide me from the crowds
Whose actions alone give numbers to the years;
But all my emotions in this savage place
This moment have a pale and hungry face:
The vision metropolitan appears.
And as I leave the crawling carcase, turning
Into the scrub, I think of rain upon
Factories and banks, the shoulders of a meeting:
And thoughts that always crouch in wait come burning –
Slim naked legs of fabulous and fleeting
Dancers, and rooms where everyone has gone.

II

Always it is to you my thoughts return
From harrowing speculation on the age,
As though our love and you were fictional
And could not ever burn as cities burn,
Nor die as millions, but upon a page
Rested delightful, moving and immortal.
This momentary vision fades. Again
You join the sheeted world whose possible death
Is also ours, and our nostalgic breath
Expires across two continents of pain.
And clearly I see the organizations of
The oppressed, their dangerous and tiny actions,
The problematic serum of the factions,
In these decayed and crucial times, as love.

Intelligent, fair and strictly moral as
A heroine of Jane's; here where the hill
Is in another country and shadows pass
Like towns, I think of you so civilized still.
And in that chaos of Europe which surrounds
Your little calm I see those leaping, rising,
Almost engendered by the times, the hounds
Of courage, hawks of vision, and the surprising
Gazelles of love. And so I run through all
The virtues, and this hopeless, barbarous space,
Which sometimes I think the future's self, can fall
Into its ancient and forgotten place.
No, I will not believe that human art
Can fail to make reality its heart.

WAR LETTERS

The letters are shockingly real,
Like the personal belongings
Of someone recently dead.

The letters are permanent,
And written with our hands,
Which crease into their lines

And breathe, but are not so
Living as these letters.
Our hands are seas apart;

A pair might cease to live
While the indestructible letter,
Turned lies, flew to the other.

The letters express a love
We cannot realize:
Like a poignant glove

Surviving a well-known hand,
They can outlast our bodies
And our love transcend.

THE COAST

In the garden of the aerated water factory
Is an iron fountain and the doves
Come to its lip to drink.
Outside the totos are begging for five-cent pieces;
Boys whose faces are done in sepia, the places
Round their eyes and the irises still running.
One of them is in the fifth class at the Government School:
He wants to be a teacher and tells me
That London is very cold.
This white town is at the mouth of a river
Which holds a star-shaped island;
And all the islands of the coast
Have satisfying shapes
As, flat and green, they float upon the water.
The palms make brittle noises in the wind;
At night they are prodigious plumes; among them
The sailing crescent moon glows,
And clouds which in the daytime would be white
Fume across the stars.
In the garden I think of things
For which these are inadequate images.
The white doves in the sunlight flutter in the blown
Spray from the fountain.
There is no substitute for the harsh and terrible
Facts of the time, which only longing
And sadness cloak,
And which have grown meaningless and commonplace.
My thoughts wander to the strong and desirable
Body of a girl shown as she arranged her blanket,
The swollen and fibrous, frightening leg of a beggar,
And on the road to the hospital
The bloody negro borne by his friends.
Round them stretch the lovely and legendary islands,
The jewel-coloured sea, and far,
Cold Europe.

NIGHT

It is the null part of the night,
And I am sick of some intense
Dissociation from the act
Of living, as I wake and fight
Dark with my eyes, and every sense
Slowly perceives its offered fact.

Here are the pillows and the bed,
And here my stretched-out limbs; here
Sharply are matches and a book, the mess,
And my ranged comrades like the dead,
Invisible but with their near
And incoherent presences.

Hamlet had more diseases than
His age, and felt them when the gun
Was silent and his mother sleeping,
His gnawing for Ophelia thin:
It was the terror in the sun;
His happy body's curious weeping.

I strike a match and reach the door –
Deep green and light-reflecting palms,
High clouds and the higher empty sky,
The chaos of stars, the unseen shore
Of all the islands, and the arms
Of sea, as brilliant as an eye:

And no dead in their millions, no
Burning or torture, no nightmarish
Slippings down the abyss of time
Backwards, but only, as long ago
He looked, man looking on the garish,
Struggling to find it the sublime.

Emotionless, the forms of nature
Confront the upright system of cells,
That ailing and inadequate
Machine, that nerve and flesh-racked creature,
Who from his spirit's endless hells
Made his reality and fate.

[77]

CRUSTACEANS

Upon the beach are thousands of crabs; they are
Small, with one foreclaw curiously developed.
Against the ashen sand I see a forest
Of waving, pink, in some way human, claws.
The crabs advance or, perhaps, retreat a step
And then like Hamlet's father slowly beckon
With that flesh-coloured, yes, obscene, incisor.
These actions in the mass take on a rhythm
– The sexual display of higher beasts,
The dance of the tribe, or the enthusiasm
Of a meeting.
                    If you go closer to the crabs
You see that with their normal claws they are making
Spheres from the sand, small perfect rounds, which they,
After a little preliminary twiddling,
Produce from beneath their bodies suddenly,
Like jugglers, and deposit by their holes.
While this goes on, that monstrous foreclaw, that
Button hole, is motionless. And all around
The shafts sunk by these creatures lie the eggs
Of sand, so patiently, endlessly evolved.

At last I stretch and wave my hand: the crabs
Instantly bolt down their holes and pull a sphere,
A trap door, after them, and in a second
The beach is still.
                    While I was watching them
My eyes unfocused with the effort, or
Maybe it was the whole activity
Which like an idea detached itself from its
Frame, background: and I thought, are these that I
Regard with such pity, disgust, absorption, crabs?

[78]

THE PETTY OFFICERS' MESS

Just now I visited the monkeys: they
Are captive near the mess. And so the day
Ends simply with a sudden darkness, while
Again across the palm trees, like a file,
    The rain swings from the bay.

The radio speaks, the lights attract the flies,
Above them and the rain our voices rise,
And somewhere from this hot and trivial place
As the news tells of death, with pleasant face,
    Comes that which is not lies.

The voices argue: *Soldiers in the end*
Turn scarecrows; their ambiguous figures blend
With all who are obsessed by food and peace.
The rulers go, they cannot order these
    Who are not disciplined.

O cars with abdicating princes: streets
Of untidy crowds: O terrible defeats!
Such images which haunt us of the past
Flash on the present like the exile's vast
    Shivers and fleshy heats;

But never coincide. Do they approach?
Upon that doubt I'm frightened to encroach –
Show me, I say, *the organizations that*
Will change the rags and mob into the state,
    Like pumpkin into coach.

The voices make no answer. Music now
Throbs through the room and I remember how
The little pickaxe shapes of swallows swerve
From balconies and whitewashed walls; a curve
    Of bird-blue bay; a dhow:

Small stabbing observations! And I know
(The cheap song says it on the radio)
That nerves and skin first suffer when we part,
The deep insensitive tissues of the heart
    Later, when time is slow.

[79]

And time has done his part and stands and looks
With dumb exasperated face. The books
Year after year record the crisis and
The passion, but no change. The measuring sand
   Is still. There are no flukes,

Like the virtuous sulphonamides, to kill
The poisons of the age, but only will:
Reduction of desires to that cold plan
Of raping the ideal; the new frail man
   Who slays what's in the hill.

The monkeys near the mess (where we all eat
And dream) I saw tonight select with neat
And brittle fingers dirty scraps, and fight,
And then look pensive in the fading light,
   And after pick their feet.

They are secured by straps about their slender
Waists, and the straps to chains. Most sad and tender,
They clasp each other and look round with eyes
Like ours at what their strange captivities
   Invisibly engender.

TODAY AND TOMORROW

Tomorrow let us drive between the hills
And visit our good friends upon the farms,
Walking among the rows of sugar-cane
To look across their tassels at the snows.

And let us say good-day to sweet brown boys
Who keep their goats beneath that sheeted peak.
Tomorrow life will certainly be simple,
As at the drawing of an evening curtain.

Today there is the body to dispose of,
The blood to try to scour from all the house:
One must give lying smiles to calling neighbours
And soothe the children in the bedroom crying.

Today there is that terrible sense of guilt
And fear of being discovered; there is still
Regret for yesterday when everything
Was quiet and loving in tomorrow's way.

THE LEGIONS

When we have pissed away the marble walls,
And turned a foreign vandyke in the suns,
And lions wander in the ruined halls
And come and lick the barrels of our guns,
And the last letter has arrived and been
Forgotten, and the nights are dreamless –

                                    Then
Shall we be free? And turn for home, as lean
And baffled wolves turn for their starving den?
Or shall we merely look upon our nails
And see what kind of beast we have become;
And weep at that: or, if our nature fails,
Shrug, and descend to dancing and the drum?

Exile has sores which battle cannot make,
Changing the sick from sound, the truth from fake.

EMBARKATION IN WARTIME

I step (like one who makes without volition
A fatal but trivial decision)
From quay to deck. At once into my head
Comes the old thought of being dead –
But freshly and strangely, as in flight one sees
Aircraft not on sky but trees.

SEPTEMBER 3, 1943

Does anyone believe in what appears –
Caught in the sights of rifles, or the flames
Blurring a city, rubble, deserts, tears,
Or photographs of statesmen, lists of names?
No; the rough years, their flotsam of events
And men and objects are to us unreal
Who have a secret, incoherent life
As deep as wrecks, and cannot think or feel:
But urge on and dissipate the hours that should
Be precious; gloat on the mounting dead; who know
There must be so much ill before the good.
So much. Oh fearful knowledge, that of time
Makes simply an unbearable suspense
Between the anniversaries of doom!

THE EMOTION OF FICTION

Reading a book of tales
Which has stirred my imagination,
I have put down the book
And stared at the congregation
Of shadows and hollows which then
Made up the world; and found
Such meaning in meaningless things –
The neutral, patterned ground,
The figures on the sky –
As made me ache to tell
The single secret that runs,
Like a tendon, through it all.
And I could promise then
An overwhelming word,
A final revelation –
The image of a seabird
With scimitars of wings,
Pathetic feet tucked away,
A fine, ill-omened name,
Sweeping across the grey.
And I knew then the purpose
Of everything; that illusion

That comes in the unexpected
Moment, an aimed explosion.
Perhaps the object of art
Is this: the communication
Of that which cannot be told.
Worse: the rich explanation
That there is nothing to tell;
Only the artificial
Plot and ambiguous word,
The forged but sacred missal.
Even the word becomes
Merely a path to meaning;
It is the plot that stays
Longest, a model of leaning
Out over raging seas,
As if our ship or longing
Could weather infinite water
Or fatal, ghostly thronging.
If one could invent a plot
Whose action was slow as life
But vivid and absorbing,
With a last twist of the knife,
Virtues of furious neatness,
Coincidence, surprise,
The loves of the old or plain
Made plausible as lies.
And all to be ideal,
Even the gross and stupid
Details of passion and death
That one can never decide
Whether nothing or everything –
And then? Would that be more
Precise than this intense
But vague emotion? Roar,
Lions of living flesh,
On bone-strewed plains! It is
The winged and semi-human
Monsters of civilized myths
Whose terrible questions, above
Familiar evil or good,
Are unanswerable, but
Whose tongue is understood.

THE STATUE

The noises of the harbour die, the smoke is petrified
Against the thick but vacant, fading light, and shadows slide
From under stone and iron, darkest now. The last birds glide.

Upon this black-boned, white-splashed, far receding vista of
grey
Is an equestrian statue, by the ocean, trampling the day,
Its green bronze flaked like petals, catching night before the
bay.

Distilled from some sad, endless, sordid period of time,
As from the language of disease might come a consummate
rhyme,
It tries to impose its values on the port and on the lime –

The droppings that by chance and from an uncontrollable
And savage life have formed a patina upon the skull;
Abandoned, have blurred a bodied vision once thought spare
but full –

On me, as authority recites to boys the names of queens.
Shall I be dazzled by the dynasties, the gules and greens,
The unbelievable art, and not recall their piteous means?

Last night I sailed upon that sea whose starting place is here,
Evaded the contraptions of the enemy, the mere
Dangers of water, saw the statue and the plinth appear.

Last night between the crowded, stifling decks I watched a man,
Smoking a big curved pipe, who contemplated his great wan
And dirty feet while minute after tedious minute ran –

This in the city now, whose floor is permanent and still,
Among the news of history and sense of an obscure will,
Is all the image I can summon up, my thought's rank kill;

As though there dominated this sea's threshold and this night
Not the raised hooves, the thick snake neck, the profile, and the
might,
The wrought, eternal bronze, the dead protagonist, the fight,

But that unmoving, pale but living shape that drops no tears,
Ridiculous and haunting, which each epoch reappears,
And is what history is not. O love, O human fears!

RETURN

There is before the night,
For us, a foreign twilight.
The grey waves rise and splinter:
We voyage into winter.
Beyond the disc of sea
Stretches our northern country.
Our blood made thin by burning
And poison is returning.
Is it too late, too late,
For dreams to approximate?
Will the port be the same,
Or have another name:
The road, the house, the wife,
Only a spectral life?

INVASION BARGES IN THE CLYDE, 1943

Like new growth pushing through dead stalks –
Barges cocooned in girders in the yard.
These are the hearses for a generation,
Impersonal as a fatal card.

Over the little houses goes,
Like silk released, a flight of foam-white gulls,
While the indifferent workers clang and weld
The soon-to-be historic hulls.

Far off, those birds fall on the waves
Where rock preceded, will outdistance, man:
Their cries, the spray, the sea-black stone proclaim
Absence of destiny or plan.

Who can help weighing loneliness
And chaos against the town's precarious order?
Life after life inexorably flies
From off the system's whirling border.

Over a haunting formless sky
Barges and men eventually will move,
Saved only from constituent dust and ore
By history's spiral, luck's last groove.

WINTER IN CAMP

I

A three-badge killick in the public bar
Voluptuously sups his beer. The girl
Behind the counter reads an early *Star*.
Suddenly from the radio is a whirl
Of classical emotion, and the drums
Precisely mark despair, the violin
Unending ferment. Some chrysanthemums
Outside the window, yellow, pale, burn thin.

Not only these strange winter flowers take on
In this dread air the meaning of a myth,
But all the common objects now have gone
Into the littoral which borders death.
The ancient sailor holds an unplumbed glass;
The girl is instantly a sculptured mass.

II

The music and the shadows in the dark
Cinema stir a huge, authentic feeling,
And, when the lights come on, the shabby ceiling,
The scarred green walls and seats confirm the stark
Contrast between the crust and infinite deeps.
I go to the canteen, ramshackle, warm,
And move among the poor anonymous swarm;
I am awake but everybody sleeps.

Outside: the moonlit fields, the cruel blue –
Which box another world; as that absurd
Material life of sonneteers contains
A second, utterly unlike, self-made,
And contradicting all experience
Except this rarest, fearfullest, most true.

III

The trees I thought so cold and black and bare
In the late afternoon sprung softest browns:
The rain had stopped, and through the perspex air
The low sun made the land as green as downs.
The country hovered on a neutral edge;
And I was startled by a startled bird
Fluttering among the bayonets of the hedge –
And this is the illusion of the word.

Beyond the word, the chosen images,
Painful and moving as they are, I feel
Unutterably the epoch's tragedies,
Beside which this scene's cruelties are real
But hopelessly inadequate; like the pities
Of living airmen borne above smashed cities.

IV

What we imagined tortuously and dreaded
Comes like a friend advancing from the dark;
The morning sheet emphatically is leaded
With news of cities gone – and left unread.
And even as I write this, overhead,
The bombers fly to Europe. As I write:
In this bare camp, in country like a park,
Where uniforms and rain make thick the night.

Who now this winter dreads and who imagines?
The years of war pile on our heads like lime,
And horrors grow impersonal as engines;
Nor can I think in discipline and slime.
Perhaps beside some blue and neutral lake
Another Lenin sorts the real from fake.

[87]

V

Day after day upon the concrete square,
Cargo for sinking iron, sweaty places,
The men assemble with their cold, cramped faces,
Then go, for me forever, into air.
Their minds are full of images of fear,
Unending lust, their bodies in the traces
Of conformation: and the brief time races.
How will they recognize the crucial year?

Now man must be political or die;
Nor is there really that alternative.
Correctly to be dedicated and to live
By chance, is what the species asks. The sky
Is smutted with migrating birds or ships;
The kiss of winter is with cracking lips.

VI

And everywhere is that enormous lie;
So obvious that it seems to be the truth:
Like the first moment of a conjurer's failure,
Or visions of love from waves of cheap perfume
In villages on Sunday afternoons.
It even penetrates this quiet room,
Where three men round a stove are talking.
'The strikers should be shot,' one says: his hand
A craftsman's, capable and rough. The second:
'Niggers and Jews I hate.' It is the squawking
Of an obscene and guiltless bird. They sit,
Free men, in prison. And the third: 'I hate
Nobody' – raising, to gesticulate,
His arm in navy with a gun on it.

VII

Defined, undazzling, paper thin, the sun
At dusk: the moon at morning with the ghastly
Brightness of violet or mere decay.
And what, unconscious, we have truly done
Is done, and there remains the girl, the gun –
Embedded, actual, in the staring day
Night's symbols almost overwhelm us. Lastly:
The world which suffers of these things subtraction.

For what is now our life is neither dreams
Nor their more intricate and sensual stuff,
But that which to posterity descends
As formulae and measurements; which seems
To diggers, tombs, to critics, words; enough
To change the role of horses, hump waste sands.

VIII

What does the robin whisper and the trees,
Expressive of wind and winter, round this coast,
The human flesh that might contain a ghost?
Only plain words like *oil* and *manganese*.
It is not that our sensibilities
Are dead: what moved and frightened in the past
Confronts us still; still we construct the vast
Network of space from small realities.

But now the rotten crimson robes are falling,
What shaped them seen as bones with common names.
Magic is smothered under bribes, concessions:
Nothing beside the war can be appalling.
The victims of the sacrificial games
Discerned no symbolism in the lions.

My working-party hacks the grass, the tall
Tubers of summer rusty as the sickle.
In camp a season, these young men have all
A respite from the battle over nickel
– Or dynasties or rubber, anything
But what is mass-induced into their heads.
And while they work they sentimentally sing:
As credulously they will go to beds
As graves.

        Their weakness is the measure of
My own; their guilt my own inactive past;
Their stormy future mine, who wish that love
Could melt the guns, expropriate a caste.
How, when my only rank is consciousness,
Can I despise them, far less pity, bless?

EPITAPHS FOR SOLDIERS

I

Passing soldier stop and think
I was once as sad as you,
Saw in history a brink
More fearful than a bayonet's blue
– And left to what I thought but birds
The human message of these words.

II

Incredibly I lasted out a war,
Survived the unnatural, enormous danger
Of each enormous day. And so befell
A peril more enormous and still stranger:
The death by nature, chanceless, credible.

WINTER NIGHT

An owl is hooting in the grove,
The moonlight makes the night air mauve,
The trees are regular as crystals,
The thawing road shines black as pistols,
And muffled by the quiet snow
The wind is only felt to blow.
Dread bird that punctually calls!
Its sound inhuman strangely falls
Within the human scale; and I
Am forced to place (besides the cry)
The moon, the trees, the swollen snow,
Reluctantly with what I know.
Even the road conveys the sense
Of being outside experience;
As though, this winter night of war,
The world we made were mine no more.

DURING A BOMBARDMENT BY
V-WEAPONS

The little noises of the house:
Drippings between the slates and ceiling;
From the electric fire's cooling,
Tickings; the dry feet of a mouse:

These at the ending of a war
Have power to alarm me more
Than the ridiculous detonations
Outside the gently coughing curtains.

And, love, I see your pallor bears
A far more pointed threat than steel.
Now all the permanent and real
Furies are settling in upstairs.

EPILOGUE

No day seems final but there must be one
When death completes what was fragmentary,
And makes a symbol from futility,
As when the curtain falls, the audience gone,
There is a meaning though was purposed none.

And even all the war-lopped lives that we
Find so grotesque have, as the prowling sea
Or bullet comes to them, a satisfaction;
Dying they turn in retrospect to art.

So in our time all art seems meaningless,
Confused with life as brain might change to heart:
Who would invent when he as well might guess?

And where the pattern in the whole when part
Is virtuous, pitiful, complete, no less?

PART THREE

Mainly from
Epitaphs and Occasions
(1949) and
Counterparts
(1954)

DEDICATORY EPISTLE,
WITH A BOOK OF 1949

To Jack Clark and Alan Ross

Here's proof – as if one needed any –
Of Fuller's classic parsimony.
One volume, two dedicatees;
So little verse and less to please.
Alan, I hear you say, behind
That manner which is always kind:
'No meat, and where's the bloody gravy?
He wrote much better in the Navy.'
And you, Jack, glancing up from Proust:
'It's compromise come home to roost.'

Hysteria is the destiny
Of those who want, insatiably,
In childhood love; and the condition
Of being wet in bed's ambition.
What kind of pasts must we have led
That now we're neither red nor dead?
We had our fill of love and hunger
When uninhibited and younger:
After we lost the initial breast
We knew a falling off of zest;
And while the workless topped three million
Read Eliot in the pavilion;
For us the Reichstag burned to tones
Of Bach on hand-made gramophones;

[95]

We saw the long-drawn fascist trauma
In terms of the poetic drama;
And even the ensuing war
For most was something of a bore.

Dear Clark, it's you to whom I speak,
As one who hovered in that clique:
A wit and cause of wit in others;
Who called the working-class half-brothers;
Easy at Lords or Wigmore Hall;
A nibbler at the off-side ball –
We would have moved, were held, alas,
In the paralysis of class.
We spoke our thoughts not loud and bold
But whispered through the coward's cold;
And all the time, with deadly humour,
Inside us grew the traitor's tumour.
Nothing I say can warn, console,
You who've survived the liberal rôle,
And in a world of Camps and Bomb
Wait for the end with false aplomb.

The nineteenth century dream of good
Erecting barricades of wood
And storming keypoints of reaction
To substitute its kindly faction,
Until what's violent and rotten
Withers like warts tied round with cotton –
Such vision fades, and yet our age
Need not become the last blank page,
And though the future may be odd
We shouldn't let it rest with God;
Confused and wrong though things have gone
There is a side we can be on:
Distaste for lasting bread and peace
May thus support a king in Greece,
And trust in General Chiang Kai-shek
Will safely lead to freedom's wreck.

Our dreams no longer guard our sleep:
The noses of the road-drills creep,
With thoughts of death, across the lawn
Out of the swarthy urban dawn.

And one by one, against our will,
The cultured cities vanish till
We see with horror just ahead
The sudden end of history's thread.
Ross, with your innings' lead of years,
Such brooding will not bring your tears.
You lived when doom was not the fashion,
What's sad for you is human passion.
Your verse is sensuous, not spare,
Somerset in, not Lancashire.
We disagree in much, I know:
I'm over-fond of Uncle Joe;
You find in Auden not an era –
Simply a poet who grows queerer;
The working-class for you's a fact,
No statue in the final act.
Yet we should never come to blows
On this – that man as artist goes,
And in that rôle, most sane, most free,
Fulfils his spacious infancy;
That truth's half feeling and half style,
And feeling and no style is vile.
About us lie our elder writers,
Small, gritty, barren, like detritus:
Resistance to the epoch's rage
Has not survived their middle age.
The type of ivory tower varies
But all live in the caves of caries.
The younger men, not long from mother,
Write articles about each other,
Examining, in solemn chorus,
Ten poems or a brace of stories.
The treason of the clerks is when
They make a fetish of the pen,
Forget that art has duties to –
As well as to the 'I' – the 'You',
And that its source must always be
What presses most, most constantly.
Since Sarajevo there has been
Only one thing the world could mean,
And each successive crisis shows
That meaning plainer than a nose.
To write what he was going through,

Sassoon to the Georgians said 'Napoo';
And Owen knew why he was born –
To state the truth and thus to warn.
The poet now must put verse back
Time and again upon the track
That first was cut by Wordsworth when
He said that verse was meant for men,
And ought to speak on all occasions
In language which has no evasions.

Dear friends, I wish this book bore out
More than the bourgeois' fear and doubt.
Alas, my talent and my way
Of life are useless for today.
I might have cut a better figure
When peace was longer, incomes bigger.
The 'nineties would have seen me thrive,
Dyspeptic, bookish, half-alive.
Even between the wars I might
With luck have written something bright.
But now, I feel, the 'thirties gone,
The dim light's out that could have shone.
My richest ambiguity
Is nightmares now, not poetry:
After eight lines the latter ends
Unless I'm babbling to my friends.
The arteries and treaties harden,
The shadow falls across the garden,
And down the tunnel of the years
The spectre that we feared appears.
Gazing upon our love or book,
Between the lines or in the look,
We see that choice must fall at last,
And the immortal, lucky past –
Thinking of bed or lying in it –
Cry out and crumble in a minute.
For such times are these poems meant,
A muted, sparse accompaniment,
Until the Wagner we await
Provides a score that's up to date,
And world and way and godheads pass
To vulgar but triumphant brass.

ON SEEING THE LENI RIEFENSTAHL
FILM OF THE 1936 OLYMPIC GAMES

The nation's face above the human shape,
Sunlight on leaf, gloved skin and water pearled
– No art can hide the shocking gulfs that gape
Even between such bodies and their world.

Art merely lets these tenants of a star
Run once again with legendary ease
Across the screen and years towards that war
Which lay in wait for them like a disease.

ON HEARING BARTOK'S CONCERTO
FOR ORCHESTRA

Instinct with the division of labour peals
The sonorous and manufactured brass:
The lonely instrument and player caught
   And transcended by the mass.

At such art in our time one cannot help
But think with love and terror of the double
Man, and the puzzling dumb notation under
   Floors of the future's rubble.

SCHWERE GUSTAV

Schwere Gustav, built by Krupps,
Was the largest of all guns:
Of thirty-one-inch calibre,
It fired a shell of seven tons.

Worked by fifteen hundred troops
Topped by a general, no less,
Gustav fired two rounds a day,
But after sixty was u/s.

The soldiers seeing Gustav's barrel
Huge against the eastern sky,
And his complicated breech,
Knew why they had got to die.

Accumulated capital
Made possible this symbol of
Our deep, ridiculous desires.
O war, O Gustav and O love!

FATHERS AND SONS

Their sons, grown-up, the spectres lay;
The house is still again and light.
And then to war were marched away
Their sons, grown-up. The spectres lay.
The sons return: once more the grey
Figures make terrible the night.
Their sons, grown-up, the spectres lay:
The house is still again and light.

THE DIVIDED LIFE RE-LIVED

Once again the light refracted through the dusty crimson air
Leaves the spaces of the evening blurred and bare.
Bats that flicker round the edges of the square Victorian lawn
Symbolize the bourgeois soul from life withdrawn.

Now the sunset blackbird touches us, upon the withered tree,
With its rather disappointing melody,
And against the chalky purple thrown by distant main-road arcs
Flow the tired suburban leaves like mouldy sparks.

Here the mower furred with grass like filings round a magnet's
                                                            pole,
Teacups left for ants to make our fortunes droll;
While we sit and try to think that everything is not too late –
Sparrows sitting on the sad outfield of fate.

Once and only once we were in touch with brutal, bloody life
When we got in or kept out of global strife;
And in desert or in dockyard met our coarser fellow men,
Wielding friendly gun or scrubber, not our pen.

How we innocently thought that we should be alone no more,
Linked in death or revolution as in war.
How completely we have slipped into the same old world of cod,
Our companions Henry James or cats or God.

Waiting for the evening as the time of passion and of verse,
Vainly hoping that at both we shan't get worse;
While outside the demon scientists and rulers of the land
Pile the bombs like fiddler-crabs pile balls of sand.

And the best that we can wish for is that still the moon will rise
Enigmatic, cracked and yellow to men's eyes,
And illuminate the manuscripts of poems that foretold
All the ruin and survival of the old.

MEDITATION

Now the ambassadors have gone, refusing
Our gifts, treaties, anger, compliance;
And in their place the winter has arrived,
Icing the culture-bearing water.
We brood in our respective empires on
The words we might have said which would have breached
The Chinese wall round our superfluous love
And manufactures. We do not brood too deeply.
There are our friends' perpetual, subtle demands
For understanding: visits to those who claim
To show us what is meant by death,
And therefore life, our short and puzzling lives,
And to explain our feelings when we look
Through the dark sky to other lighted worlds –
The well-shaved owners of sanatoria,
And raving, grubby oracles: the books
On diet, posture, prayer and aspirin art:
The claims of frightful weapons to be investigated:
Mad generals to be promoted: and
Our private gulfs to slither down in bed.

Perhaps in Spring the ambassadors will return.
Before then we shall find perhaps that bombs,
Books, people, planets, worry, even our wives,
Are not at all important. Perhaps
The preposterous fishing-line tangle of undesired
Human existence will suddenly unravel
Before some staggering equation
Or mystic experience, and God be released
From the moral particle or blue-lit room.
Or, better still, perhaps we shall, before
Anything really happens, be safely dead.

STANZAS

In the year's autumnal rage
When nations and leaves are rank
And with great tenderness
Horses stand head to flank,
Motionless under stress,
Upon their plinth of green,
I burrow through my age
To the cause of what has been.

The cause of what has been
Is fixed in the sensual past.
It was then that the deed or thought
Fulfilling the pattern was cast.
But the memory that ought
To give release from guilt
Hides in the stone ravine
That culture and time have built.

Culture and time have built
Their state upon a flaw:
The anguished faces gaze
From cold, symmetrical law.
And the happy beasts still graze
In their instinctive wood
Who have never plunged to the hilt
In their prince and father's blood.

Their prince and father's blood
In trivial, terrible guise
Returns to ferocious youth.
The sane cannot recognize
Their dreams, nor the mad the truth.
And into darkness the age
Whirls its pathetic good
In the year's autumnal rage.

1948

Reading among the crumbs of leaves upon
The lawn, beneath the thin October sun,
I hear behind the words
And noise of birds
The drumming aircraft; and am blind till they have gone.

The feeling that they give is now no more
That of the time when we had not reached war:
It is as though the lease
Of crumbling peace
Had run already and that life was as before.

For this is not the cancer or the scream,
A grotesque interlude, but what will seem
On waking to us all
Most natural –
The gnawed incredible existence of a dream.

VIRTUE

In these old hackneyed melodies
Hollow in the piano's cage
I see the whole trash of the age –
    Art, gadgets, bombs and lies.

Such tunes can move me to confess
The trash moves, too: that what offends
Or kills can in its simplest ends,
    Being human, also bless.

EPITAPH

Whoever you may be,
Killed by the times or time,
Lie underneath this rhyme
And feed the berried tree.
We cannot outlast verse
And verse lives best on this.
But stone can split. No worse
Chance of continuance is
The change to vegetable,
Immortal on the rubble.

THE LAKE

Once more the meditative poem. Léman,
Its peacock and turquoise in the random shapes
Of birthmarks, laps the shore where all the famous
Wrote in a storm of sails and alps and grapes.

The French side lifts its dark and green-pored face:
The train runs through the terraces to war:
Northwards the weather speaks: only upon
This sunlit hub is reason any more.

Chess-like, political energy, exerted
Across the squares and diamonds of states,
Gradually drove those masters to a corner
In which the obsessive thought was human fate.

Rousseau and Gibbon found in history
And love small freedom for the personal will:
And next the revolving clock-arm swept the blue
On Shelley, and pushed Byron farther still.

Then action ended: there was merely sadness –
Arnold returning to a *fait accompli*.
Around the lake the world fell twice in ruins.
The lake became anachronistic simply.

The trunks of plane trees dappled like giraffes;
The six blurred cygnets and the crystal swans;
The ancient gravel; peaks that float at night,
Veined with the peach of blood their skeletons;

Lizards, damp lashes, on the sun-dry stone;
Beyond the morning blinds the swallows shrieking
Like silk in skeins; the steamer's innocent missions –
Of these it is quite pointless to be speaking.

For all the symbols which the poets used
While the fires quivered and the needle turned,
Have lost their aliases, and can be uttered
Here only, where the century has not burned.

Perhaps there are new tropes for our own world
Where, in their madmen's stupor, empires wait,
The flies of factions on their rigid masks,
Lost in a dream of homicide and fate.

I do not know. I feel the lake preserved
For some new Gibbon's mildly-stirred repose,
In which, long after, lake-bound, he translates
Our frightful end to ornamental prose.

KNOLE

Inside the sombre walls the neat quadrangles still are green
As though a light shone on them from a sun, grey-masked,
                                                        unseen.

And some remoter light leans through the embrasures of the
                                                        house
And frees the colours of the hangings – crimson, lime and
                                                        mouse.

The firedogs dangerous weapons, beds tents, rooms an insect's
                                                        maze,
But nothing burns, loves, spies, through rain- or history-nervous
                                                        days.

An ancient painted Sackville down the chamber from the frame
Looks over what has lost its meaning yet is still the same.

He stares and will stare pointlessly, stiff in his mint brocades,
Hair reddish, bearded, white of hand, until our living fades.

His face the worried, capable, Elizabethan face,
He stands with the fresh-created ruler's half self-conscious
grace.

Of savagery, the codpiece in the fairy's clothes remains;
All else the civilizing new discovery of gain.

Vestigial organs in their jars his stuffs and filigree:
The capital he started now explodes spontaneously.

But still outside, upon the deer-striped lawns, the trees are
caught
Spread in the sheltering crystal of the mansion's stored-up
thought;

And like those dreams of treasure only stir to accumulate
Their golden leaves in natural rhythms, endless, sad, sedate.

In this calm magic island in tempestuous seas, the plan
Holds yet: the spirits of earth and air still serve the passionate
man.

CHEKHOV

Chekhov saw life as a series of departures;
Its crises blurred by train times, bags, galoshes.
Instead of saying the important word
The hurried characters only breathe Farewell.

And what there was of meaning in it all
Is left entirely to the minor figures:
Aged or stupid, across the deserted stage,
They carry, like a tray, the forgotten symbol.

EMILY DICKINSON

A few old props, a few new words –
  The drama breathes again:
And in the parlour, on the lawn,
  Blood ambles from its den.

The simple, solitary life
  Imagining, feeling all,
Postures and dabbles in the red
  Behind the bedroom wall.

And from those withered lips there come
  The world-deceiving cries:
'Love has no need of flesh.' 'The soul
  Perceives eternities.'

POETS

Of course, it's not a demon which possesses
Poets at that wild moment when the verse
Admits the saved-up image like a purse.
It is the id which has arranged its cesses
So as to season the prim ego's guesses.
Whether the thing goes better then or worse
Depends upon the gift or on the curse,
The poet's public life and private messes.
What wonder then that in the authentic go –
Romantic woolly hit or austere miss:
Running on nylon legs or broken castors –
Is some huge ambiguity, as though
The last line of a poem such as this
Were dead gold leaves against the garish asters.

EPITAPH FOR A SPY

Because his infancy was fixed on prying
His fated choice of a career was spying:
And so what father threatened was fulfilled –
The curiosity for secrets killed.

THE HERO

When the hero's task was done
And the beast lay underground,
In the time that he had won
From the fates that pushed him round

He had space to contemplate
How the peasants still were bled
And that in the salvaged state
Worms continued at the head.

Little space: already, where
Sweetly he enjoyed his fish,
Seeing through the shouldered hair
Loosening sails and dirty dish,

Gasped a pale new plea for aid.
Cleaning his gun later, he
Felt with awe the old beast's shade
Fall across the wine-dark sea.

IMAGE AND FOSSIL

The infant innocently thinks the adult free from error,
Free from anxiety and lacking in the dark his terror.

The father wonders how the son can break the imprisoning
                                                    pattern
Of cells that over generations stretch unaltered, slattern.

The ageing poet thinks: 'Shall I continue to find strange themes?'
As he removes himself from action and forgets his dreams.

The civilization which observes its fatal symptoms asks:
'When I am gone will the barbarians set themselves my tasks?'

Through ice-ages of space the dubious particles move on,
Till the round destinies rise in them, brilliant, one by one.

Image and fossil undefeated lie among the lives
That fell in tragedy or plain despair upon their knives.

[108]

To worlds undreamt of in the shrinking orbit of our fears
Fly and take root like vivid grass the marvellous careers.

THE FIVE HAMLETS

The murdered king was Hamlet, and his spectre.
Hamlet, the son, a copy of the dead.
The sacrifice, foreteller and protector;
Dragon and guilt and hero in one head.

But this was only art: my child I called
Hamlet, who breathed and clung about his mother,
Remembering that former son, appalled,
Who saw his darling taken by another.

For I am that real Hamlet who endured,
And gave his rival all for which he burned:
Whose love collapsed in wrinkles, though uncured;
Whose ghost returned, returned, returned, returned.

LITTLE FABLE

The mouse like halting clockwork, in the light
A shade of biscuit, curved towards the right

And hid behind the gas stove, peeping out
A sickly moment with its pencil snout.

Its run was blocked to keep it in the wall
But at the time it was not there at all.

The food is covered and a penny trap,
Being bought, is baited with a bacon scrap.

Its back is guillotined and seen to be
Grey and not brown, its feet formed properly.

Thus the obscene becomes pathetic and
What mind had feared is stroked by hand.

THE FAMILY CAT

This cat was bought upon the day
That marked the Japanese defeat;
He was anonymous and gay,
But timorous and not discreet.

Although three years have gone, he shows
Fresh sides of his uneven mind:
To us – fond, lenient – he grows
Still more eccentric and defined.

He is a grey, white-chested cat,
And barred with black along the grey;
Not large, and the reverse of fat,
His profile good from either way.

The poet buys especial fish,
Which is made ready by his wife;
The poet's son holds out the dish:
They thus maintain the creature's life.

It's not his anniversary
Alone that's his significance:
In any case mortality
May not be thought of in his presence.

For brief as are our lives, more brief
Exist. Our stroking hides the bones,
Which none the less cry out in grief
Beneath the mocking loving tones.

TO MY SON

When you can understand
This endless paper that I cover,
With what strange feeling will you find
That I feared and loved, was sensitive, not clever.

For it's to you I write
(My only true posterity)
This verse that seems not to better what
I seized from environment and ancestry.

I should not mind your smile
At all the crudities and gaps –
By that less likely yourself to fail
To raise up character and living's lapse.

Critic and art in one;
Not tied by fate and yet unfree;
The classic killer, loving son;
Yes, you'll know each word I add is irony.

THE GAZE

Catching myself obliquely in the glass,
I thought I saw my father.
He died at my age now, but the years that pass
Do not destroy him – rather
Make him resume his dense forgotten mass.

Although the memory of his face has gone
I know mine different,
And what I see in mirrors is the wan
Dwarf that the orbit bent –
The Dog-star's mysterious companion.

How well I understand what he transmitted!
The gaze that travelling
At will through the generations sees the pitted
Mask of the timeless thing,
And knows itself both weak and dedicated.

[111]

SLEEPING AND WAKING

I

I saw her tiny figure at the end
Of that tremendous, bare room of my dream.
During the swift but hours-long journey, penned
To one thought and one look, there did not seem

Another life to which this was the key.
Desire was of intolerable weight
And tenderness beneath the anxiety
That she would go and I should be too late.

Her slender back towards me slowly grew
Into the copy of reality.
But then instead of that clear face I knew
She turned the future's sunken anguished lie.

Waking or sleeping now I see no more
What we imagined, only what we are.

II

My sleep stopped like a play. The lights came on,
And there was only normal life again:
The first birds tapping at the lawn, the rain
Still mottled on the glass. The shapes had gone
That woke me with their mimic of the past,
And showed too real for consciousness the meaning
Which, by the unremembered act and leaning
Wish, is upon the ambiguous present cast.

And yet the terror stayed. Inside these walls,
And coloured by the livid wash of dawn,
The darling sleepers copied death. I lay
Beside them, like an aeronaut who falls
To worse from danger, till the drapes were drawn
Upon the safe caged savagery of day.

BALLAD

Father, through the dark that parts us,
Through the howling winds I hear,
Come and drive away this dabbled
Ghost I fear.

But I've crossed the dark already
And am part of all you hear,
I shall never leave you, darling,
Do not fear.

NURSERY RHYME

Than the outlook of the ulcer
Nothing could be falser,
And the way of living of
The psychosis is not love.

In the good society
Morbid art's not necessary.
It's a sick subhuman voice
Comes from Kafka, Proust and Joyce.

After much analysis
Freud found he could not tell lies.
But in most there is no truth
After the initial tooth.

Though among both poor and rich
Are found the bully and the bitch,
Only those who haven't got
Can be free of what they've not.

Round the massive legs of man
Scuttle all the little men,
Busy planning for what's great
Their own ludicrous charred fate.

SONG

The blonde who reads *Prediction*,
The curate who reads Marx,
The poet who writes fiction,
The dog-lover who barks,
The dying who feel better,
The girl who buys quinine,
The wrist inside the fetter,
The bed behind the screen;

To such the ultimatum,
The test-tube in the rack,
The advertised pomatum,
The weakness of the back,
The psychopathic leader,
The laisser-faire of God,
The parent who's a bleeder,
The sergeant who's a sod,

Provide a normal setting
For runners in an age
Where life's not in the betting
And love's not on the stage,
Where there's no neat solution
For melting wills or gold,
And hope is revolution
And revolution's sold.

HYMN

Tell us how we can arrive at
Secrets locked behind the veil –
Byron's foot and James's privates,
Why Pope was pale.

Why we cannot still recall
What we did in bed with father –
Or what nurse said through the wall,
If you'd rather.

Put us in the way of knowing
Why we work our hair to toupees,
While the idle rich are flowing
In drop-head coupés.

Tell us why we wish for peace
While our nation swells its forces,
Why in others lust to crease
Us madly courses.

Now from all the ghastly land
Rise the swirling tea-leaves of
Rooks, and syphilitic stand
Stone boys of love.

Over bile-hued fields of May
Shines the day-time moon, a bone,
From them in this sad today
A light has flown.

While the leaders point, enraged,
And their people groan like ice,
Quietly sit the mad, engaged
With phantom lice.

Teach us thus to live in patience,
If you cannot teach us more,
Till progressive cerebration
Stops with war.

THE CIVILIZATION

By their frock-coated leaders,
By the frequency of their wars,
By the depth of their hunger,
Their numberless refugees,
And the brevity of their verse,
They were distinguished.

Their revolutions
Were thwarted by kisses.
The cold mathematicians
Aged into blurred philosophers.
Their poets choked on
The parallel of past calamities.

Their funeral customs, art,
Physique, and secret
Societies, unequal:
Their doom inevitable.
Ambiguous as dreams
Their symbolic poetry.

Yes, it had happened
Before. Ill-pictured leaders,
Food-queues in foodless places,
Migration to areas
Of moderate terror,
Monotonous poems.

Then horses galloping
Over burned foundations,
Ascetic communities,
The improbable moon,
Death from a cut,
Bleak, eroded spaces;

And eventually the strangers,
With the luxury of spices,
Effective weapons,
Their tales of travel,
Their ikons of leaders,
Their epic verse.

OBITUARY OF R. FULLER

We note the death, with small regret,
Of one who'd scarcely lived, as yet.
Born just before the First World War,
Died when there'd only been one more:
Between, his life had all been spent
In the small-bourgeois element,
Sheltered from poverty and hurt,
From passion, tragedy and dirt.
His infant traumas somewhat worse,
He would have written better verse,
His youth by prudence not so guided
His politics been more decided.
In the event his life was split
And half was lost bewailing it:
Part managerial, part poetic –
Hard to decide the more pathetic.
Avoiding China, Spain and Greece,
He passed his adult years of peace
In safe unease, with thoughts of doom
(As birth is feared inside the womb) –
Doom of his talent and his place,
Doom, total, of the human race.
This strange concern for fellow creatures
Had certainly some pathic features.
He could not understand that death
Must be the lot of all with breath,
And crudely linked felicity
With dying from senile decay,
Finding no spiritual worth
In guided missiles, torture, dearth.
Quite often he was heard to babble
'Poets should be intelligible'
Or 'What determines human fate
Is the class structure of the state'
Or 'Freud and Marx and Dickens found –
And so do I – souls not profound'.
These views were logically a feature

Of his rude, egotistic nature –
So unemotional and shy
Such friends as he retained would cry
With baffled boredom, thankful they
Were not part of his family.

If any bit of him survives
It will be that verse which contrives
To speak in private symbols for
The peaceful caught in public war.
For there his wavering faith in man
Wavers around some sort of plan,
And though foreseeing years of trouble,
Denies a universal rubble,
Discovering in wog and sailor
The presages of bourgeois failure.
Whether at this we weep or laugh
It makes a generous epitaph.

RHETORIC OF A JOURNEY

The train takes me away from the northern valleys
Where I lived my youth and where my youth lives on
In the person of my parent and the stone walls,
The dialect of love I understand
But scarcely speak, the mills and illnesses.

In Trollope's novel open on my knee
The characters are worried about money:
The action revolves round the right to a necklace.
I have only to bend my head and immediately
I am lost in this other reality, the world
Of art, where something is always missing.
In *The Eustace Diamonds* life is made tolerable
By standing away from time and refusing to write
Of the hours that link the official biography.

I think of the poem I wrote on another visit –
A list of the poet's hoarded perceptions:
The net of walls thrown over waves of green,
The valleys clogged with villages, the cattle
Pink against smoking mills – and only now
Experience what was delayed and omitted.
For those were rooms in which we dared not look
At each other's load of emotion: it was there
Our past had to die: and where we acknowledged
With pain and surprise our ties with the disregarded.
I would like to renounce the waking rational life,
The neat completed work, as being quite
Absurd and cowardly; and leave to posterity
The words on book-marks, enigmatic notes,
Thoughts before sleep, the vague unwritten verse
On people, on the city to which I travel.
I would like to resolve to live fully
In the barbarous world of sympathy and fear.

Says his life to the poet: 'Can you make verse of this?'
And the poet answers: 'Yes, it is your limitations
That enable me to get you down at all.'
The diamonds glitter on his paper and
His sons sail unloved to the Antipodes.
Those whom a lack of creativeness condemns
To truth see magazines in the hands of the patient
And realize that the serial will go on
After death; but the artist becomes ill himself.
For only the fully-committed participate
In the revolution of living, the coming to power
Of death: the others have always some excuse
To be absent from the shooting, to be at home
Curled up with a book or at the dentist's.

Sometimes I find it possible to feign
The accent of the past, the vulgar speech
Which snobbery and art have iced; but feel no longer
The compulsion of hills, the eternal interests
Which made my fathers understand each other.
That mockery of solidarity
Some of the civilized always experience,
Waiting half hopefully for the dreaded barbarians,

Sick of their culture, traitors to the division
Of toil and sensibility. Yet really
I can speak easily only to myself.
The tears meant for others are wept in front of the glass;
The confession is never posted; and the eye
Slides away from the proffered hand and discovers
An interesting view from the window.

The ridiculous mottled faces pass in stiff
Procession: relations, friends and chance encounters.
And the asinine minds that lie behind the gestures
Of goodness I can never reciprocate
Repel me with their inability
To escape from the grossest errors. Is it weakness
That sometimes imagines these shaped as heroes?
That cannot conceive of happiness as other
Than the apotheosis of the simple and kind?
That refuses to see how the century rises, pale,
From the death of its dream, ignoring the gains
Of the cruel, the different wishes of slaves?

The train removes me to another set
Of evasions. The valleys disappear. The train
Bolts through the central plain. I shall discover
Whether Lizzie Eustace retained her diamonds,
How far the hordes are from the city,
And my end will make significant for me
A casual place and date. My own child
Will grow from the generous warmth of his youth and perhaps
Discover, like me, that the solemn moments of life
Require their unbearable gaucheness translated to art.
For the guilt of being alive must be appeased
By the telling observation, and even feeling
Can only be borne retrospectively.
Bending over to kiss, the sensitive see with alarm
That their selves are still upright: the instant of death is
                                                    announced
By a rattle of tin in the corridor. Meaning is given
These disparate happenings, our love is only
Revealed, by conventions: 'Dear Mother, I hope you are better.'
Or 'Lizzie resolved that she would have her revenge.'

[120]

The lilac will last a fortnight if the rain
Arrives, the sparrows will always turn to let
Their lime drop over the gutter, the gardener
Will lift the chickweed, and the clots of nests
In the elms disappear in the whirling green of summer.

At the end of the twilit road a figure is standing
Calling us to go in, while the far-off rumours
Of terrible facts which at last may destroy
Our happiness spoil our play. In the place we go to
The kettle boils on the fire, the brasses are polished,
But people are busy with pain in another room.
One night I shall watch the city and black sky meet
In the distance, the car lights stream on the heath like tracer,
And in such moments of lonely and mild exultation
This rhetoric will be forgotten, and the life of omission go on.
Behind me will lie the sad and convulsive events
As narrative art, and as fated, immortal and false.

TEN MEMORIAL POEMS
N.S. 1888–1949

Illness is to reconcile us to death – André Gide

I

Week after week, month after month, in pain
You wrestled with that fiendish enemy –
The thing that tried in vain
To drag you from the room to its own territory.

Each day renewed the duel and our grief
Until at last upon the crumpled bed –
To our unwished relief –
The strange emaciated brown-faced fiend lay dead.

II

The image of the times that hurt me most
Were those blanched crawling creatures of the camps
        Whose flesh was carved away
        By fools and cruelty.

What horror that the object of our love
Should take that terrible symbolic shape
    And guilt and fear release
    From Europe to this house.

III

Your illness changed your life into a dream;
Its habits and its furniture became
The symbols of despair, our faces maps
Of odd utopias to which collapse
Had not as yet extended. In your head
Trembled the foreign language of the dead.

And yet you feigned an interest in our acts
As though the living were the permanent;
Like us, pretended to ignore the facts
That make the nightmare really what is meant.

Sometimes to please us you stretched for a cup
And smiled from that vile place where you lay bound:
Until you had to give our crude world up
And whisper what we couldn't understand.

IV

To think of your suffering and bear it,
The thought not the suffering:
That is the duty you gave me – unwittingly,
For you patiently took on the thing
To save me the sting.

To call forth a poem or so, it turns out,
Was your only appeal:
Perhaps you were conscious, fondly, that there too the gap
Between the idea and the real
Was too great to feel.

V

To understand the story
The innocent child assumes
A knowledge of jealousy
Or love. What ignorance looms,
What terrible feigning rages,
When death for us turns its pages!

Drug, legend, amulet,
Aphorism, prayer and tear,
To the truth approximate
Like scaffolding. The fear
Lives in the central lack
When the spars have been put back.

We can see dimly then
The hereditary fate
That comes to every man
In accidental shape,
Whose grotesque senselessness
Adds the sole sense to us.

VI

What irony that I can speak like this
Who rationed feeling when you were alive
To the half-felt but always studied kiss,
Dumb with the fear of those who run from love.

Now I can see, of course, our casual
But deep and strange relations from my birth,
How children must deny at every call
The embarrassing blood that links them to the earth.

My thoughts draw back like infinite generations.
Your parents do not know that you have died:
And now you have passed on to me the patience,
The loss, the care that one must try to hide.

Hoarding his gift for who must take it later,
The heir knows all the pangs of his testator.

VII

A year already since you died:
And I look back and see the vain
Lines I have written since the hour,
Frightened to turn to art that pain.

Art must create from human filth
And history's stupid lesson, hope.
Even in these atrocious days
Your death remains beyond my scope.

VIII

I imagine that simply to live is heroic,
Thinking of your death,
Forgetting the age will add to living
Its putrid breath.

IX

What first we feared for you we wished at last,
And death became a mentionable name,
As of an efficacious drug. So past
Ages preserved by love must in the shame

Of their decay call down an hourly curse.
And yet the age itself, in ignorance,
Desires to live; in its descent to worse
Heroic beyond the watcher's anxious stance.

O courage more than mine, you know a hope
That leaden evil days cannot offend:
For you death is unthinkable, its scope
Being no less than human suffering's end.

X

A long tense shadow falls across my page.
I flick the insect off the edge and know
What frightful light projects me on the age.

Between this south-east suburb and the glow
Of evening London turns a pitted face
Beneath a sky the colour of a blow.

Thinning and broadening as they check and race,
The ruins-loving birds that have returned
To haunt our cities take their resting place.

The horror of your pain and death that burned
Like acid in my chest now merges with
The duller but more constant gnawing learned

Through two long decades of a tragic myth.
The individual sorrow shrivels, leaving
Grief round the general sphere like bitter pith.

And in the larger body, also, heaving
Cells form irregular patterns that destroy
A hard-won alimentary achieving.

Yet since I found how pain supposes joy
I measure against man our long-drawn Troy.

THE SNOW

The morning of the snow I walked alone
Through the deserted park, the bushes stone,
The snowless grass green shadows under yews,
Each footprint quick and violet as a bruise.

Empty of thought as was the sky of colour,
I saw the dead shoots blur the frozen pallor,
And turned into a narrow path between
The dirt of branches loaded with the clean.

What was it then that pierced my inmost self,
Walking alone along that little gulf:
What archetypal memory of cold,
What wolves, what forests, what unquiet child?

YOUTH REVISITED

The hastening cloud grows thin; the sun's pale disc
Swells, haloes, then bursts out and warms the stone,
Pitching the yew's black tent on brilliant green.
A dozen years have gone since last I saw
This tiny church set on the parkland's edge
Between the glistening hunters and the cattle,
A Sunday exercise for week-end guests,
And I approach it conscious that emotion
Ought to be suffered, as indeed it is.
Did I live here and was I happy then?
A war more innocent, an age of man
Removed, my poems thick with formal doom
And baseless faith in humans. Years that now
Pass with the clarity of hours then
Record the degeneration of the nerves
And the world situation, make a golden
Time from that decade of infirm belief.

I am half glad to find the place has marked
Dramatically my absence. All the roof
Has gone, grass flutters on the broken stone,
A notice says *These walls are dangerous.*
Through unglazed windows marble monuments
Are glimpsed like modest spinsters in their baths.
Bombs or neglect, informants are not sure:
In any case the church will now decay
With other luxuries. The horses are
Not here, no doubt the mansion house beyond
The lake is requisitioned by the state,
And furrows creep across the pleasure ground.

I wonder if my son completely fails
To grasp my halting reconstruction of
My youth. Here, where we brought him in our arms
Was neat then, facing time with fortitude.
The statues in the gloom stood for their moral,
The wicked viscount's smoke rose from the house,
The evils of the epoch had not quite
Made rational the artist's accidie.   ·

And yet, the clock moved on another twelve,
He would have something still to put to his son.
The jet planes slither overhead, a frog
Throbs in the dust half-way across the road,
Over two fields a saw scrapes like a bird.
Creatures, machines and men live yet among
The partial, touching ruins of their world.

PSYCHOANALYST TO POET

The child's insatiable desire for love –
Destiny of hysteria: presences
That watch and terrorize –
Forgotten wishes of the infant past.

Now that the dream no longer guards his sleep,
The patient feels the truth of night, and wakes
To moonlight on crumpled sheets:
The image crude, interpretation vast.

Only the truly mad take on themselves
The guilt for every murder in the State,
Who loved so fiercely once
They lock their dangerous bodies up, aghast.

Yes, you're observed, but merely by yourself;
Yours are the gestures with significance.
The fated have no need
To seek the road the oracles forecast.

On the rats still the multiplying plague;
Its second crime has not yet made the life
Of innocence meaningless:
As far away as death the waves of blast.

Tear up the warnings. Your derangement falls
Behind the world's. The pain is not excessive,
The mask presentable.
Even the next relapse mayn't be the last.

HUMANS

The trait of speaking to the fire or window,
The moustache, the walking-stick, the deep-set eyes,
The love of Haydn, constitutional leanness,
Large size of headgear, ulcer, fear of mice –
These are the elements that make a person,
Who densely occupies a space, then dies.

The puzzle's not behind the stubborn shyness,
The taste for farinaceous food, the mole,
But in those trivialities themselves –
Erased by dying with such ease – the whole
Chekhovian or Dickensian apparatus,
With death its single though unconscious goal.

But never, as will disparate dots on paper,
Such humours a reasonable portrait fix:
The owner is too busy with the building
To see the pattern in the slapped-down bricks;
And others cannot know the thing remaining
Inside the illusionist's box of simple tricks.

DIARY ENTRY IN THE FIFTIES

A razor wind today – from some far land
Of furs, breath like acid fumes, and ice-locked culture.
Today bought this notebook, lit a cigarette
While writing my name in it. Fed only by
Permission of remote and rural worlds:
The racial breakfast orange, cruel beef.
And read how someone said that a communist agent
May by a special indulgence be permitted
To attack the party line: thus anything
Anti-communist should be taken as proof
That the utterer is, in fact, a communist.
Today saw that the Head of State himself
Had tested a new rifle's accuracy and power.
Wrote to my son at school. Played a record of Brahms.
Before retiring wedged the rattling door
With newspaper. But had insomnia. Felt cold.

TIME

Stretched in the sun, I notice through my skin
A few and tiny violet veins, like worms –
Not shocked, but as the sceptic viewer in
The lenses sees the plasm laced with germs.

The sun climbs on, the body's pigmentation
Darkens and, just as gradually, the man
Accommodates the frightening situation,
The unlived years that fold up like a fan.

Time moves through matter at so queer a pace
One seldom sees it truly – sheer and vast.
Only in corners of the human space
Bruises reveal the struggle to hold fast:

Until time's final effort to be free
Involves the whole in stains and agony.

CÔTE DES MAURES

J.L.F., his poem

The azure marbled with white and palest grey:
The cactuses with buds like hand grenades:
The roman-candle palms: a lonely house
Against a hill, a wrong piece of a jig-saw.
The terraces descend in armour plating,
The grapes a violet shadow in their vines.
The gorgeous cobalt runs its washes up
Sienna bays. 'Colibris,' 'Les Flots Bleus,'
'Canadien's' – the memory retains
The *plages* like cheap tunes of a fatal year.

Two warships anchor in the gulf. The town
Suffers. A dog is begging by the sea,
Wearing a wrist watch, trousers, spectacles.
The images, instead of happiness,
Show once again the old compulsive shape:

The drama of unpurposed lives whose climax
Cannot evade the conventional pistol shot.
And the return to autumn: leaves that strew
Glass pavements under trees like ruined lace;
Reports from cruel, sentimental empires.

The traveller finds water, brings his own
Disease. The poet's eye, impervious
To all except his fears, gives back a world
Dark, coloured, miniature, attractive, false.
The town that scabs the summit looks across
A land as densely folded as a pelt:
Below, the tide brings in its curious art.
Holding a knot of sea-turned wood, the bronze
Nude being sees through shores of culture bones
Of unadaptable enormities.

THE IMAGE

A spider in the bath. The image noted:
Significant maybe but surely cryptic.
A creature motionless and rather bloated,
The barriers shining, vertical and white:
Passing concern, and pity mixed with spite.

Next day with some surprise one finds it there.
It seems to have moved an inch or two, perhaps.
It starts to take on that familiar air
Of prisoners for whom time is erratic:
The filthy aunt forgotten in the attic.

Quite obviously it came up through the waste,
Rejects through ignorance or apathy
That passage back. The problem must be faced;
And life go on though strange intruders stir
Among its ordinary furniture.

One jibs at murder, so a sheet of paper
Is slipping beneath the accommodating legs.
The bathroom window shows for the escaper
The lighted lanterns of laburnum hung
In copper beeches – on which scene it's flung.

We certainly would like thus easily
To cast out of the house all suffering things.
But sadness and responsibility
For our own kind lives in the image noted:
A half-loved creature, motionless and bloated.

SENTIMENTAL POEM

In misty still October evenings
At the garden's end, attracted by the spade
Or mower, a bird comes on the fence and sings,
Prompted by whistling noises I have made.

Or so it seems – but one must guard against
The trap of the robin's sentimental name.
Maybe without me this soft throaty tensed
Recitative would go on just the same.

Because the bird half disappears upon
The dusky orange sunset sky, and will
Spring like a shade at solitary men
When others fly before the darkening wheel,

Do not imagine it can sympathize
Or love: no more than equal hope
These flowers with their yellow feline eyes
In lashes of unlikely heliotrope.

A brown leaf on a filament revolves.
Across the now-grey lawn the house lets fall
Its oblong lights: there human emblems move,
More plausible but no less strange and frail.

POEM TO PAY FOR A PEN

On the aeroplane from Nice I lost my pen,
That instrument of poetry and affairs.
Nor do I miss the coarser symbolism
The minor drama so naïvely bares.

In this the thirty-ninth year of my age,
Returned from those historic shores, it seems
That any old subject fits into my verse,
And there will stand for something else, like dreams.

The needle of the gramophone induces
The mood essential for the poet's art:
The sense of happiness, the huge ambition,
Last the few minutes to the record's heart.

The tides throw up the broken bits of culture
Perished when wine and oil gave way to coal:
The centre shifted to the provinces,
Drizzling and dull. The sun is to console.

And now the fecund centre shifts once more,
As all the life of capitals wears thin:
In gnawed rain-blackened buildings poets sit
Through wars of wanting neither side to win.

It shifts to where? Far from the world of pens,
And under suns too strong for wine or oil,
The tribes keep pure their healing savagery
And animal empires multiply and boil.

I do not know which are the most obscene:
Poets, profoundly sceptic, scared, unread:
The leaders monolithic in their mania;
Or the unteachable mass, as good as dead.

The solitary gramophone's entire
Repertoire is romantic; in the garden
The moonrise summons from its sullen fire
A yellow face that hurts but cannot pardon.

Moonlight, dark vegetation, ageing glands –
Those centuries-recurring aids to thought –
Bring up the never far away idea
Of humans shining virtuous as they ought.

This idealization somehow is the real;
True like the fabulously moving strain
That with the grossest means, pen, gut and brass,
Resolves and then transcends the mortal pain.

THE TWO POETS

The one was witty and observant,
Words and translucent form his servant.
The other counted beats, weighed vowels,
His verse as thick and coiled as bowels.

The first died young. The second aged,
And, though officially he raged
Against the former, privately
Envied the light lost poetry.

Envied but never ceased to hope,
Thinking it still within his scope,
That unsought carelessness and truth
– The lucky manner of his youth.

TO A NOTEBOOK

You always open at unfinished pages.
Behind, the failures: daunting blanks ahead.
Here and not elsewhere my emotion rages.
Hungry for dreams you lie beside my bed.

An enemy to life, you give it hints
Of how to live: it still returns to you.
Yet your neglect means that my living stints
My life of all I feel, consider true.

You are the brilliant portrait that has made
Uneasy the nonentity it hired.
I'd like to end you but I am afraid,
Knowing that entry must be undesired.

Will you survive me? That's my constant care,
Living a miser for a doubtful heir.

[133]

PREFACE TO AN ANTHOLOGY

Don't be deceived, some poems printed here
May merely illustrate the condemnation
Of the anthologist: omission were
Too vague a sign to show his detestation.

Nor has he chosen of the verse he likes
That he thinks quite the best: he aimed to prove
A theory in this volume, as one looks
On an old wife with warm complacent love.

With quiet pride he added just too few
Examples of his own successful work:
If the thing as a whole should fail he knew
There was at least one signpost in the murk.

Anthologists not always have the wit
To see it is their passion that abets
The gradual ruin of their choice: that what
Their pages fail to stale history forgets.

ON READING A SOVIET NOVEL

Will not the Local Party Secretary
Prove that his love of men's not innocent:
The heroine at last be blown off course
By some base, gusty, female element:
And the grave hero be eventually torn
By a disgraceful infantile event?

No, in this world the good works out its course
Unhindered by the real, irrelevant flaw.
Our guilty eyes glaze over with ennui
At so much honest purpose, rigid law.
This is not life, we say, who ask that art
Show mainly what the partial butler saw.

And yet with what disquiet we leave the tale!
The mere appearance of the descending Goth,
So frightful to a sedentary race,
Made him invincible. It is not wrath
That breaks up cultures but the virtues of
The stupid elephant, the piddling moth.

The threatened empire dreads its rival's arms
Less than the qualities at which it sneers –
The slave morality promoted to
A way of life: naïve, old-fashioned tears
Which once it shed itself by bucketsful
In nascent, optimistic, long-dead years.

ANDRÉ GIDE

After a night of insomnia I read
In the morning paper of the death of Gide,
Who by allowing smaller men to share
Such nights of his made theirs the less to bear,
Even to answer to creative need.

Himself an instrument through which events
Become translated into measurements,
His death makes, like a father's ending or
The long-anticipated start of war,
An alteration in the epoch's tense.

Whatever routes the intellectuals haunt
Around the action of their times will want
The practical travel notes of Gide; and feel
The spirit of the illusory and real
– That figure, thin-lipped, passionate and gaunt.

A general hope hung on him with the weight
Of intimate anxieties; and yet
He carefully made plain the consolations
Of an earth colonized, he knew, by nations
Pregnant not with amelioration – hate.

All contradictions were resolved in art:
Utopias in bad taste, the gulfs that part
The individual life from what it sees
As fated but grotesque realities,
Writer from age which yet must feed his heart.

Now he becomes the earth he praised, in spite
Of art: but as when in the desperate night,
Sleepless, we switch the lamp out finally,
To our unwished and sad relief we see
Behind the curtain leap another light.

IBSEN

Some of the symbols are ridiculous.
The drain, the tower – these do not even mean
      What one expects them to.
      They clump across the stage
      As obvious as wigs.

A minute later one is not so sure.
The drain transmits blood laced with spirochetes.
      The tower is not ideals
      Nor sex but one of those
      Emblems without a key:

And all the high stiff collars and the ledgers
Shine out with their own intense interior meaning:
      The names like fiords, the
      Chorus of doctors, take
      Their place in consummate verse.

Ibsen revealed that the symbol had a past,
That crude interpretation could be stripped
      Of rings of time, to find
      Inside the foliate five
      Acts the small pulsing germ.

ON SPALDING'S *HANDBOOK TO PROUST*

Like life the novel's just too long to grasp:
Perhaps an index will show what they mean.
Over a hundred entries deal with LOVE –
Alas! – almost two hundred ALBERTINE.

The index drives us back into the text,
The text to life; until we see again
How they both hover on the edge of what
The entries of an index would explain.

NECROPHAGY

The jelly baby is a kind of sweet,
    It actually has eyes;
And held up to the light its little corpse
    Bears the transparencies
    And flaws of realer size.

These soft smooth bodies lie in heaps, and if
    One is picked up the rest
Tend to cling to it in mixed attitudes,
    So first you must detach
    The victim from the batch.

Some eat the jelly baby whole but most
    Dismember it at leisure,
For, headless, there is no doubt that it gives
    A reasonable measure
    Of unexampled pleasure.

About the jelly baby other things
    Occur to me: the fact
That eating it brings back the feelings of
    Our infancy; the act
    Of choosing black with tact;

And finally that in its rigid arms
    Held close against its side,
And absolute identity with others,
    Its pathos and fate reside,
    That else it had not died.

TRANSLATION

Now that the barbarians have got as far as Picra,
And all the new music is written in the twelve-tone scale,
And I am anyway approaching my fortieth birthday,
    I will dissemble no longer.

I will stop expressing my belief in the rosy
Future of man, and accept the evidence
Of a couple of wretched wars and innumerable
    Abortive revolutions.

I will cease to blame the stupidity of the slaves
Upon their masters and nurture, and will say,
Plainly, that they are enemies to culture,
    Advancement and cleanliness.

From progressive organizations, from quarterlies
Devoted to daring verse, from membership of
Committees, from letters of various protest
    I shall withdraw forthwith.

When they call me reactionary I shall smile,
Secure in another dimension. When they say
'Cinna has ceased to matter' I shall know
    How well I reflect the times.

The ruling class will think I am on their side
And make friendly overtures, but I shall retire
To the side farther from Picra and write some poems
    About the doom of the whole boiling.

Anyone happy in this age and place
Is daft or corrupt. Better to abdicate
From a material and spiritual terrain
    Fit only for barbarians.

INACTION

Writers entrapped by teatime fame and by commuters' comforts –
Marianne Moore

A strange dog trots into the drive, sniffs, turns
And pees against a mudguard of my car.
I see this through the window, past *The Times*,
And drop my toast and impotently glare.

But indignation gives way to unease.
Clearly the dog, not merely impudent,
Was critical of man's activities,
Mine in particular, I'm forced to grant.

And so the entertainment of the morning
Headlines is temporarily spoiled for me:
During my coffee I must heed their warning,
The fate of millions take half seriously.

Inadequate, I know, this old concern,
Only productive of a quickened pulse,
A hanging jacket that gives one a turn.
The sneering dog demanded something else.

A WET SUNDAY IN SPRING

Symptoms at high altitudes:
Emaciation and overstrain.
Life at high latitudes: small wingless flies
Capable of living for long periods
In a frozen state.

I sit in the inventive temperate zone,
Raised only by the city's floors of culture,
Watching the rain bombard the lilac, feeling
The radio come in round me like a tide.
Deafness let Beethoven escape the tyranny
Of concord: some such mutation should exclude this age
From having to admit the possibility
Of happiness.

The ivory-horned chestnut
Effortlessly assumes its task; the rain
Is perpendicular and horribly fertile;
The embattled green proliferates like cells.
I think feebly of man's wrong organizations,
Incurable leaders, nature lying in wait
For weakness like an animal or germ,
And aircraft growling in the summer air.

TIMES OF WAR AND REVOLUTION

The years reveal successively the true
Significance of all the casual shapes
Shown by the atlas. What we scarcely knew
Becomes an image haunting as a face;
Each picture rising from neglected place
To form the dial of our cursor hopes,
As that undreamt-of frontier slowly writhes
Along the wishes of explosive, lives.

The pages char and turn. Our memories
Fail. What emotions shook us in our youth
Are unimaginable as the truth
Our middle years pursue. And only pain
Of some disquieting vague variety gnaws,
Seeing a boy trace out a map of Spain.

WINTER ROUNDEL

From shapes like men fog thickens in the street
And London grows as lonely as a fen:
A muffled shout, a dangerous sound of feet,
        From shapes like men.

The solstice nears, the armistice again
Recedes; the pavements of our world retreat,
And lovers huddle closer in their den.

The deadly particles of matter greet,
Less hypothetical, the physicist's ken:
Paralysed cities wait a solar heat
        From shapes like men.

THE FIFTIES

The wretched summers start again
With lies and armies ready for
Advancing on that fast terrain.

Like those of China, Poland, Spain,
With twenty territories more,
The wretched summers start again.

The rumours and betrayals stain
The helpless millions of the poor
Advancing on that fast terrain.

Asian and European rain
Falls from between the blue of yore:
The wretched summers start again.

And rubble and the jungle gain
A foothold on the cultured shore,
Advancing on that fast terrain.

Short youth was shortened by the pain
Of seasons suitable for war:
The wretched summers start again,
Advancing on that fast terrain.

THE MEETING

At the ineffective meeting is received
    The letter: 'From your guilt
I resign. I exculpate myself from all
    Your pistols and libels.

'I shall devote myself henceforth to God
    And the investigation of freedom.
I write from a country cottage where the chestnut
    Makes miniature

'Images of itself with its sea-scum blossom.
    Your world is urban and evil.
My cat advises me: remove my name, please,
    From your list of dog-lovers.'

[141]

The committee composes its reply: 'We, too,
Have seen that tree in Spring
Making pink blotting paper of the lawns.
      And as for the shootings

'They were of those who would have let art die
   With lovely anaemia.
Your cat is right: his name has been embossed
      On our notepaper.

'Consider: we need your support who are able even
   To formulate the questions.
Try to recover the original impulse
      That led you to join us.

'For the season now is nearly over and
   The orators put away
Their stools. The belting slows. The tubes are about
      To leap from their racks.'

PANTOMIME

Steeped in a mouldy light, the frightful Witch
Proclaims excessively the power of evil.
Surely there is no need to emphasize
The eventual triumph of the cyst and weevil.

And yet the Fairy seems quite confident,
Promising that good will eventually reign
In the divided kingdom, rising superior
To tattered tinsel and blue pathetic vein.

True enough, the foolish but kindly Prince is restored,
The lovers promise to live happily ever after,
The chorus of agricultural labourers
Is heard in apparently genuine laughter.

Is there no epilogue of realism?
Do the trapdoors which led to lower regions
Remain fast shut upon the destructive thoughts
And heavily armoured and most fatal legions?

FREUD'S CASE-HISTORIES

Not the real people in my life
But the Rat Man and Little Hans,
And other text-book creatures have
Supplied me with romance.

In these the repetitive motives of
The family were convolved,
Though I myself from duty, hate
And affection seemed absolved.

From these my forgotten infancy
I saw was not forgotten
But steamed behind the ordered man.
Rich-smelling, live and rotten.

I realized that in his dreams,
His illnesses and love,
The human makes for all below
Great symbols from above;

And that the poet, lonely in
A cold society,
Is the true archetype of man,
Loneliest when most free.

To see your father as a horse,
The penis as what devours,
Is art without the stigma of
The artist's ivory towers.

And though the hand that wrote them down,
To understand and heal,
Was not entirely guiltless, these
Strange histories are real.

Yes, real the pince-nez blinkers, real
The rats that gnaw the heart –
Emblems of human longing to
Approximate to art.

THE DOPPELGÄNGER

Dear son, you said you thought to write about
A hero's search for his twin brother, lost
At birth – or as to whom, perhaps, some doubt
Existed whether he was born at all.
I mean these stanzas not for what had crossed
Your mind but rather what you can't forestall.

We shan't be the first to use the curious theme
Of man's irrational knowledge of a twin
Whose life consists of what we only dream
And yet is us, and will in some far place
Confront us with our vile and furrowed sin,
Liker than we are to our proper face.

You know why I was moved by the idea,
That equally the ageing father must
Be haunted by such archetypal fear
Though long contemporaneous with his shame;
For a new twin was summoned by his lust
Whose shade he then involuntarily became.

A DYING DICTATOR

The children years ago made their escape
Out of the father's tense, oppressive field:
His moral scheme was of too strict a shape
To hold the freedom that their growth revealed.

Now he lies bound and senseless up the stair,
Drowned by the failing channels of his flesh,
They momentarily return and wear
The old familiar pressure of the mesh.

They wait among the ugly furniture,
Rich with the poignant memories of their youth:
Once more they feel that agonizing blur –
The hopeless falsehood merging into truth.

And still perceive a sprig of what their hate
Grew up with and then choked – but all too late.

NINO, THE WONDER DOG

A dog emerges from the flies
  Balanced upon a ball.
Our entertainment is the fear
  Or hope the dog will fall.

It comes and goes on larger spheres,
  And then walks on and halts
In the centre of the stage and turns
  Two or three somersaults.

The curtains descend upon the act.
  After a proper pause
The dog comes out between them to
  Receive its last applause.

Most mouths are set in pitying smiles,
  Few eyes are free from rheum:
The sensitive are filled with thoughts
  Of death and love and doom.

No doubt behind this ugly dog,
  Frail, fairly small, and white,
Stands some beneficent protector,
  Some life outside the night.

But this is not apparent as
  It's forced to serve, alone
In the spot-light's glare, absurdities
  Far beyond its own.

PART FOUR

From
Brutus's Orchard
(1957) and
Collected Poems 1936–1961 (1962)

SPRING SONG

Behind the plate glass of hotels
Old ladies watch the savage sea;
The adolescent casts his spells
On ignorant reality;
And every girl is made by time
Tragic beyond her silly power;
And still the poet in his rhyme
'Accept, accept,' cries from his tower.

Upon a gate in carven stone
Two armoured torsos sneer with pride;
The empires riddled to the bone
As sick men stand, who stand and hide
A mortal sickness; and the poet,
Like the great apes, in childhood gay
Morose thereafter dare not show it:
'Accept, accept,' his verses say.

Irises point indecent buds
Beside the withered daffodils;
Tender lascivious feeling floods
The veins that show, the heart that kills;
And where the wry-mouthed fledgling crawls
With busy termite citizens
The sentimental poet bawls
'Accept, accept,' through blinding lens.

The 'cellist from between his knees
Sends out a transcendental chord;
Suddenly cherry branches freeze;
The captain points across the ford;
Conception lags behind the world
That dreams and poetry reveal:
The grub within its shining curled
'Accept, accept,' *is* heard to squeal.

SUMMER

From estuary to channel
White explosions of cloud;
The charming cyclists tunnel
Through the leaf-shadowed road.
Fate's motto theme suspended
Under long arpeggios
Of warmth and light; unhanded
Unjustly-sentenced youth.
Each bill and torrent cries
An indubitable truth.

All living matter's power
To reproduce its form
Includes occasional error:
In air and water swarm,
Gorgeous beyond their title,
The creatures; and the mother
Sends out into the battle
Past her retreating force
Fresh notions of brow and feather
To perpetuate the race.

Desire could gaze for ever
Where in the dark meniscus
Sparkles the imaged river.
O lovers, fabulous maskers,
Enjoy your day: too soon
Swans whitening the dusk
Above the magician's fane
Will announce the long dominion
Of loss. What shall you ask?
To see in your companion,

If only for a curt
Moment, potentials as moving
As the materials of art.
The universe of loving
Is not this summer, even,
Where far into the night
Blossom and owl make known
Perfume and grove, but wrong
Cells that the strange create
From which the conquerors spring.

PICTURES OF WINTER

Whips, river systems, hands of mandarins –
With trees on skies the inventive mood begins.

After the gallery's rich, vivid hoard
The still, grey river stabs me with its sword.

Behind the city the unmoving west
Burns smoky-orange like a robin's breast.

At four o'clock the living-room window frames
A faded photograph of roofs and flames.

Stepping outside the muffled house I freeze
Beneath calm, radiant immensities.

In the cold air the breath clouds of a horse
Fade, whiten, fed by two cones from their source.

Under my feet the snow cries out like mice,
Its feathers left behind compressed to ice.

Night, and the snow descending on the high
Branches now scarcely darker than the sky.

Décor of wolves and puppets, swan and dreams –
A snow-hung garden in a street-lamp's beams.

Closing the curtains, through the yellow light
I see a whiteness where it should be night.

The tangerine belies its glowing form,
But shivering bodies find each other warm.

Strange this new colour of the world I know;
Strange as my ginger cat upon the snow.

A general weeping from boughs still severe
Moves the heart with the turning hemisphere.

The puffed white blossom in the garden urn
Dissolves to earth that holds a queen's return.

I dig the soil and in its barren cold
Surprise a bulb-bomb fused with palest gold.

But still the knouts and veins divide the air,
Save for their swelling buds of sparrows, bare.

AUTOBIOGRAPHY OF A LUNGWORM

My normal dwelling is the lung of swine,
   My normal shape a worm,
But other dwellings, other shapes, are mine
   Within my natural term.
Dimly I see my life, of all, the sign,
   Of better lives the germ.

The pig, though I am inoffensive, coughs,
   Finding me irritant:
My eggs go with the contents of the troughs
   From mouth to excrement –
The pig thus thinks, perhaps, he forever doffs
   His niggling resident.

The eggs lie unconsidered in the dung
   Upon the farmyard floor,
Far from the scarlet and sustaining lung:
   But happily a poor
And humble denizen provides a rung
   To make ascension sure.

The earthworm eats the eggs; inside the warm
   Cylinder larvae hatch:
For years, if necessary, in this form
   I wait the lucky match
That will return me to my cherished norm,
   My ugly pelt dispatch.

Strangely, it is the pig himself becomes
   The god inside the car:
His greed devours the earthworms; so the slums
   Of his intestines are
The setting for the act when clay succumbs
   And force steers for its star.

The larvae burrow through the bowel wall
   And, having to the dregs
Drained ignominy, gain the lung's great hall.
   They change. Once more, like pegs,
Lungworms are anchored to the rise and fall
   – And start to lay their eggs.

What does this mean? The individual,
   Nature, mutation, strife?
I feel, though I am simple, still the whole
   Is complex; and that life –
A huge, doomed throbbing – has a wiry soul
   That must escape the knife.

ON GRAZING A FINGER

In time and place such wounds are staggered;
Healing, too, holds them in dominion.
I am most thankful: under the surface
A ghastly thing moves on its skeleton.

ELEMENTARY PHILOSOPHY

White blossom in the room:
And, stepping in the gloom
The pallid garden wears,
I watch the glowing disc
Indigo cloud unbares
And feel the human risk.

Four thousand million years
Have hatched these staggering fears,
And years that lie ahead
Of equal amplitude,
With man alive or dead,
Can never heal the feud.

Planets and stars alone
To destinies unknown,
This universe and more
For monstrous, alien reasons,
Journey beyond our four
Senses and local seasons.

I go back to the flowers,
The house's love and hours,
But still I see this Spring,
That buds with final wars,
Foam from some heaving thing
Blown over endless shores.

THE DAY

At the time it seemed unimportant: he was lying
In bed, off work, with a sudden pain,
And she was haloed by the morning sun,
Enquiring if he'd like the daily paper.

So idle Byzantium scarcely felt at first
The presence in her remoter provinces
Of the destructive followers of the Crescent.

[154]

But in retrospect that day of moderate health
Stood fired in solid and delightful hues,
The last of joy, the first of something else –
An inconceivable time when sex could be
Grasped for the asking with gigantic limbs,
When interest still was keen in the disasters
Of others – accident, uprising, drouth –
And the sharp mind perceived the poignancy
Of the ridiculous thoughts of dissolution.

A day remembered by a shrivelled empire
Nursed by hermaphrodites and unsustained
By tepid fluids poured in its crying mouth.

ON A TEXTBOOK OF SURGERY

Dear fellow-humans, what
Inhuman deformities
And highly-coloured growths
Your colourless flesh can suffer!

Keepers of fish in ponds
Sometimes clip off with scissors
The fungus that exudes
From those dumb swimming creatures.

I would not, myself, keep fish.
Or, if compelled, would at
The term of their bright youth
Kill or not visit them.

TO A GIRL IN THE MORNING

Hair blurred by slumber still;
The dreams in which you moved
Towards such prodigies
As loving and being loved
Slow like some gentle hill
Your limbs; and in your eyes
I see myself transformed
To what Circe once charmed.

[155]

Before your innocence
And infinite desire,
Wisdom and age will stagger
And start to doubt their power,
While you recite the tense
That drives a yearning dagger
In those who know what scar
Future and past must score.

The thought that generations
Spring to infinity,
Could formerly sustain
Such death-racked men as I,
But now the state of nations
Threatens a burnt-out strain,
And you may be the last
Of those who have moved my lust.

ECLIPSE

January 19, 1954: 12.50–4.13

So last night while we slept the moon
Crawled through the shadow's long black spear,
Finding in all that sun-ruled void
The darkness of the human sphere.

Our dreams were as incredible.
The little bodies froze, and then
Their longing soared and fell on worlds
Too distant for the years of men.

Tonight across the unflawed moon
Clouds like the ribbing of a shore
Pass endlessly, and life and planet
Take their far stations as before.

I pass into the house which wears,
As architecture must, its age:
Upon the rotting floor the moon
Opens its pure utopian page.

[156]

DISCREPANCIES

Even smooth, feared executives have leisure
To show the inadequacy of their love:
    The longest day must end
    In animal nakedness.

And in the city what amused our fathers –
Sledgehammers wielded by dwarfs to mark the hours –
    Move us as emblems of
    Something quite terrible.

Gazing upon us as we cross the courtyard
Of the exchange, on our legitimate business,
    Are frenzied masks of stone
    With clutching human hands.

And we imagine what unthinkable shape
A girl's slim velvet shoe conceals that strolls
    The pavements of boulevards
    Carrying intestines of sewers.

A man at the floor of his destination finds –
Inexplicably for a moment – the same defect,
    As at the start of his journey,
    In the lift's inner gate.

And the emperor, drenched in scents from realms too far
To visit, cannot know that history
    Will fail to record the name
    Of his son, teasing the peacocks.

But eras when the sensitive reported
Doom through the deformation of a pot,
    False quantities, and sounds
    Too harsh for memory,

Were secretly incubating even then
Bravery out of freaks, ethics from hate
    And valid economies
    Of starving theorists.

Our systems hunt in trying to be just:
Too violent man's feed-back. Hector's shield
　　　Lies under a massive floor
　　　Of hideous ornaments.

The sublimations of the poets rise
From their renunciation of coarse hair
　　　And the inanities
　　　Of ravishing crimson lips.

EXPOSTULATION AND INADEQUATE REPLY

*I wish you would write a poem, in blank verse,
addressed to those who, in consequence of the
complete failure of the French Revolution,
have thrown up all hopes of the amelioration
of mankind, and are sinking into an almost
epicurean selfishness, disguising the same
under the soft titles of domestic attachment
and contempt for visionary* philosophes. –
　　　　　　　Coleridge to Wordsworth, 1799

Alas! dear Coleridge, I am not the man,
After a century and a half, to write
That poem – of another Revolution
And yet another generation of
Poets who, since the age holds out no hope,
Abjure the age and its attempted changers,
Trying to find in personal love their tropes
For poetry and reason for their lives.
It will not do: their verse is sloppy and
Their beings trivial or meaningless.
For still the active world maintains the turn
It took when you were young, and posed against
Its harsh demands for truth and sacrifice
The useless poet must arrange himself
With care if he is not to be an adjunct
Reactionary or irrelevant.
Of course, my only difference is I know
How weak I am, what strength the times require:

Attempting to disown the spurious virtue
That springs from guilt and from the making out
Of paths I dare not tread.

                          Writing these lines
Beneath the gentle gold that streams obliquely
From branches soon to show entirely their
Essential structure, I wonder how precisely
You, Coleridge, regarded that autumnal
World which arrived so quickly after Spring.
Could you imagine yet another chance
For tyranny to die, for men to make
An order of equality and right?
You did not sink, I know, immediately
Into acceptance of the status quo,
The old lies and the old injustices.
And history, although you could not tell,
Was gathering up the scattered elements
To make in time another grand assault
Upon the barricades of privilege,
Islands of class, the beaches of selfish atoms,
And will again, though it's our tragedy
– And opportunity – that history
Is only the totality of action
By many men who each alone are blind
To what they do, and may do.

                               Seen far off
The forest's million bones are smudged with bands
Of bistre, raw sienna, faded green.
Sad season of the end of growth, the start
Of cold that seems, in this faint sun, will be
Unbearable! And yet it will be borne,
And those who can survive will find the new,
Delicate but sure republic of the crocus,
The warm fraternal winds, the growing strength
Of wheat and apple's equal luxury.
This could not be the poem you desired.
We grow to understand that words alone,
The visionary gleam through which the poet
More and more consciously, less frequently,
Renews his youth, are, like all art, condemned
To failure in the sense that they succeed.

You, who so early lost that power, know best
How men forever seek, not quite in vain,
Sublime societies of imagination
In worlds like this, and that no more exist.

A SONG BETWEEN TWO SHEPHERDS

1. *Shep.*   Upon this pasture scarred and brown
    I find it hard to feed my flocks:
    What's left by the invading town
    Between the factory and the rocks
      Has been the battered shore
      Of swinging tides of war.

2.*Shep.*   Why trouble to sustain the breed
    Since soon the heat and aims of hell
    Released from that exploding seed
    Will change the pattern in the cell:
      Rich chops, wool thick and frore,
      Be born to you no more?

1. *Shep.*   Though shepherds always will complain
    Of shepherdesses and of grass,
    Hoping for love without its pain,
    Fat sheep from hills of hidden brass,
      Only they will ensure
      Survival of the poor.

2. *Shep.*   The inorganic shapes that prank,
    Fortuitously, monstrously,
    Our mineral star's indifferent flank
    Already count their tenancy
      In years of famine or
      The first armed hours of war.

1. *Shep.*   My sheep are no more strange than this
    Blue planet that now winks above
    The dusky wood; my shepherdess
    No briefer than the craving love
      For magnet of the ore,
      Of orbit for the core.

2. *Shep.*   Shepherd, I see in you the dupe
            Of happiness, the weakling who
            Finds warmth in huddling with the group,
            And wishes what he felt were true.
                This lank flock, withered ear,
                Accept for what they are.

1. *Shep.*   Shepherd, I must survey with sorrow
            My pasture trenched with arms and street,
            Yet I will hope to see a morrow
            When sheep and town will join to meet
                Real enemies – the four
                Seasons, man's last half score.

PLEASURE DRIVE

Children play on the by-pass, with the peaks
Of gasometers haunting them, and factories
Like lingering shapes of the past. Beyond, in fields,
Are massive artificial animals
And haystacks like Tibetan hats – the strange
Art of the simple. Lanes lead to villages
Selling beer and petrol as stores to mad explorers:
Behind the walls are superstitious rites,
Performed under pious mottoes worked in wool.

And so to higher land whose fortifications
Date back to fathers with somewhat smaller brains.
The roads and churches in the valley sink
Beneath old vegetation: farther still
The opposing line of downs is menacing
As a rival system.

Now we descend, the wind
Fresher, tinctured with chemicals, through
Light industries, across the estuary's bridge.
The point of this provincial city is
A tower that kept the river from the sea,
Particular from general. Like a rotten tooth,
Its walls disguise an empty centre where
Hundreds of birds festoon the greyish air,
Their droppings falling through the rooms of state
To pile up in the dungeons. In the squares
Of battlements fit sections of the city:
The railway's claws, the suburbs spread like fans,
And in a moat of green the similar
Cathedral stone, a different kind of ruin.

Time has irregularities, its grain
Leaves knots where the unfortunate remain,
Hacking against irrational designs.
Let us return to the metropolis
Whose fuming lights the sky, whose galleries
Blaze with ingenious art, whose sewers flow,
Where those in love are glad and soldiers only
Polish euphoniums and horses' rumps;
And not despise its anachronistic pleasures.
Even when classes do not slay each other
And generations accept their heritage,
In times of monolithic calm, the single
Life must enjoy its happiness between
Atrocious thoughts: the smiling driver who
Forever nears that unwished destination
Where his road ends in blood and wrecked machine.

WINTER WORLD

A clouded sky at dusk the dirty red
Of grazed skin: slightly furred, the trees, as though
Drawn with a fine pen on a still-damp wash:
    The river slow.

Over the black and echoing viaduct
Golden-barred trains stretch out and glide like snakes.
The swans precede converging, crimson and grey
    Dissolving wakes.

Some by the lapping brink assume the long
Contorted shapes of heraldry or dreams,
One swelling to the myth that forced out girlish
        Half-frightened screams.

Their beaks are rough and chill: I let the bread
Fall to the gravel which contains the bones
Of birds and men, coins of dead dynasties,
        And ice-age stones.

The poem should end here, its *trouvailles* all
Exhausted, but there still remains the moral –
The aggregate of all the lives in time,
        That reef of coral.

The lyricist in a technician's age, the castle
In the cathedral's, and the single life
Born in an era of universal doom,
        Still, like a wife,

Look to an eventually happy time, in the teeth
Of the evidence. And during Rome's most dread
Decline the barbarians were enjoying themselves,
        As Whitehead said.

The Faustian image: I am one of those
Whose skull will be discovered; but its whole
Consciousness then sucked out, long since surrendered
        Its gloomy soul.

Tonight the swans, tomorrow the marble leader
Disfigured with tears of droppings – everywhere
Poets of the final period find themes
        For their despair:

Always they see their bodies, not their work,
Consorting with that vanished world which must
Present itself noble in pathos, inevitable, to
        The sifters of its dust.

FLORESTAN TO LEONORA

Our shadows fall beyond the empty cage.
The Minister has gone and I am left
To try to live with your heroic age.

I spare a thought, my dear, for you who must
Go home to change the jackboots for a skirt
And put the pistol on its nail to rust;

But mainly think of my impossible task.
My own love might have tried what yours achieved:
It cannot bear the gift it did not ask.

After the trumpet I felt, in our embrace,
I had been cheated of the captured's right
To innocent inaction and to face

A suffering unjust as a sarcoma.
Did you never conceive that it was possible
To like incarceration? In this trauma

Of the imprisoning era there must be
Some prisoners – for torturers to visit,
To wear the pallor and the beards of free

Philosophers, and tap on streaming walls
Their selfless ineffective messages
Concerning liberty to brutish cells.

When the mob sang of brotherhood and joy
I was embarrassed, more so when I saw
The near-erotic answer in your eye.

You take my hand as though I ought to live;
And lead me out to that alarming world
Which, the oppressor dead, the sensitive

Can find inimical no longer. Yes,
Our values must shrivel to the size of those
Held by a class content with happiness;

And warmed by our children, full of bread and wine,
I shall dream of the discipline of insomnia
And an art of symbols, starved and saturnine.

THE IDES OF MARCH

Fireballs and thunder augment the wailing wind:
A vulgar score, but not inappropriate
To my romantic, classic situation.
Within the house my wife is asleep and dreaming
That I, too, am cocooned inside the world
Of love whose fear is that the other world
Will end it. But I wait uneasy here
Under the creaking trees, the low dark sky,
For the conspirators. This is the place
Where I come, in better weather, with a book
Or pen and paper – for I must confess
To a little amateur scribbling. Love and letters:
One ought to be content – would, if the times
Were different; if state and man were free,
The slaves fed well, and wars hung over us
Not with death's certainty but with the odds
Merely of dying a not too painful death.
Yes, I have caught the times like a disease
Whose remedy is still experimental;
And felt the times as some enormous gaffe
I cannot forget. And now I am about
To cease being a fellow traveller, about
To select from several complex panaceas,
Like a shy man confronted with a box
Of chocolates, the plainest after all.
I am aware that in my conscious wish
To rid the empire of a tyrant there
Is something that will give me personal pleasure;
That usually one's father's death occurs
About the time one becomes oneself a father.
These subtleties are not, I think, important –
No more than that I shall become a traitor,
Technically, to my class, my friend, my country.

No, the important thing is to remove
Guilt from this orchard, which is why I have
Invited here those men of action with
Their simpler motives and their naked knives.
I hope my wife will walk out of the house
While I am in their compromising presence,
And know that what we built had no foundation
Other than luck and my false privileged rôle
In a society that I despised.
And then society itself, aghast,
Reeling against the statue, also will
Be shocked to think I had a secret passion.
Though passion is, of course, not quite the word:
I merely choose what history foretells.
The dawn comes moonlike now between the trees
And silhouettes some rather muffled figures.
It is embarrassing to find oneself
Involved in this clumsy masquerade. There still
Is time to send a servant with a message:
'Brutus is not at home': time to postpone
Relief and fear. Yet, plucking nervously
The pregnant twigs, I stay. Good morning, comrades.

AFTER THE DRAMA

DUKE: Bear him away. This villainy will be
Remembered only as a moral tale
To warn our children. Come, my delicate pair:
To bed. Your pleasure's long been waiting there.

The curtain falls, the Duke removes his whiskers,
And there is no controlling force to ensure
That wrong is punished, and that happiness
Discovers youth and beauty powerless.

In the wings the gaolers have unhanded Cano,
The lovers separate with indifference,
And no philosophy can dissipate
For the tired Duke the sordid cares that wait.

The blue sky is dismantled: the lights go out.
Actors and audience become congruent.
And in the freezing street the newsboys cry
The frightful art that all must live and die.

The play's rich ambiguities assume
A rule of conduct in the viewer's mind;
Its subtle music fades as soon as uttered.
Now the great portals of the place are shuttered,

And the playbills flap to nothing in the wind.
Has here, too, some wise ruler lent his power
To an ambitious devil that at last
Will face the formal gathering of his past;

And find prevented his high-sounding rapes,
His avarice unmasked he named the social
Order, and see what half he always feared –
The unconsidered man resume his beard?

NEWSTEAD ABBEY

Birds on the lake; a distant waterfall:
Surrounded by its lawns, a vandyke shawl
Of woods, against the washed-in sky of March,
The abbey with its broken wall and arch,
Its scoured and yellow look, has power still
To move.
       The Nottingham Corporation will
At the converted stable block provide
Postcards and teas, and in the house a guide.

Impossible to doubt that he foresaw
The fate of the stately home, the social law
Which now ropes off his manuscripts and bed;
That pathos and joke were clearly in his head
When for the sentimental lookers-over
He reared the conspicuous monument to Rover,
Designed the too-heroic helmets for
His tripped-up entry in the Grecian war,
Made the monks' mortuary a swimming bath,
Loved those dim women.

[167]

                              Lout, girl, polymath,
Stare at the puzzling relics of a life:
Grapplings with action, blind turning to a wife.

In bed he could gaze out across the scene
Where now the trees are heavy but not green
With Spring, and see perhaps the rowing boat,
The little broad-beamed *Maid of Athens*, float
At her rope's end, past the blue toilet jug,
The tumbler of magnesia.
                              And the bug
That impregnated then this habitation
And kept it quick despite the abdication
Of all it served, of that for which it was planned,
I know too well but really understand
No better than the guide.
                              'The table that you see
Is where the poet Byron wrote his poetry'.

ONE AND MANY

Awake at five, I am surprised to see
Across the flocculent and winter dark
Windows already yellow; and am touched
By the unconscious solidarity
Of the industrious world of normal men
With art's insomnia and spleen,
As unaccountably as when
A long-dead negro plays through a machine.

I think of galleries lined with Renaissance man's
Discovery of physique, and jealously wonder
Why now it is impossible to show
Human existence in its natural stance –
The range of burgher, tart and emperor,
Set among withers, game, brocade,
Merely as themselves, not emblems for
A stringent world the artist never made.

Did the imagination then proceed
Quite naturally with a cast of men
Resembling the creator, who played out
Not anguish at the prospect of a deed
Ending a loathed society, nor that
Consideration shown by fear,
But were ambitious, usual, fat,
Pugnacious, comic, worldly, cavalier?

Not really so: the eye of art was cocked
Always from low and lonely vantages,
And the great boots and thighs, the glittering chests,
Taken for granted by their owners, blocked
A sky full of desired irrelevant stars
Whose enigmatic message lay
In wait until the rogues and czars
Fell ranting in a dynasty's decay.

And now art's only living figure broods
On the ensanguined falling moon until
The opposite horizon cracks and lights
Go out: over sapped and far-transported foods
I read of crises and prepare for living
In that strict hierarchy of
A miser body made for giving
And which prepares for war desiring love.

TO SHAKESPEARE

I turn your marvellous pages like
An invalid regarding birds,
Envying, too, your power to strike
Soft centres with a blow of words.

But more: within the words a myth
Resides that poets have to use –
Shamefacedly, as children with
Baths that their siblings first infuse.

And time removes from round the plot
Implausible or obvious coats.
I learn now, for example, what
Obsessional jealousy denotes

And think of all Leontes felt
Unknowing for Bohemia's king;
Why the short sword of Brutus dealt
A thrust at its beloved thing;

What made Cordelia dread to tell
Her love; and that compulsive feud
When the flat land of Denmark fell
Into a classic attitude.

No end to these great symbols of
The shapes that human life must take:
And moving from the sphere of love
I see the wider claims you stake.

The dynasties parade of weak
Crowns, strong usurpers, on that course
Of twistings set by history's bleak,
Impersonal, even mystic force.

Fickle, emaciated mobs
Rage, and the common soldiers die;
By the rich coronation sobs
The fat rejected coward 'I'.

Your simple but mysterious life,
Its sexual ambiguities
Moving within a reign of strife,
Determined and experienced these –

Which now and till the end of our
Society and tongue will keep
Their verbal, archetypal power
To make the lonely Gellies weepe.

THE PERTURBATIONS OF URANUS

Such fame as I have drops from me in a flash
When the girl behind the café bar sends back
A candid gaze. I judge her by the lack
Of overt imperfections in her flesh
And by her youth, but fear she will advance
Such standards to me. I open my book and read
That the sole sin is human ignorance,
Through mind must stretch the future of the breed.

I agree, without reservations I agree;
But glance occasionally where the urn
Distorts the image of her whom I confirm
Is not distorted, and again I see
How still the world belongs to the obtuse
And passionate, and that the bosom's small
But noticeable curve subtends its tall
Explosions and orations of mad abuse.

A fraud, then, this concern about the fate
Of the supposedly less rational?
No, but the powers that dissuade from all
Libidinous action rise from our weakest part.
And I go out into the urban grey,
Where one vermilion bus sign hangs as though
Placed by a careful painter, and array
Again my lust with the armour of outward show.

The planet Neptune's existence was revealed
Only by the perturbations of Uranus.
Crabbed lines of poetry, pigments congealed
Insanely on a little canvas train us
For those transcendent moments of existence
In which the will is powerless, and the blind
Astonished flesh forgets that it is kind
And drives in love or murder with its pistons.

Our art is the expression of desire,
Yeats said; and one who buys a landscape for
Its beauty takes home in his arms the bare
Outrageousness of an uncaring whore –
Among this trivial brick such rhetoric seems
Irrelevant to the short degraded lives
For whom the artist plans, the prophet dreams,
Perversely, virtuous law and golden hives.

Girl, through young generations still unborn
You will induce again and yet again
Disturbances within the learned men;
And they will feel brain from spare body torn,
Whether they hear, in ruins that their pity
Failed to prevent, their fear knew they would meet,
Or in the intact and reasonable city,
The disrespectful giggles of the street.

AMATEUR FILM-MAKING

A cold, still afternoon: mist gathered under
The distant black-lead avenues of branches;
Above our heads the drizzle ready to fall
Through greyness uniform, crepuscular;
And where we wander with the camera,
In the empty park, they have been felling trees
                And uprooting the stumps.

This is a portion of that film which proposes
To show the poet posed on various backgrounds,
Accompanied by his own voice, perhaps,
Reading a poem. The words will reinforce
The image only fortuitously, as
A crisis of one's life is impregnated
                With a cheap tune.

You say: 'This is ideal: I'll pan along
The horizontal trunks and you, near me,
Will be standing by the biggest of the roots.
The shot will end with you in close-up, leaning
Gently on your stick, expressionless, against
The complicated tendrils, stones, dried clay,
                Of the upturned root.'

[172]

The root is like a monstrous withered flower,
A Brobdingnagian mole or tumour, or
Some product of the microscopic eye
Of a romantic painter: and I stand
Beside it conscious, like a boy snapped with
His feared headmaster, of an incongruous
        And awful presence.

'I'm shooting now,' you say. 'Prepare your face.'
The camera purrs; you swivel slowly round,
Recording first the black recumbent forms,
Like shattered marbles, then the gasping root,
And finally I face the little eye –
Behind it yours, which watches in the glass
        The impersonal image.

'I'm holding this,' you say, and so I continue
To gaze, and decide it is impossible
Really to be expressionless. I feel
The initial cobwebs of the rain, and think
What jam I shall choose for tea, and of a book
I am reading on psychiatric art, and then
        Of myself, the poet.

I suppose I must be grateful that I am
Unlike the vast world of the sane and mad –
Not ill enough, or too ill, to create.
The camera stops. 'We've got,' you say, 'a great
Motion picture here.' 'You said it, dear boy,' I say.
And demonstrate the indubitable rain
        And that tea will be waiting.

POEM OUT OF CHARACTER

Rapidly moving from the end
To the middle of anthologies,
The poet starts to comprehend
The styles that never can be his.

The dreams of tremendous statements fade,
Inchoate still the passionate rhymes
Of men, the novel verse form made
To satirize and warn the times.

[173]

And yet at moments, as in sleep,
Beyond his book float images –
Those four great planets swathed in deep
Ammoniac and methane seas.

He walks the ruined autumn scene –
The trees a landscape painter's brown,
And through the foreground rags, serene
The faded sky, palladian town.

Or thinks of man, his single young,
The failure of the specialized,
Successful type; the curious, long
Years before earth was dramatized:

The West Wind Drift, that monstrous belt
Of sea below the planet's waist:
The twenty-one world cultures felt
Like fathers, doomed to be defaced.

Yes, these vast intimations rise
And still I merely find the words
For symbols of a comic size –
Ambiguous cats and sweets and birds.

Viewed through such tiny apertures
The age presents a leaf, a hair,
An inch of skin; while what enures,
In truth, behind the barrier,

Weltering in blood, enormous joys
Lighting their faces, is a frieze
Of giantesses, gods and boys;
And lions and inhuman trees.

SITTING FOR A PORTRAIT

To Raymond Mason

I

Committed to your impersonal scrutiny,
The searching eyes that look at mine unseeing,
I fear your verdict on my anatomy:
'There is a growth upon your inmost being.'

You work with that controlled, alarming haste,
As though an anaesthetic set a date.
I hear the pen's incisions, and my face
Tries to assume a calm, a mood, a fate.

Tries to assume what it has lost, in fact –
Identity: but now your strokes impart
That image to the paper; more an act,
I feel, of primitive magic than of art.

So this is what I am. Or rather what
I hoped I was – and wished that I was not.

II

Using as images my lineaments,
You have to make the poem come out right;
Attempting to arrange what life invents
In forms more meaningful, in better light.

Do you encounter stretched and clotted parts,
Or feel obliged to improvise, despair
Of reconciling textures with your arts,
Or long to end the quest before you're there?

Be comforted: it is not you who fail
But the intractable subject. I could wish
To have for you the satisfactory soul,
The certain shape, of apple or of dish.

Although I know you want to see, like me,
Always the human in reality.

AT A WARWICKSHIRE MANSION

Mad world, mad kings, mad composition – King John

Cycles of ulcers, insomnia, poetry –
Badges of office; wished, detested tensions.
Seeing the parsley-like autumnal trees
Unmoving in the mist, I long to be
The marvellous painter who with art could freeze
Their transitory look: the vast dissensions
Between the human and his world arise
And plead with me to sew the hurt with eyes.

Horn calls on ostinato strings: the birds
Sweep level out of the umbrageous wood.
The sun towards the unconsidered west
Floats red, enormous, still. For these the words
Come pat, but for society possessed
With frontal lobes for evil, rear for good,
They are incongruous as the poisoner's
Remorse or as anaemia in furs.

In the dank garden of the ugly house
A group of leaden statuary perspires;
Moss grows between the ideal rumps and paps
Cast by the dead Victorian; the mouse
Starves behind massive panels; paths relapse
Like moral principles; the surrounding shires
Darken beneath the bombers' crawling wings.
The terrible simplifiers jerk the strings.

But art is never innocent although
It dreams it may be; and the red in caves
Is left by cripples of the happy hunt.
Between the action and the song I know
Too well the sleight of hand which points the blunt,
Compresses, lies. The schizophrenic craves
Magic and mystery, the rest the sane
Reject: what force and audience remain?

The house is dark upon the darkening sky:
I note the blue for which I never shall
Find the equivalent. I have been acting
The poet's role for quite as long as I
Can, at a stretch, without it being exacting:
I must return to less ephemeral
Affairs – to those controlled by love and power;
Builders of realms, their tenants for an hour.

DIALOGUE OF THE POET AND HIS TALENT

Poet

I give you this calm, star-thick night of Spring,
A hooting owl that freezes in mid-air
The foreleg of the cat; a garden where
You may make courteous contact, like a king,
With lower life; and in the house an earth
Of anxiety and love, with some escape
Through sleep into that country of your birth
Where the desire can summon up the shape.

Talent

And these could be enough: I want to use
That almost-face, those other worlds; the small
Existences that parody the tall;
The holy family, the dream's excuse.
But I demand from you an attitude –
What Burckhardt called the Archimedean point
Outside events, perhaps – in which the crude
World and my words would marry like a joint.

Poet

How well I know your wish! It is my own.
To be committed or to stand apart:
Either would heal the wound. Alas, my heart,
Too cowardly, too cold, is always blown
By gusts of revulsion from the self and aim
Of simple man, yet sharing in his fate
It cannot calmly watch the stupid game
With the moon's irony, the orbit's state.

Then I must be content with images:
At worst the eye's own coloured stars and worms,
At best all the reflective mind affirms;
Wishing to people steppe, metropolis
And littoral, yet only finding room
To note inadequately on my pages
The senseless cataclysms of their doom;
While coiled in others sleep new words, new ages.

THE FINAL PERIOD

I watch across the desk the slight
Shape of my daughter on the lawn.
With youth's desire my fingers write
And then contain an old man's yawn.

At first my only verb was 'give',
In middle age sought out a god:
Ugly and impotent I live
The myth of a final period.

I see within the tetrastich
A jealousy as gross, intense,
As ulcered that real love of which
Art's tragedies alone make sense.

He pulses still the man of force –
The armoured chest, the boar-thick yards;
And here the woman-nature, coarse
Beneath the dainty silks and fards.

Appalling that should still arise
All that is dead and was untrue,
That my imagination flies
Where now my flesh may not pursue.

Life goes on offering alarms
To be imprisoned in the cage
Of art. I must invent more charms
To still the girl's erotic rage:

[178]

Frozen in their betrothal kiss,
The innocent boy will never move
To loose the codpiece, and his miss
Stay spellbound in her father's love –

And yet the actual girl will sigh
And cross the garden with her flowers;
And I will leave the desk, and try
To live with ordinary powers.

Bermuda or Byzantium –
To some utopia of forgiving
And of acceptance I have come,
But still rebellious, still living.

The first absurd haphazard meeting
With one loved unrequitedly,
The insurrection caused by fleeting
Words of my own, while I stood by –

Those fatal and recorded times
Return like heartburn, and I see
Behind heroic plangent rhymes
Unutterable deficiency.

Even this noon of greens and blues;
June's badges, roses of human red;
Birds in the cavern of the yews;
A lark's quaver figure in my head;

The car in the lane that circumvents
The archipelagos of dung –
These trivial concomitants
Of feeling, these, too, must be sung.

And in the song all will be whole,
Immortal, though the author pass –
Ended his little speaking rôle –
On to the doomed and venal mass.

She comes whom I would marble through
Her painful and tumultuous years,
So she would wake at last in true
Epochs, to music of the spheres.

TO POSTERITY?

I wonder, putting down this opening line,
If what will follow's that unlikely freak –
The verse that must outlast my life and speak
To those unborn and send along their spine
The chill delicious hand that now I feel,
Truth in its ravishing mask of the ideal.

So that the composition need not show
The velvet nude or great empurpled sky
But merely what at present meets my eye:
The promising pen and paper in the glow
Of lamplight wars occasionally permit;
The books unburnt; the living flesh unhit.

This moment – reaching out towards the box
Of cigarettes, the brass-augmented theme
Announced upon the radio – is the dream
That I would wish to cheat the racing clocks,
Dials that mark the vital seventy years,
The culture's thousand, the coming lustrum's fears.

Though in such moment there of course will be
A sense of time undreamt of even by these:
Ages piled on the planet's flank that freeze
With inconceivable immobility;
And far back in the wastes the tiny span
Of the erect and big-brained Primate, man.

TO A FRIEND LEAVING FOR GREECE

From the Tin Islands' autumn where the foliage hangs
In green and yellow tatters like an old
Set on a provincial stage, you go
To burgundy seas, white harbours, empty skies –
Greece, with its islands like discovered bones,
Its names of our neuroses and its youth
Made dark 'with fabulous accounts and traditions'.

To disinter the universal crime
Of the legendary past is possible.
Possible, too, the survival of the once
Tormented and warring centre of the world
As fallen columns, terribly eroded
Decapitated bearded heads – ignored
By the quite happy and unimportant heirs.

You visit a country where the unclean being
Who brought disaster has already been expelled
And far back in its history the gloomy date:
'Twenty-eighth year of the War. Blockade of Athens.'
Will you return with hopeful messages
For the new victims of the Theban king
And of the destroyers of democracy?

MYTHOLOGICAL SONNETS

To My Son

I

Far out, the voyagers clove the lovat sea
Which fizzed a little round its oily calms,
Straw sun and bleached planks swinging, the
Gunwale ribbed with a score of tawny arms.
Nursing a bellyache, a rope-rubbed hand
Or a vague passion for the cabin boy,
Accustomed to the rarity of land
And water's ennui, these found all their joy
In seeing the hyphens of archipelagos
Or a green snake of coast rise and fall back.
And little they imagined that in those
Inlets and groves, stretched out as on the rack,
Their girls were ground under the enormous thews
Of visiting gods, watched by staid munching ewes.

II

There actually stood the fabled riders,
Their faces, to be truthful, far from white;
Their tongue incomprehensible, their height
Negligible: in a word, complete outsiders.

Why had they come? To wonder at the tarts,
Trade smelly hides, gawp at the statuary,
Copy our straddling posture and our arts?
How right that we had not thought fit to flee!

'Join us at cocktails, bathing?' No reply.
'Let's see your wild dances, hear your simple airs.'
No move save the shifting of a shifty eye.

Trailing great pizzles, their dun stallions
Huddled against the hedges while our mares
Cavorted on the grass, black, yellow, bronze.

III

The legendary woman he had sought,
Whose name had been as threadbare and remote
As God's, whose awful loveliness was taught
With participle, peak and asymptote,

Now lay below him smiling past his gaze;
The breasts a little flaccid on their cage
Of ribs, her belly's skin as speckled as
A flower's throat. She had been caught by age.

And he could see that even in the past
The pillars that enclosed the myth concealed
A slippery stinking altar and a vast
Horde of lewd priests to whom all was revealed.

Yet she was fair still, and he cried out in vain
To reach and own her far complacent fane.

IV

Beneath a bit of dirty cloth a girl's
Thin severed hand; a portrait of a man
Streaming with blood from badly painted curls;
A withered heart just pulsing in a pan.

Even though these have been displayed to us
Can we believe them or the cause of their
Existence, comically anomalous?
Here under peeling walls, a sceptic stare,

The hand writes its seditious words of love,
Belief goes on being painfully expressed,
And pity flutters at its far remove
From the historical tormented breast.

Did God intend this squalid spuriousness
To mean both what it is and purports? Yes.

V

A granulated, storm-blown, ashen sky
Behind blanched, still unruined columns where
Monarch and queen, prophetic sister, dry
Old statesman still descend a marble stair.

'You are my destiny.' 'Do not go forth
Today in combat.' 'This whole realm is sick.'
Their voices rise into the breaking light
And die away towards the barbarous north.

These could not, though half conscious of their plight,
Grasp the extent of time's appalling trick
That stole the flesh that was so sweet and thick,
Broke wall and bones, saved from the gorgeous site
Some kitchen pot, discarded and obese,
And gave the great names to horses and disease.

VI

The sage cut an orange through the navel, dwelt
Upon the curious pattern then revealed.
Breaking a habit makes the world, he felt,
Burst out with meanings usually concealed.

Experimenting later with that girl
Who cooked his rice and dusted all his books,
He saw what he had never seen – a curl
Soft in the well where the neck's sinews rise,
And yearned in pity that with no rebuke
She lent herself to these perverted grips.

But as for her, she never thought her lot
Called for emotion. This strange exercise
Came with the rice and dust – the habitual cut
Of a world small and dry and full of pips.

VII

Well now, the virgin and the unicorn –
Although its point and details are obscure
The theme speeds up the pulses, to be sure.
No doubt it is the thought of that long horn
Inclined towards a lady young, well-born,
Unfearful, naïve, soft, ecstatic, pure.
How often, dreaming, have we found the cure
For our malaise, to tear or to be torn!

In fact, the beast and virgin merely sat,
I seem to think, in some enamelled field;
He milky, muscular, and she complete
In kirtle, bodice, wimple. Even that
Tame conjugation makes our eyeballs yield
Those gems we long to cast at someone's feet.

VIII

Suns in a skein, the uncut stones of night,
Calm planets rising, violet, golden, red –
Bear names evolved from man's enormous head
Of gods who govern battle, rivers, flight,
And goddesses of science and delight;
Arranged in the mortal shapes of those who bled
To found a dynasty or in great dread
Slept with their destiny, full-breasted, white.

But long before stout Venus, clanking Mars,
What appellations had the eternal stars?
When, cheek by jowl with burial pits, rank dens
Lay open to the dark, and dwarfish men
Stared under huge brow-ridges, wits awry,
What fearful monsters slouched about the sky?

IX

Naked, the girl repelled his lustful hands:
Her shining skin exuded awe, like art.
The visiting god held out his simple gift
And, stepping modestly across the sands,
The innocent fool played her predestined part
And clad herself in the lubricious shift.

Years later and from that same place their child,
Lugging his vessel to the sheltered reach,
Started on his heroic bloody fate.
The ancient motive of his father bent
His gaze towards the ocean, wine-dark, wild:
He never saw upon the trampled beach
The thing that had assumed, but all too late,
The hard epidermis of a succulent.

X

Girls fight like fiends in paintings to defend
Themselves from centaurs: envious, outraged,
We never think (our feelings too engaged)
The crisis through to its surprising end
When the sad, baffled beast with clumsy hooves
Paws impotently at the delicate
And now relenting limbs. So Hercules,
Whose lovely wife the centaur Nessus got,
Should not have loosed at him the angry shot
That stained the shirt that brought the hero's fate.

I do not know what this conclusion proves
Unless it is that honest lust will freeze
To piteous art, and subtle jealousy
Must poison needlessly what has to be.

[185]

XI

Mysterious indeed are epochs, dates
And influences: how a woman springs
Into a painting of organic things
And gradually moves forward till the great
Shoulders and flanks blot out the foliate
Sepia. Then once more the fashion swings:
Among a tempted saint's imaginings
A thin pot-bellied virgin emanates.

Even the most serene and opulent
Goddesses rise from the sordid life of man,
Who catching, say, a girl in stockinged feet
Arranging a shop-window sees the event
Translated to a new and staggering span
Of art, the previous pantheon obsolete.

XII

That the dread happenings of myths reveal
Our minds' disorder is a commonplace.
Myths, too, are history's half-forgotten face
Remoulded by desire, though we will feel
Compared with myths contemporary life unreal.
Tower and wall may sink without a trace
But the strong sense of lust and of disgrace
Lives on.
        Ourselves have seen Prometheus steal
The fire the overlords denied to man,
Which act enchained him to Caucasian rocks.
We still await the hero that must free
The great conception whose ambiguous plan
At once brought to the world its evil box
And the sole chance to share felicity.

XIII

Once brought indoors the leaf-eyed cat became
An emblem disproportionately odd.
Its blunt head, much enlarged but looking tame,
Displaced the human lineaments of God.
The teasing beast that squatted on her rock
And ate the duffers had a feline face,
And even he who turned the riddle's lock
Went on to symbolize mankind's disgrace.

Down corridors of night an awful thing
Brushes against us softly like a wing.
Our hands that reach across the bed for her
We love meet unexpected, frightening fur.
And looking in the glass we find at last
The claw-made lacerations of the past.

XIV

Discovered in this vine-ridged, rounded land
In which its tutelary goddess, tanned
And huge, had spent her slender mortal youth –
A number of ancient men. Old age, old age!
Wine, evening sunshine, philosophic truth –
Nothing can still that agonizing rage
For what was never ruled but for an hour
And now lies far beyond the sceptre's power.

Towards the temple stride young girls whose dress,
Taut with the zephyr of their passage, shows
The secret lack which men initially
Despise, then eye with tragic covetousness,
And lastly envy, conscious of the blows
Time hammers on their superfluity.

XV

Even (we think) the heroes cracked at last –
Great lumping extroverts with shields that pelts
Of only fabulous beasts could cover, vast
Lickerishness and canyons of half-healed welts.

[187]

The man of ordinary valour, size,
Finds it impossible to visualise
These others – who had been alone with girls
On islands, with their deeds like daydreams, curls,

Hawk profiles, iron paps – that these could creep
Far from the friendly tents, the invading hordes,
And throw themselves upon the ground and weep
Or, growing mad, attempt to eat their swords.

Such were the flaws their sires could not foresee,
Blinded by marvellous human nudity.

XVI

How startling to find the portraits of the gods
Resemble men! Even those parts where we
Might have expected to receive the odds
Are very modest, perhaps suspiciously.

For we cannot forget that these aloof and splendid
Figures with negligible yards and curls
Arranged in formal rising suns descended,
With raging lust, on our astonished girls –

No doubt because they were intimidated
By their own kind (those perfect forms that man,
Ironically, has always adulated)
And craved the extravagance of nature's plan.

So that humanity's irregular charms
In time fused with divine breasts, buttocks, arms.

XVII

We read of children taken by the heel
And tossed over battlements; a sharp hot stake
Sizzling in a giant's eye; and near a lake
Two tender virgins lying naked while
Unknown to them four indescribable
Monsters approach. That world, we much would like
To think, is simply an artistic fake,
Nothing to do with that in which we dwell.

But could mere images make even now
Ears drum with lust, the chest run secret shame?
The myths are here: it was our father's name
The maiden shrieked in horror as she turned
To wrinkled bark; our dearest flesh that burned,
Straddling her legs inside the wooden cow.

XVIII

The stench hung even in the garden: down
The corridor it thickened: in the room
It strangled us. The visage, cramped and brown,
Seemed to belong already in the tomb.

'How long has he been at this dreadful point?'
– Idle remark to try to hide our fears;
But the astonishing reply was: 'Years.'

And as the sheet was lifted to anoint
The noisome wound we shudderingly turned
And tried to understand what we had learned:

That this old squalid hurt was done some bright
Day when it seemed there was no end to truth,
And the large heroes wandered in the sight
Of gods still faithful, through the planet's youth.

XIX

Stone countenances, bearded, ill with time;
The screeching class of starlings, dissident,
In cultured cities; crooked wigs of lime
That contradict the famous masks' intent –
The nervous images that haunt an age
Bud in the unremembered past and flower
In that long battle art and history wage:
And epochs compressed in childhood and the womb
Breed the regalia of the public hour.
The murdered father's head leans by those doors;
The brothers' quarrel stands behind the doom
Of one life's sickening and recurrent wars;
And the smooth tongue that offers love is built
On teeth ground flat in violent dreams of guilt.

[189]

MONOLOGUE IN AUTUMN

With yellow teeth the hunter tears and crunches
Whole boughs of the quince, then walks away,
His hind legs on a mannequin's straight line.
The clipped back (ample as a bed, unyielding
Save for a slight threat like an anchored ship)
Returns what always astonishes – the warmth
Of a new embrace.

                    And you arrive. I help
To raise your body in its carapace
Of steel and leather. Then I see you move,
A centaur, down the slopes towards the plain
Where in the mist the sun already hangs
Its monstrous copper and autumnal shape.

You fade. I turn across the leaf-crumbed lawn:
Under the mulberry the gales have torn
A cat gnaws the purple lining of the pelt
It emptied yesterday.

                  And now the house:
First the twin balustrades and then the busts
Whose formal curls and noses are as rough
As if their existence truly were marine
Under the window's random lights. Inside,
The books propound what all books must propound:
Whether man shall accept the authority of God
Or of his senses.

                  In the drawing room
The fire sadly burns for no one: soon
Your guests will descend, taste tea on Sunday tongues;
Their lives and mine and yours go on with talk,
The disposition of chairs and lamps, the opened
Doors to the terrace, the order of good-nights.

Hard to imagine that the ambassador,
Your cousin, lives at this same hour among
Furs, fuming breaths, ardours of moral striving;
That such half world exists for which our own
Has manufactured all its cruel swords and faces
Whose profits surround us here as love affairs,
Portable sketching outfits, hair arranged
Like savages and scented with the whole
Resources of science.

                              Yet this must account
For what I feel, in love with you, within
This house and season – that residual sadness
After bare rooms and trees have been subtracted
And love has learned the trick of suffering
Its object's relative indifference.
Why, as you always ask, should I so dread
What threatens from the rivalry of two
Crude ways of life, two grotesque empires, whose
Ideals, diplomacy and soldiery
We must despise? But merely to formulate
The question seems to me to answer it,
And show that shameful collective death as quite
Other than what we think of in the dawn –
The torturer that will test us in our cell.

I open the piano, sound a note,
Remember dreams. How could you come to grow
In my imagination (that must have been
My wish) so sallow and in such a place –
As strange and circumstantial as the future?
You said the words too wild to be recalled,
Lay back and gently died.
                              You will return,
Your horse not sweating quite enough to mark
The lapse of time. I shall forbear to ask
The question that makes pain a certainty,
But merely look with the avoiding eyes
Of a Cesario or Cordelia.

And dinner will stretch into drowsiness,
Owls swing like theatre fairies past the moon
Whose battered lantern lights the tops of woods
And shines along the calm, dividing sea,
Painting with fire the armour in the harbours
Which lie encircled by their snowy lands
And multiplicity of helpless wills.
The uninvited images invade
The separate and sleeping heads: dead branches
Threading the sockets of those equine skulls

Whose riders perished in the useless war,
Whose teeth are rattled in their open jaws
By tempests from sastrugi, and whose foals
Stream through what whitens their brazil-nut eyes
Towards savannahs where the planet holds
Only inhuman species to its pap.

ON THE MOUNTAIN

I

Why red, why red? I ask myself, observing
A girl's enamelled nails, not understanding
The convention – an unrealistic art.

I live in a suburb of the capital,
A hill of villas, and sometimes note such things;
Old enough to remember better days.

The stoics have virtually disappeared.
I like to think myself the last of them,
Shaken but not devoured by ghastly omens.

The theatres are given up to leg shows
And gladiatorial games. The savage beasts
Are weary with the number of their victims.

In poetry the last trace of conviction
Has long since been extinguished. Round the temples
Are crowds of flautists, eunuchs and raving females.

The decoration of the baths and other
Edifices of importance is assigned
To those same careless slaves who mix the mortar.

The so-called educated classes share
The superstitions and amusements of
The vulgar, gawping at guts and moaning singers.

Atrocious taxes to 'defend' the frontiers;
Fixing maximum prices yet deploring the black market
– These the preoccupations of the state.

And the alarming aspect of imperial
Succession! The imperial madness! O
My country, how long shall we bear such things?

I find a little comfort in recalling
That complaints of evil times are found in every
Age which has left a literature behind:

And that the lyric is always capable
Of rejuvenation (as is the human heart),
Even in times of general wretchedness.

II

In my garden, at the risk of annoying my cat,
I rescue a fledgling: as it squeaks, I see
That its tongue is like something inside a watch.

They would not find it odd, those Others –
Mysterious community, not outside
And not within the borders of the empire;

Not the barbarians precisely nor
The slaves: indeed, from their strange treason no
Mind is exempt . . . even the emperor's!

Could I believe? Surrender to the future,
The inevitability of the future – which
Nevertheless can only come by martyrdom?

Respect those priestly leaders, arguing
Whether the Second Person of the Three
Is equal or subordinate to the First?

While in their guarded monasteries they lift
Their greasy cassocks to ecstatic girls –
Under the bed their secret box of coin.

I suppose their creed must conquer in the end
Because it gives the simplest and most complete
Answer to all men ask in these bad years.

Is there a life beyond this life? Must art
Be the maidservant of morality?
And will the humble triumph? Yes. Yes. Yes.

Disgusting questions, horrible reply;
Deplorable the course of history:
And yet we cannot but regard with awe

The struggle of the locked and rival systems,
Involving the entire geography
Of the known world, through epochs staggeringly prolonged.

To name our cities after poets, or
To hasten the destruction of the species –
The debate continues chronic and unresolved.

III

How rapidly one's thoughts get out of hand!
With my unsatisfactory physique
I watch the blossom through the blinding rain,

Cringe the while at the shoddy workmanship
Of the piddling gutter – typical of the times –
And stroke with skeleton hand the mortal fur.

It is as hard to realize where we are
As for the climber on the famous peak
For whom the familiar outline is no more

The record of a deadly illness or
The tearing organs of a bird of prey
But merely boredom, breathing, prudence, stones.

FAUSTIAN SKETCHES

Faust and the Dancers

I saw their skirts' inverted petals
All frail and overblown,
Their heads of various shining metals,
Their arms that would have flown
Save for the dovetailed bone.

I saw the tights, chalk-white, unwrinkled,
Full of their fated shapes,
The dark or sparkling beasts' fur sprinkled
Down deeply-valleyed napes,
The breasts unround as grapes.

I wanted privately to whisper
Their fragile public name,
Become the tease, the pet, the lisper,
Transformer of their shame,
The partner in the game.

Sick of my years' renunciations,
Pretence of calm at joy
Bequeathed to following generations,
What soul would I destroy
To be again a boy!

Indeed, I deny that soul lives after
The power has gone to bend
These slanting spines beneath one's laughter
Till dancers all contend
Against the dance's end.

Faust Bathing

Standing with girded loins beside
Thalassa, watching in the tide
The bathers white as halibut,
There comes the feeling in the gut

[195]

For piteous humanity.
These faces, vulgar, gay, unfree,
These bums divided like a root,
These breasts impossible or cute,
And varied, as signatures, these howls
As from absurd displaying fowls,
Remind me of my superior brain,
My aptness for intenser pain,
And my paralysis before
That bleeding accident, the core
Of living.
          Now I plunge. The cold
Deludes me that I am not old.
The stringy limbs are galvanized
Like one of my own frogs, surprised
By current from the jars, and speed
Through foam, turds, condoms, bootlace weed.
Soon spent, I turn upon my back:
The billows nicely weigh the slack;
Above their syrup greens a slow
Sea-bird, brown-smudged like urban snow,
Sails skies as soft as towelling.

On land again I feel that wing,
The symbol of creative power,
Hang rotting from my neck. The hour
Has come when all philosophies
That seek mysterious unities
Of number, element and force
In stuff of air, star, gold and horse,
And those utopias of rich
Gardener, exiled tsarevich
And moral poetry, are able
No longer to console the fable-
Seeking imagination of
The sensitive, the starved of love.
Now only magic can reverse
The impetus towards the worse
And halt the atom in its rage
To burn the world, bring on old age.

Magic

It's magic that has ravished me.
Study to magic, magic to desire,
And magic is to set me free.

Though haunted by the poetry
That shows the age its mask of ire,
It's magic that has ravished me.

I serve that plain philosophy
Whose world is merely air, earth, fire –
And magic is to set me free.

In impotent maturity
I see afresh love's lewd attire:
It's magic that has ravished me.

Power to transcend the sad toupee,
The miser heart, I shall require.
And magic is to set me free

To range the kingdoms of the sea
And pluck the salt rose from the brier.
It's magic that has ravished me
And magic is to set me free.

Dreams in the City

The luxury of cities prompts
Deluded dreams. Of accumulating
Intaglio rings depicting, say,
The sauromatic virgins or
A tiny priest with golden bough.
Of cornering the market in
Rhinoceros horn or yellow pepper.
Of being done in terre-verte
Or bronze by some heroic artist.
Of selling against the frightful future
Or buying against the certainty
Of the exploiters' immortality.

Fluently I write astounding words:
The force that bends missiles to the brain
Equals the wave that pulls maroon
And brown from the uncoloured moth;
And all this substance of the world
Was not created, yet lacked being
Before it flew away as stars.

Or: Faust abducted from her Duke
The grave clever beauty, starved of love.

In certain streets there seems to be
A scattering in the air – not starlings
Or dust or abandoned wrappings but
The very sordidness of the city,
Though here might stand the famous piles
I long to inhabit in the roles
That need a purple wig or huge
Cuirass with simulated paps.

But in dreams I feel myself at one
With my times and think it no disgrace
To share the lust for the principate;
And after all what great quintets
Were written for the viola-playing king!
Besides, the status quo can only
Be altered by devout ascetics
Independent of the enormously
Expensive life of cities,
Where under awnings metal ticks
On porcelain through the general sound
Of laughter, wheels and wheeling birds.
And yet how fresh the air in gardens
Whose boundaries heraldic cats
Conventionally signify,
And through whose trees there sometimes thread
Dead boughs whose canvas gently bears
Poppy and muskets to the heart!

Fresh on the skin, that envelope
Bulging with emotion, truly fresh,
So that with curiosity and passion
I watch the chalked and empty crescent
Fill slowly with golden light,
As though its meaning had been devised
By man – 'A good evening for verse
Or love or happiness or money' –
And not, as it is, an eye that sees
Even the disasters of its own
Order with complete indifference –
As: the collision of galaxies;
Life starting on primeval shores.

In the Wolf's Glen the seventh bullet
Killed a pale deer with flaxen hair.
The portents are sufficiently grisly,
No doubt, for all who sell their souls.

I hear a terrifying aria;
Flames send their giant shadows on
Tawdry and flimsy scenery.
Human ambition elevates
The humble, introspective self
To unimaginable cruces;
Where citizens actually see approach
The flat-nosed riders of the steppe.
Can I be that improbable
Singer, this the unlikely song?

Faust's Servant

I'm quite the opposite of my clever master.
He's at his books all day. I spy on ladies
And think of naught but filth, though there's no faster
Road for a chap to Hades.

I wish I had his brains to take my mind
Off of the feminine anatomy.
He reads at Greek and Latin till he's blind,
Doesn't see the things I see.

[199]

Today the girls seem bigger there than ever:
Not that I ask for anything so young.
It's just I find it hard that I shall never
Again slip home the bung.

A widow thirty-five or so would do –
But what's the use of dreaming when my chin
Says to my nose 'How are you?' as I chew,
And buttocks are so thin.

When bladder gets me up at four I'd give
My soul for sweeter breath and tighter pills,
And sometimes for a second really live
With magic's miracles.

Jottings of Faust

I

Assuming spectacles enables me
Better to eye the pulchritude of girls;
But joy is dulled by realizing that they see
In turn an ageing man in spectacles.

II

Straight from my study's stupor I awoke;
Walked through the curtains to the dazzling sky;
Saw on a flower a frightening butterfly –
A long-horned devil in a battered cloak.

III

A thought occurs to me
As I comb my hair and see
The pistils at my crown
Of silver in the brown.
Not the familiar one
Of what the years have done;

Not terror nor regret
At all this coronet
Announces; but a quite
Impersonal sense of white
And coarse in common fate
With soft and chocolate –
Some creature of the snows
And mould that briskly goes
Before the aiming guns –
The sense of how life runs
In harness with another,
Its pale and powerful brother.

IV

The fountains only play
On Wednesday and Saturday,
But the momentary spray

Is caught by the camera
Of the lucky visitor,
Which also records the blur

Of Faust crossing the square,
To puzzle the developer:
'Who is the figure there,

That with ambiguous mission
Ruins the composition
Of the dolphins' ammunition

Against the sea nymph's arse?'
– A dweller in this farce
Of myth that will never pass.

V

That humans should engender ivory
Is Faust's, to him, surprising reverie
As magical day ends and through the dusk
Light gleams on Helen's even little tusk.

Helen

It staggers me to find between her thighs
The gold that struck me with such awe when first
I saw it like a halo round her head.

That I am kneeling here, that from her rise
The imperfections that make passion cursed,
That all the Grecian and the Trojan dead

Are dead indeed, that now I must despise
The breathing wish that from my old age burst
And stretched itself upon the crumpled bed,

That youth and lust are lies and are not lies,
That no man who's alive has met the worst –
These propositions fill my heart with dread,

Pressed though it is upon a breast whose guise
Was fashioned by a swan, himself immersed
In love profane, by human nymph misled.

Questions to Mephistopheles

I

'Why did I choose this trivial shape,' you ask –
'The rouge, the plumpness and the mincing gait?'
I answer: is it not appropriate
For one whose Master laid on him the task

Of undertaking that the Paphian flask
And the Circassian dancing girl await
The soul's vendor? Besides, one can't equate
The real me with any human mask.

I mean, think how God's hate must change the entire
Expression, serving Satan hump the back;
Imagine further how the holocaust
Of hell dries up the flesh, that devils lack,
Like angels, sex and therefore must perspire
In vile self-love. Perhaps imagine Faust.

[202]

'If Mephistopheles in serving Faust
Can bring on dancing girls and get him soused
Why doesn't Mephistopheles thus serve
Himself?' It's not that I haven't got the nerve,
And obviously not because I think
There's any turpitude in sex and drink.

Why then? Remember that my former state
Was perfect innocence, without desire
Except to praise my God. Then came the dire
Notion He fell in love with to create
A being of moral cowardice and great
Pudenda. From that time His angel choir
– Thirst still unknown to them, groins still entire –
Were set to shaping man's disgusting fate.

Gretchen

He didn't talk of love at first,
But all he'd read and thought about.
A blackbird sang as though he'd burst,
And then the rosy sun went out.

It still was sultry in the garden,
And when at last he took my hand
I thought I'd have to ask his pardon
For sweating, burning, like a brand.

He told me I was innocent
And very beautiful and young,
But his best flattery wasn't meant –
Being the seriousness of his tongue.

He asked to kiss me. Oh I gave
My lips to him with all my heart.
Close to my ear I heard his grave
Voice vow that we should never part.

And when he gently went to lift
My breast, my only qualm at all
Was that he should regard my gift
As too ridiculously small.

[203]

This was not like those other cases
When boys have fumbled, brawny, red,
And I've stared at their indrawn faces
A puzzled breath before I fled.

Though as he slid beneath my skirt
My voice cried 'No' and 'No' once more
When staggeringly his hand begirt
What had been only mine before.

How could he like what I myself
Had, save for nature, quite ignored:
The part thrust on me by some elf
Forgotten at my christening board?

I'd put on new the drawers that fashion
Decreed that smart girls ought to wear.
They were not meant to rouse his passion
But to make ugliness lovely there.

He never saw their style or hue,
For with a surgeon's deft dispatch
He bent me to the pose he knew
Would let him make the outrageous scratch.

And in a moment all was done:
The pain, the dagger's bulk and range;
And the assassin looked upon
His murder's mess, emotion's change.

His love was gone: I said as much.
Again his hands sought out their goal.
He said: 'To have the right to touch
You there I've given up my soul.

'Perhaps it was precisely this
Was lacking as we closely fought.
I might have pressed a father's kiss
On one more guilty than she thought.

'And need not have exchanged for love
What lives on love's renunciation,
And shared with you the burden of
The cries of human tribulation.'

The Princes

A reckless use of fur and cloth of gold,
Wastage of peacocks, boars and apple fool,
Enormous men with hired tights and pig
Eyes who surround descending princes,
Bargaining at impossible hours amid
Small tipsy trebles and Mongolian
Acrobats – this is how fate is ordered through
The world's inhabited and cultured regions.

At such a weighty congress Faust arrives –
Another wizard (though a famous one)
Among decipherers and economists
And experts in the ailments of old men.
Having passed all his life through want and wars,
Innumerable wrong decisions, tyrannies,
And bluff field-marshals, he has always dreamed
Of finding a second youth and reckless power.

Two or three kings are playing in the garden
With variable skill at cup and ball.
'Peru, this is the celebrated Faust . . .'
'How interesting to meet a real magician . . .'
'Do you read palms or entrails?' 'What success
In the alchemic line?' The trumpet sounds.
All pass into the specially built hall
Which cost ten architects and many masons.

Platoons of pallid secretaries surround
Each place, at which are set the texts of long
Insulting speeches. The morning's business starts.
'Before we can permit our boiling oil
To cool we must be sure your catapults
Are pointing from our frontiers.' 'If your spies
Disguise themselves as dervishes, our kites
Will tumble fire-balls on your mausoleums.'

Faust makes himself invisible and gives
The Duke of Seville a buffet on the ear.
This potentate turns to his deadly foe, the Grand
Mufti, and dabs him with his withered arm
And overturns that paralytic Turk,
Whose allies, rushing for the door, collide
With the false friends of Spain. Thrombosis, rupture,
Incontinence of urine, rife in the hall!

Then Faust ignites some Chinese crackers, which
Explode among a group of experts in
Fearsome ballistics. They take flight. And soon
The gorgeous chariots and litters move
Along the dusty roadways of the world.
Faust is alone, and dares the planet's wars
To wound him more than his unease of soul,
Gazing upon the empty towers of man.

Finale

The lid is taken off the flames of hell,
An angel chorus opens in the sky,
Its fatal twelve the clock begins to tell,
Power and ambition see that they must die,
Irrelevant love is weeping where she fell
And Faust prepares to act the final lie.

Faust's life before the Change was all a lie:
To him the world about as bad as hell
Appeared, since he unduly feared its fell
Rulers, and he was quite prepared to die,
Could the affair be painless. In the sky
There was no father he might kiss and tell.

The only good, so far as he could tell,
Was to find pretty girls with whom to lie,
But him they saw as one about to die.
To have your thoughts on earth is perfect hell
When earth imagines that they're on the sky.
No wonder, tempted slightly, that he fell.

With profile, wealth and vigour, it befell
That his great moving moment was to tell
A simple girl that pie lurked in the sky.
And when this specious statement proved a lie
And he had left her to reside in hell,
He thought he'd find it easy just to die.

But see, the moment comes when he must die.
The pit appears in which the angels fell.
At last he truly grasps the idea of hell –
Despite his past, before he could not tell
Precisely how existence was a lie
Measured against the spite of earth and sky.

Is he by love, or something from the sky,
To be redeemed and never really die;
Or is the optimistic art a lie?
–Faust being right when in his grizzled fell,
Immured among his books, he used to tell
His fellow humans human life was hell.

Hell! a great legend spreads across the sky:
'Tell Faust he's dead but shall not ever die.'
Fell Gods sustained by weak men rarely lie.

THE HITTITES

Short, big-nosed men with nasty conical caps,
Occasionally leering but mostly glum,
Retroussé shoes and swords at oblong hips –

Or so the stone reliefs depicted them.
But how trustworthy can those pictures be?
Even in that remote millennium

The artist must have seen society
From some idiosyncratic vantage point.
Short, big-nosed, glum, no doubt, but cowardly,

For him, as always, the time was out of joint;
And his great patrons as they passed the stone
Would turn their eyes and mutter that complaint

Whose precise nature never will be known.

VERSIONS OF LOVE

'My love for you has faded' – thus the Bad
Quarto, the earliest text, whose midget page
Derived from the imperfect memories
Of red-nosed, small-part actors
Or the atrocious shorthand of the age.

However, the far superior Folio had
'My love for you was fated' – thus implying
Illicit passion, a tragic final act.
And this was printed from the poet's own
Foul papers, it was reckoned;
Supported by the reading of the Second
Quarto, which had those sombre words exact.

Such evidence was shaken when collation
Showed that the Folio copied slavishly
The literals of that supposedly
Independent Quarto. Thus one had to go
Back to the first text of all.

'My love for you has faded' – quite impossible.
Scholars produced at last the emendation:
'My love for you fast endured.'
Our author's ancient hand that must have been
Ambiguous and intellectual
Foxed the compositors of a certainty.
And so the critical editions gave
Love the sound status that she ought to have
In poetry so revered.

But this conjecture cannot quite destroy
The question of what the poet really wrote
In the glum middle reaches of his life:
Too sage, too bald, too fearful of fiasco
To hope beyond his wife,
Yet aching almost as promptly as a boy.

THREE BIRDS

Pigeon

A cropped, grey, too-small, bullet, Prussian head
Leading a body closely modelled on
A silly clay model for the sporting gun.

One shoos the other from the scattered bread,
Prolonging needlessly a marital
Irascibility. The bill could well

Support a pair of spectacles: instead,
All who will closely look at once espy
A geometrical and insane eye.

Starling

Abandoning looks to art like a diva, the young
Starling opens its bill at an obscene
Angle, and squawks.

Not art but wrath, no doubt, at seeing the wrong
World: felines sprawled across his green-
Crusted pie of worms.

Was it this bather-sleek and quartz-flecked rowdy
Who later lay upon his back and showed
That beneath his arms

The upholstery in fact was dun and dowdy:
Disdained except by one extended bored
Tea-sipper's claw?

Budgerigar

Head, miniature helmet
Of steel-white armour plate
To hide and facilitate
An apparatus for spying
Danger from every sense.

The eye, a camera lens
At its tiniest aperture
Whose bead of jet is closed
By an incredibly neat suture.
Mask, god of Nilotic lands;
Like an old semite, all nose,
With the beard tucked well beneath:
Twin nostril holes above,
Punctures of some dread syringe.
One's finger is clutched by the hands
Of a Lilliputian orphan,
While on its agile hinge
The blunt tongue juggles with
Regurgitations of love.

ANATOMY OF THE POET

I

Mantled with hair, walled in with bone,
The skull breeds its terrific notions.
And then the little windows groan

Their shutters up to let the oceans
Gush through their tender apertures,
Blue shires round currents green as lotions;

Or black-pored mountains, gorse-egged moors;
Or rivers where weed trails like snot
On the white flanks of herbivores.

And thus the soul combines with what
It thought indifferent to its mad
Destiny, and with foolish hot

Optimism and in language bad
And gorgeous speaks to the object of
Its wish. The godly iliad;

The eighteenth attitude of love
Of second-rate Rachmaninov.

II

How liable to ulcerate,
The mouth where poems form! This hole
To succour and regurgitate,

This soft, sharp, empty, giving goal
Of other mouths – we utterly fail
To keep it for the vaporous soul.

What staggering words may we exhale
From rottenness; and even when
The structure like a lowered sail

Collapses on itself, yes even then
The orifice goes on reciting
Noble trochees, and seeks to fasten

Its sucker upon all inviting
Firmness, regardless of repulse.
But see the poet's actual writing –

No strings of lust or chancred hulls.
There all is sunlight, flower-decked bulls.

III

Some agile ancestor bequeathed
To the poet his poet's modern hand.
Round boughs coal-destined it was wreathed,

Or moved adroitly on the sand.
The limb that scribbles presupposes
A skinless and a suffering gland

Whose baby's great mouth never closes
Upon its speechless scream. To touch
The epidermis of white roses

With tentative love and then besmutch
Itself is what the hand requires,
Running blots into tears. How much

It longs to be the cook's or dyer's
Hand, whose deft motions demonstrate
A way of living with the fires

And hues of commonplace estate;
But this was not the sad claws' fate.

IV

And who decreed that it should be
Heart-shaped, the heart? And crimson, clenched
Around the strong machinery

Which warrants that the man is drenched
In blood from top to toe? And hard
If, as must be, the thing is wrenched

From where in happy disregard
It leans upon its beating side?
The seat of passion is this scarred

Muscle, but soon it may provide
Merely enough of that to keep
Its own gigantic needs supplied;

And sacrificial girls who creep
Naked, with naked steel, towards
The breathing breast will burrow deep

And find in the tangled mass of cords
No pulsing love but love's dead words.

V

It seems to concentrate the gaze –
A famous monument or flayed
Scar. Sometimes important: days

Of slogan, oratory, grenade.
At other times it shocks: the place
Where we were negligently made,

So crude as to call out for grace
Or pathos. And this dog-like trait
Is what engenders in the race

The power of spelling out the great
Unutterable aims of art.
For when we write about the fate

Of champions or of God's wide heart
What wells up in our throats and flows
Through our trembling pen is that strong part –

As though the angel and the rose,
Like love, must use the things most gross.

VI

A joke, the belly. Angels, possessing
No digestion, being fed on God's
Nutrient but deliquescent blessing

Model the serious life we clods
Should aim for, when, our paunches gone,
We must match up to periods

Of endless love and inspiration
Without a single belch or stab.
All that enwraps the skeleton

Suffers the canker and the scab,
And fears its change to pain and fust.
And when we contemplate the drab

Liver and wrinkled tripes, how must
We long to be entirely song
And dazzling feathers, or, like a bust,

All intellect and calm, its wrong
Cut off above where it might long.

[213]

MEREDITHIAN SONNETS

Incredulous, he stared at the amused
Official writing down his name among
Those whose request to suffer was refused.

W.H. Auden

I

To suffer, yes, but suffer and not create
The compensations that will cancel out
The thing: to crawl alone in the redoubt
Of suffering, like an animal – too late!
Even the ruined life deceives itself.
He looks in the glass: the handsome features show
Nothing of that foul spell cast long ago
By some malicious uninvited elf
Who ordered him to love a purple flower.
Even desire re-touches what it bares,
Removing all that's human – creases, hairs
And likelihood. A poet in a tower
With rapture watched an army dye the ford
And paper swans upon the stormy glooms:
Man's love is more primeval than a bloom's,
Another wrote, slain by a rose's sword.

II

Great suns, the streetlamps in the pinhead rain;
Surfaces gradually begin to shine;
Brunettes are silvered; taxis pass in line
On tyres that beat through moisture like a pain.
Doubtless upon such evenings some at least
Of those events that shaped his soul occurred:
Against the streaming glass a whispered word
Whitened and faded, and the shapeless beast
Drank from the dripping gutters through the night.

But all the child expressed and feared is long
Forgotten: only what went wholly wrong
Survives as this spectator of the flight
Of lovers through the square of weeping busts
To happiness, and of the lighted towers
Where mad designs are woven by the powers;
Of normal weather, ordinary lusts.

III

Rising as moisture in a cloven print,
Eventually it bears upon its bronze
A miscellaneous life of hulls and swans.
In puddles on the wharf reflections glint
Of leaning mariners almost on land,
And a red setting sun far out at sea.
Its purpose may have always been to flee
The bright temptations of the city: and
If man will follow, here he must embark.
And take the gulls in pennants to the deep,
And leave the gulls and journey through his sleep,
And sail into a harbour in the dark,
Wakening upon an unimagined scene
To strange confused remembrances, as though,
His wealth left to the poor, he were to go
With sensual body to a virgin queen.

IV

The worker columns ebb across the bridges,
Leaving the centre for the few ablaze.
In bars, fox terriers watch their masters raise
Glass to moustache; and rain streams from the ridges
Of blackened balustrades and capes of girls.
To death and rubbish theatres resound:
Dummies in shops imperfectly expound
The nude: throats raise the temperature of pearls.
Luxury and moderate gaiety disguise
The flight of coin, the absence of ideas.

Doomed certainly, he thinks, and feels the spears
Upon his flesh as he upturns his eyes
Towards the yellow face of time against
The racing sky. So this is the thing it is,
He says aloud, to live in mortal cities –
Haunted by trivial music, stomach tensed.

V

'You would not be surprised if I could show
Myself to you who thought that you were fated
Always to become one of the celebrated.
And yet with what amazement would you know
The man so different from his answered wish.'
Thus he addressed his childhood in the minutes
Of calm, when the unfrightened lamp within its
Cone holds the sleeping tablets, book, and dish
For ash, and still in unimportance stand
Mirror, mahogany and hanging shirt –
Fairy tale characters that squeak and hurt
At some clandestine hour. 'From your far land,
In fact, comes the pallid thing that in the night
Starts at its image and the glimmering shapes.
Concomitants of youth, the rumoured rapes
Of queens: what now is threatening my sight?'

VI

Mouths pallid mauve, eyes in mock sleepless rings –
However strange the style, the heart responds
To each new generation's browns and blondes
With chaste illegible imaginings.
Girls cluster at the corner of the street
With feathered heads of birds, on legs of birds:
Their high indifferent voices utter words
Whose spell the meaning cannot quite defeat.
Behind, in concrete neutral as a gull,
The slavish windows of the epoch stare,
But through those lips the corresponding air
Emerges with romance ineffable;
And he desires that what he sees will be
Uncovered by a future plough in tense,
Glittering and perfect terms – false evidence
Of fleeting fashion, of his lunacy.

[216]

VII

The autumn wind had sounded through the night,
But stepping in the garden after dawn
He sees the flowers round the wounded lawn
Like posters, all their valleys filled with light;
Considers that the season is no more
Fitted to hold the cardinals and mauves
Than mind what it had called up in the groves
Of moonbeams at the dreadful hour of four.
The world begins to turn towards the task
Of living, and those self-destructive vows
That coincide with distant gear and mouse
And others' sleep recede: a formal casque
Replaces ghastly head and serpent hair.
Barred by the antechamber's ceremonies,
Who guesses that within is one whose cries
Ask no reply because they do not dare?

VIII

Some figures representing history,
Myth, comedy and tragedy are making
An offering to another, who is taking
All calmly as his due. Undoubtedly
This happened at a period remote
From ours. But what *most* gives him the blues
Is that the group includes the comic muse.
How could he, with his constant pains to note
The deadly parallels of time, bring on
Louis the Fat, say; or, his mind obsessed
With kings who find close relatives undressed,
Dwell on some lucky, sheep-dunged simpleton?
And surely he stays unheeded and unknown
Because he cannot grasp that laughter came
Before the daughters spat the searing name,
And the uncovering of the jester's bone.

IX

Is it the tongue enslaves him to the land?
Turning the pages of a dictionary,
He finds the snail serrates the strawberry.
On chocolate furrows birds like snowballs stand,
While horses scissor pieces of the skies;
The ploughman's lips are dreamt of in a garden
Where spheres and spheroids in the light unharden,
And shadows tremble in the shapes of eyes.
Under the birch, the peasants and the deer,
The hills run chalky fingers to the waves
Where blue bays lead into the gantried naves
And smoking spars of cities. Seasons here
Contend with brick and iron, yet in Spring
Frost goes away on waggons with the coke,
And larks rise through disintegrating smoke
And see it is an island that they sing.

X

You are required to utter what is true
By gulping insane amounts of water: or
You are cast up upon a burning shore,
And there the sister whom you never knew
Cradles your head across her naked thighs.
Such things may run in secret through his head
While he bisects a piece of breakfast bread
Or drives his motor car with careful eyes.
He thinks: my life and thought – stupendously
Incongruous. And then he sees the fat,
Bogus entablatures and columns that
Enshrine the god, the law, the currency,
Which to break down will cost the death of some
– Perhaps the girl who, loping down the stair,
Recalls to him his frame of flesh and hair
That at the least must hurt by being numb.

XI

Returning, sees his footsteps dark as blood . . .
The snow itself seems to illuminate
The sky, whose jaundice the branches separate
With Rouault lines. A night like this, one could
Imagine that one still was in the age
Of imagination, and that warriors massed
Upon the snow – their hairy bosoms vast
With romantic love – like printing on a page.
Oh then, a marble temple was of marble,
And soaring colonnades apparently
Supporting porticoes in verity
Supported them. How did we come to garble
The message to the hands of what they make?
Though no less cruel, evanescent, blind,
Our cheap, scarred times have bred the usurious mind
And substituted fresco for mosaic.

XII

Yes, the dun monsters that loom up and pass
Are the celebrated buildings that in youth
Held those great heretics who spoke the truth
Even when, half consumed, the fire was
Removed from under them: and in middle age
Sent out the pirates in their little ships
To rob the gold from realms that robbed the lips
And ears of negresses. And now the stage
Is come when no one knows the noble tune
Embedded in the dull, unplayed toccata.
How different from the captain and the martyr
Is he who walks, this rainy afternoon,
The streets of monuments deformed by time,
Stopping at photographs of girls with flowers
For nipples and with thighs beyond his powers,
Racking his memory for a useless rhyme.

XIII

He reads a poem in a railway carriage
But cannot keep his glance upon the tropes,
And asks himself what is it that he hopes:
Criminal contact, fatherhood or marriage?
The child's grey eyes and tiny, dirty nails;
Its other sex; its beauty, unflawed, slim;
Its unembarrassed consciousness of him –
In which, however, he completely fails
To make out any element except
A curiosity sublime: is this
A human commerce far beyond the kiss
Such as awakened goodness where it slept
Inside the hairy capsule, or invented
Incredible ideas of innocence –
Conception lacking flesh and prurience,
And orifices marvellously scented?

XIV

The princess took the baton in her hand –
So small a hand, the handful huge enough –
But the vile beast, instead of casting off
Its hideous pelt, pressed forward to the land
Where evil never longs to be transformed,
And good is raped in every filthy ditch.
– Completely changed for him the story which
In youth had caused his cockles to be warmed.
Then is it that the world can really come
To be in three short decades what it seems –
A place of utter hopelessness? Are dreams
Of justice wakened by uranium
Beyond recall, and is goodwill from men
Quite flayed by torturers? Or has a new
Young innocent the castle well in view,
Prepared to try to love the beast again?

XV

The chill of autumn on a summer date
Reminds him, up at dawn through nameless fears,
How, due to uneventful happy years,
Man seems to suffer a precocious fate.
His dreams were of the time that crept on feet
Of tortoises, when love meant jealousy:
He sees now what he once tried utterly
To own, caged in a customary sheet.
Why should he rise from that lascivious nest
His whole youth yearned to make and frolic in?
Not that he loves the less nor that his skin
Has ceased to be astonished by a breast;
Rather, he's come to recognize today
How right love was to struggle to be free,
And in the softness captured by his knee
To dread to find the seed of its decay.

XVI

The wife was in the bedroom: in the attic
The servant slept, her cheek still smeared with ashes.
Diaphanous, the bedroom's shifts and sashes:
Around the servant's body, unemphatic
Calico. Yet the evening found his feet
Creaking the attic stair. At first she thought
To hide the hard ebullient flesh he fought
To show, and left him straddling the narrow sheet
The master of her inwardness and tears.
But later nights she was already bare
When he ascended merely to declare
How wild the wind, his loneliness and fears.
Soon he was visiting no more that room,
Preferring to continue to make cower
Beneath its silk the form he lacked the power
To waken, and speak freely of his doom.

XVII

Stands upright close to tree trunk during day;
Avoids men; somewhat gregarious in long
Winters; shows great affection for its young;
Comparatively silent; startled cry,
Like a laugh. He reads at night about the owl,
And sees through the uncurtained window blue
Emptiness, with only the argent moon in view
And one branch and the humped and hairy fowl.
And shuts the book and passes through the house
To where a woman is already sleeping,
Mortality upon her almost weeping
Eyelids. The owl is said to bring a mouse
Each quarter of an hour to its nest.
What can he lay before her vanished brood?
He holds some time his upright attitude,
Then with a kind of laughter gets undressed.

XVIII

The grass looks like some old and tousled head,
Each blade outlined with frost. A single tear
Rolls down a sunken cheek. The sun is a smear
Of ochre on the ice, itself like lead.
Inside the wool the body shivers round
Its shivering skeleton. No doubt, he thinks,
Somewhere a jolly god in musquash clinks
A pot of ale, and thumps a panting hound,
That whitens with its breath a marrow-bone.
Or out against the palace-sugaring snow
The queen whose gelid lips are death to know
Glides on extensive legs and tiny zone.
And trains with tall funnels steam on Europe's plain
Past groves of birch, a drypoint's black and white,
Taking the wife and lover to the quite
Fictional life of ecstasy and pain.

XIX

Slipping on peach blossom in their drunkenness,
The Chinese groped for brushes to indite
A last epistle to their friend. At night
They started awake and saw the empty dress
Thrown on a painted screen – itself depicting
Some bridge where civil servants say farewell
When leaving for the distant capital.
And in the sober morning, contradicting
The flood of tears, the poignant characters,
A little housemaid, hitherto unseen,
Carries the steaming tea towards the green
Willow that shades the customary chairs.
This gown is far from empty: should it climb
Idly beneath, one's hand will find twin boughs
That bear divided fruit, furred as a mouse,
As though the peach had come before its time.

XX

The largo fades and what must follow comes
In its rightful place. The pauses are observed.
The tune proceeds from tree and mineral curved
In throats and bellies, urged by the proper drums.
The visiting presences obey the rules:
Mopping and mowing, conjure forth his tears;
Reduce to snarling mottoes all his fears;
Pretending folly to amuse the fools.
These mathematics deal with golden fruit,
Wild the successive halvings of the string,
Commonplace objects tick, explode and ring
To underline the prince's hopeless suit.
He thinks of dotty questions that the sage
Employs to seek the meaning of the rose:
What solid does a pair of sides enclose?
The Turkish rondo in a classic age.

If galaxies are travelling away
Not quite so quickly as the light they send,
Earth's telescopes may fly around the bend
Of time and see the start of things some day.
He listens to the weather from the room,
And later is surprised to find the sky
Swept clear of clouds which now transfigured lie
Along the street, reflecting human doom.
For him these ursine, warrior lights possess
No other meaning than the stuff they are;
His task is not to beg the distant star
Out of its white majestic dust to bless
The small affairs that stab him to the heart,
But with blue weeping eyes discern the cause
And use his alphabet to state its laws,
Leaving the words to childish gods and art.

PART FIVE

From
Buff
(1965) and
Off Course
(1969)

TO X

I

How tedious the night before you came!
The moon was standing there, a ragged glow
Of a lamp behind red curtains. To and fro
I walked with my indifferent fame

Beside an ocean, darkling, jellied, tame,
And suddenly among the chimneys, low
(How tedious the night before you came),
The moon was standing there, a ragged glow.

But since your very face and curious name
Were impenetrably masked in a tomorrow,
Expected, stale, I could not really know,
Even in my longing for a human aim,
How tedious the night before you came.

II

The car arrived that brought you to the place:
As you got out I saw your very groin.
Thus goddesses, nude, upon a distant quoin
Reveal their chaste religion to the race.

The aged, usual guests who sit or pace,
By chance I casually wandered out to join:
The car arrived that brought you to the place;
As you got out I saw your very groin.

Later it seemed impossible to trace,
As you politely spooned your macedoine,
That I had known the dark skin near the loin;
Already in another time and space
The car arrived that brought you to the place.

III

I watched you, from the window, slouch away:
The season, treacherous spring; occasion, sporting
– Or probably your garments were importing
Your homage to the spirit of the day.

On long green legs, in something thick and grey
That to your youthful bust was not quite thwarting,
I watched you, from the window, slouch away:
The season, treacherous Spring; occasion, sporting?

Could I, the window-watcher, really play
That game with you whose strenuous contorting
Would peel the grey, reveal the mysterious courting
Of green and its sequel? With amused dismay
I watched you from the window slouch away.

IV

Elsewhere inside the cellular hotel
You had a being other than idea;
Rang for the maid, took off that bandolier
That must have held your stockings up, said 'Well'

And 'Really' to your husband, while the knell
Against my bosom told off year on year
Elsewhere inside the cellular hotel.
You had a being other than idea,

No doubt, but time had failed to parallel
My love with any stuff that could cohere,
Let alone bring me, as a concept, near:
Though place need not have acted to repel,
Elsewhere inside the cellular hotel.

[228]

Advice: write of emotions not your own.
The trivialities of that affair,
When in the long calm culture of your care
For someone else I landed like a lone

Barbarous invader from a starving zone,
Seemed certainly to want this not unfair
Advice: write of emotions not your own.
The trivialities of that affair

Consisted of your kind indifferent tone
And of a yearning I did not declare.
Once, I saw your anachronistic hair
And uttered an old played-out poet's groan.
Advice: write of emotions not your own.

VI

To find oneself still capable of pain
Was direly reassuring, being old;
As though an organ long thought spent had told
Of its strong presence through the chemist's stain.

Your beauty promised scorn, your youth disdain:
Perhaps I let you think of me as cold.
To find oneself still capable of pain
Was direly reassuring, being old.

Truly malignant, to have longed in vain
When a mere sentence might have let me fold
In scrawny arms your vigorous white and gold –
Precisely as though it were sufficient gain
To find oneself still capable of pain.

VII

I never thought time's fatuous whirligigs
Could touch my own accumulated years.
A rational century dissolved in tears
Playing at Carthaginians in wigs,

But that absurd and adolescent sprigs
Might suddenly blossom from long-dead veneers
I never thought. Time's fatuous whirligigs
Could touch my own accumulated years.

Taking your arms, as chill and slim as twigs,
Awkward, I drew you from your cavaliers.
Able to raise the Sidonian queen's compeers
(Revolving in the dance's barbarous jigs),
I never thought time's fatuous whirligigs.

VIII

Painfully wounded in the sleepless dark
I heard the ocean thumping at the land.
How could this end – unmutual passion banned
By forces that would not deter a clerk?

You left me – with a casual remark
And led by the marital, familiar hand –
Painfully wounded in the sleepless dark.
I heard the ocean thumping at the land

And thought incongruously of the barque
(Symbolic of what always must command
Transgressors) that informed the knight who scanned
The harbour, of the rightful, unscathed Mark;
Painfully wounded in the sleepless dark.

IX

One might imagine dreaming, too, would change,
Seizing your self for its ambiguous powers;
But falling asleep at dead-beat, silent hours,
Only my next day's waking brought the strange.

Since near your veritable youth my range
Of life took suddenly in once-withered flowers,
One might imagine dreaming, too, would change,
Seizing your self for its ambiguous powers.

The lovely captive in the cruel grange
Who from the tumid marquis nudely cowers –
Such still the night-time from my bedrock scours
And not the true, the sterile spirit's mange.
One might imagine dreaming, too, would change.

X

I didn't think that you had feelings, too,
In that affair, and doubtless I was right.
Since I saw what I saw of you was white,
That really left you little else to do.

Remarks you uttered were extremely few
That shed on the murk between us any light:
I didn't think that you had feelings, too,
In that affair, and doubtless I was right.

It was sufficient that you raised the brew
Of vodka to a mouth immensely bright
With fingers faintly work-worn, bitten, slight,
And wished my body health far from its due.
I didn't think that you had feelings too.

XI

And suddenly I saw that, after all,
It was imperfect your thought perfect face.
Not in the second or the third embrace,
When I discovered you were far from tall,

But sitting idly in the mirrored hall
Which showed an image awkward, almost base,
And suddenly I saw that, after all,
It was imperfect your thought perfect face.

Such a swift revelation must appal,
To think that merely this might bring disgrace.
Though even art is only commonplace
Since human weakness is its wherewithal;
And suddenly I saw that, after all.

XII

Shaken by longing, how can one conceive
That longing is the essence of it all?
Before some unemotional damsel, tall
And ample as a goddess of the sheaf,

Impossibly youthful, destined to receive
The seed of one's descendants, one will fall,
Shaken by longing. How can one conceive
That longing is the essence of it all?

Even in this case I must still believe
(Seeing you, commonplace, pledged, adult, small)
That joy could only come with you in thrall.
That one can ever do much more than grieve,
Shaken by longing, how can one conceive?

XIII

At times I told myself that it was yours
Not just the incidence of my desire,
The pretty skin in its diverse attire.
Neither a doll whose odourless rondures

And ductless cavities you must of course
Dully undress and dress. This snake, snow, brier –
At times I told myself that it was yours,
Not just the incidence of my desire.

An introspective middle-age ensures
That even if the membrane meet the fire
Nothing much matters save the cry and crier;
And yet the flesh was of such piteous force,
At times I told myself that it was yours.

XIV

The long road greyly striping scarp and vale
Ran from the city to our meeting place.
You came by quieter and more devious ways.
Like beasts, our two cars rested head to tail.

I left a lie behind to smudge the trail,
And, conjuring up your speculative embrace
(The long road greyly striping scarp and vale),
Ran from the city to our meeting place.

Whose lie it was that made the sunlight fail,
Who knows? It was a fairly equal case.
Rain started, as I set out to retrace
(Passing at first your face, returning, pale)
The long road, greyly striping scarp and vale.

XV

I rediscovered during our affair
Perceptions that in my Dark Age had gone.
How, say, astonishingly high upon
The spine the fastening of a brassière.

That every trivial thing in earth and air
Can constitute a mysterious eidolon,
I rediscovered during our affair.
Perceptions that in my dark age had gone

(The prurient disproportion of the bare:
Pinks, so conceived of, nearer cinnamon),
But that the gift of the youthful simpleton
To make dearth richness was in disrepair,
I rediscovered during our affair.

XVI

Spring was propinquity of the unfree:
The summer brought a far more close farewell.
In the puce public room of that hotel
I could do little more than clearly see

The thigh shown by a verdurous settee
And your obedience in another's spell –
Spring was propinquity of the unfree.
The summer brought a far more close farewell

[233]

As, to unsuitable song of lark and bee,
I proved I could your cautiousness excel.
How wrong to think that nothing could impel
A wish for what the unsatisfactory
Spring was: propinquity of the unfree.

XVII

That was the summer of the growing nail:
Its stigma marked me till the summer died.
Slamming the door, I left my thumb inside:
The wish to quit you could not quite prevail.

Your car was open: though your face was pale,
In fact the sun shone ever in that tide
That was the summer of the growing nail.
Its stigma marked me till the summer died.

Of course, I could not understand the scale.
Nursing the mangled joint, I turned aside
And thought no one could be as hurt, but lied
To your concern. Thus followed the travail
That was the summer of the growing nail.

XVIII

I knew how mean and ludicrous the thing,
Not only in itself but on the age.
Daily I opened a disturbing page
And cringed to think that very day must bring

Our confrontation. That I could not wring
Good from the storms that private man engage,
I knew how mean and ludicrous. The thing
Not only in itself but on the age

Seemed an irrelevance truly staggering
– Which period has itself a lineage
As far as ours from the fabled rage
Of passionate queen and perspicacious king.
I knew how mean and ludicrous the thing.

XIX

At first, sufficient just to drive so far.
The factory like a mosque, Eileen's Café,
The roundabout garage, the tents of hay,
The last descent below the chalk-bright scar,

Became excitingly familiar
And yours although you'd never been that way.
At first sufficient just to drive so far . . .
The factory like a mosque, Eileen's Café

And all the rest, eventually proved a bar
It called for more than driving to essay.
No need to meet to experience the dismay
Of knowing things were quite dissimilar
At first – sufficient just to drive so far.

XX

At last you'd simply omitted to arrive:
The lay-by's litter welcomed me alone.
And when I'd plucked a leaf and kicked a stone
Or two, I saw what so used to connive

With pleasure – sun where trees undying thrive –
And that I realized I must bemoan
At last. You'd simply omitted to arrive.
The lay-by's litter welcomed me alone,

But then it wasn't long before my own
Company worked its power to revive.
Fantasy, finding the body still alive,
Madly began to stalk a love unknown.
At last! you'd simply omitted to arrive.

XXI

From the great distance of the end of caring
I saw our weak attempt at happiness;
Of you recalled a certain buttoned dress,
Cringed at my characteristic lack of daring.

[235]

The tortuous machinery of pairing
In our case seemed of utter pointlessness
From the great distance of the end of caring.
I saw our weak attempt at happiness

Related only to the lust for sparing
Our lives the terror of complete success.
And gone the absorbing, vital kind of chess
I played to try to bring about your baring,
From the great distance of the end of caring.

BAGATELLES

Too self-indulgent, poetry.
Stepping outside this morning, a drop
Fell from the gutter on my pen,
Subsequently diluting these words.
Or who could want to hear about
My boring love, myopic eye
That blurs the world of kings, examines
A portly spider tickling its navel
With the arms of a Hindu deity?
*

Geranium petals, finger nails
Of little oriental whores,
Scattered on summer stone.
*

This mole beneath her hair in the nape
Might be a deformity were she not
Lovely: is a deformity.
*

I stop my car to let a girl,
Carrying a dog, cross the road;
And think 'Girl with a Dog', but wonder
If in fact art is better than life.
*

Stain the stuff lightly with umber,
The eyes and foliage wash in
With running brown, and scumble breasts,
Thighs, belly, with a famished brush.
Closeness to life depends on the scumbled hand,
Distance from art upon the running eye.
*

[236]

Early morning: my cat at first refuses food,
Wishing to be reassured, no doubt, after the night.

*

    Distinguishing in the glasses birds
    From autumn leaves by an occasional shrug
    Instead of the waving and revolving,
    A greater glossiness of speckle
    Even in the continuous rain,
    I know I unfairly evaluate
    The world's life, placing first myself,
    Whose curiosity and love
    Discover how birds make out in winds
    That strip the boughs and shake my house.

*

    Does a big nose go with playing Bach?
    No more than a collection of Van Gogh
    Postcards with the breasts of fourteen.

*

The chromaticism of '04
That almost anachronistically
We heard encased in whalebone on small
Gilt chairs in rows in gas-lit rooms,
Became the unrelieved agony
Of composers idly shot by soldiers
While taking the air at the end of wars.

Then cascades of notes in the right hand
Against old tunes composed for money,
Improvised beside the sea by negroes
To woo little ears nestling in poignant hair-dos.

*

    I saw a lady in a car
    Stop the machine and sound two pips
    At which a bow-legged milkman quit
    His meaner vehicle and, leaning
    Where she had thoughtfully let down
    The window, kissed her lips.

    I walked on jealous of that swain,
    Touched nonetheless by the resource
    With which he'd left his sturdy heart
    With bottles at her exalted door,

Making their passion mythical
Simply by being coarse.

*

I disturbed a hedgehog with the garden light.
I saw a conker from a giant tree
Whose dusty dark-grey armour frightened me
Until it took more reasonably to flight.

*

Useless to the lover, the breasts of his beloved.
His inordinate admiration arises
From unsexual wants in his infancy
And physical hatred now of his mother.

*

A pale leaf floats and falls, and instantly
Is pasted on the concrete by a tyre.
The world betrays its wobble from the fire;
The giant orbit deigned to cut the tree.

THE ZOUAVE

Lent by some organization that provides
Art to adorn commercial offices,
A reproduction hangs upon my wall
Of Van Gogh's *Zouave* – a low-bred, beetle-browed,
Unprepossessing individual
In baggy pantaloons. One is not meant,
However, to endow this coloured oblong
With attributes appropriate to life.
Art serves the social man, who at this moment
Writes a report on how a certain law
Affects the being of the corporation
(Which hired the office and the reproduction)
In the world of its rivals and its profitable
Scope. What is a zouave? Why, an arm
Of empires to enforce colonial rule:
A rather unconfident proletarian
Beneath a patchy beard and darkling squint:
A harsh but happy marriage of tomato
And arsenic: an inexpensive counter
In the ordering of the city's million minds –
Which else might well hack off their ears with knives.

[238]

FAVOURING THE CREATURES

Tapering icicles hang
Like the conventional rays
That beard cartographers' suns.
A sudden gust explodes
The edge of a snow dune. The eye,
At first amazed, finds nowhere
To heal its splintered lens,
Except in the brittle dark
Of spreading boughs where pants
An expiring, invisible race.
This well might be a world
On a more remote ellipse,
But for the distant slopes
Where figures insect-like
Drag spars with insect-like
Deficiency of purpose.
Their cries, surprisingly human,
With scarcely a diminution
My solitariness invade.
As also does a man
Fragmentarily through the trees:
Whiskered and leaden-locked,
Long coat a relic of some
Campaign. He addresses me,
Perceiving my mission, too,
Is feeding the pitiable fauna.
Tells me of the habits of deer,
Of a certain one-eyed squirrel,
Descries in the bushes a brilliant
Jay and reminds me that tits
Will take a crumb in flight.
Shying off at first (as is
My custom from all encounters,
Even Wordsworthian),
I search the sugared twigs
And pneumatic paths for vain
Escape. But finally
Surrender to the notion
That this eccentric, far more
Than half his life unwound,
Was worked on by the same

Disastrous times as I:
The coat from the war, perhaps,
Of my own unwilling collusion;
The repetitious speech
Of proletarian tones
Such as my former dream
Conceived as announcing the law
Of an altruistic future.
'What are ye gi'ing them today?'
Shamefacedly I reply:
'Almonds.' 'A wonder they'll come
To me for these peanuts, then.'
Farther along the path,
Having left my companion at last,
I think how I favour still
Some of the creatures: bequeath
My almonds more to the small
Or deformed – unlike, no doubt,
Him of the khaki coat,
Whose rough, indigestible fare
Spread impartially over
The mass helps to increase
The odds against extinction.

Such daylight as filtered through
The blanched, thick sky now begins
To fade. Beyond the park,
One yellow window already
The otherwise universal
Black-blotted white transcends.
Irreversible, this turning:
Days follow mistaken days.
Incredible to have seen
In fifty years' destruction
Afternoons of timid paws
And comical conversations.

LOGIC OF DREAMS

Waking to the scarcely-lit curtain, the plop
Of a letter, the worn familiar mask,
It is hard to imagine how dreams contrive
To deposit one nude before mad girl-faced apes.

Five minutes after waking I remember it
And, hung over the bowl, am lost in strangeness.
A moment later it has gone beyond recall
In my head reflected in the dusky mirror.

How much more convincing, the time of dreams.
Here are my mother and my son's child together;
Here I am still shattered by jealousy
In a passion that only time has changed.

I realised I loved my long-vanished friend
And showed him clumsily the vanished love,
Feeling a warm bulk in his dead shoulders
That for me they never had in life.

Once more, since miraculously she was still alive,
I had to wish my suffering mother dead.

The age's disaster we had always escaped
At last engulfed us and ghastly it was.
Yet because we lived still in the burning and torture
We knew it in our hearts to be simply a dream.

So often she told me she was chased by lions;
We smiled at the involuntary symbolism.
But to be with her, failing to save her from lions,
That is a terrible fate and meaning.

I was sure it was not her getting in the window,
Because I heard her moving about in the kitchen.

Turning into the corridor and finding
In the embrasure a waiting, silent figure,
And fleeing . . . the influence of art:
But an art rooted insanely in life, not dreams.

Astonishing that my cries should wake her,
Since they were powerless in the dream.

Impoverished wakening to unrecalled dreams:
Start of a day empty of dreaming's source.

HOMAGE TO DR ARNOLD GESELL AND TO MY GRAND-DAUGHTER SOPHIE

Even a doting grandfather must give
A point to the perspicacious pediatrist:
Yes, there's a suggestion of the primitive
In her physical anthropology – the span
Of the stance and the residual stagger; too
Stubby the velvet legs, and the lovely head
Over-large; and yes, in pantomime symbolization
She was excelled by Neanderthal man.

However, our author admits a precocity
Of speech in advance of those the jungle tree
Gave birth to; though myself I can't but feel
The 'Ba-ba's s'oes', 'Find pussies', sadly remote
From the exchanges life acknowledges as real.

Though when he asks rhetorically what
Has happened to the jargon of eighteen months,
I sense the awesome culture of two years old.
Jargon has almost entirely disappeared
(Though sometimes she excitedly may sing
Jargon and words together). It has sunk,
The jargon, according to this psychologist,
To deep subconscious levels of functioning
Where, as a sort of language orderer,
It will, for some time certainly, persist.

Odd, all the same, that we find her genius
In doing badly what all do pretty well.
The noseless, crop-eared, mad-wigged sketch of 'ba-ba',
The circular automobiles and circular horses,
For instance, are measured by us indulgently
Against a tradition of naturalistic art
(Which nonetheless expired prior to her).

[242]

And touched at being impersonated with
So few and such diminutive resources,
We disrecall the disaster of adulthood.

In fact it's the jargon that we should admire.
The best part of my life is bringing out
Jargon with words – but how minute a part,
Since ordered language is most loath to admit
The excited dream-soaked gibberish of its start.
Therefore must be preserved, if possible,
A struggler with the uncommunicable,
A chanter of enchantment, underneath
The honoured inventor of a unified
Field theory or detector of gravitons
Or prince's perfectly proportioned bride.

FIFTEEN FOOLISH ENCOUNTERS

Her going left behind her in the room
A girl-shaped cloud of unalloyed perfume.

One of those creatures made with nuts and matches –
Her slim neck, and head, and hair in piled-up swatches.

How does she know, where did she learn, so young,
To bend to her hair an arm undrawn, unsung?

He saw her in the street and did not know
The sepia cap, the naked face below.

The task of living with perfection is,
He thinks with sudden pity, hers not his.

The face naïve; antique and enigmatic
The lure: the skin unfarded, lips hepatic.

Once his train bore her and incredibly proved
It was his rut in which she also moved.

No doubt she only feigns the commonplace
To help the world incorporate her face.

He lifts the telephone one day and hears
A faltering plebeian voice that could be hers.

It's as though, like quattrocento brushes, he's
Not seen before lids filled with convex eyes.

What are her irises in their arcs of black?
Stones, soft-grained, azure, pale, from Attic wrack.

Each meeting shows a tiny change: a bangle;
Sweater; breasts gathered at another angle.

Strange her frank smile should answer to a smile
That breaks from, and masks, emotions that defile.

Her recognition – goddesses' benign
But fitful meddling in mundane design.

As her departure left him in the hell
Of loss, he wished her, and all the species, well.

A WIFE'S UNEASE

It proved to be the inhuman that she loved.
Her beauty kept her from the commonplace.
She chose the noble melancholy face,
Though came to find the clasp she reached for gloved
With the perpetual chill of self-regard,
And pressed her lips against the mask of art.
She never could resign herself to part
From what embalmed her youth. At last the scarred
Mirror revealed that she'd become unfree
For other loves to alter her. But he
Presented still a countenance sublime
Whose furrows only seemed historic grime
Shading the marble of a boy exhumed
By water where a single flower bloomed.

She saw that he was still in love with her –
The self that loved him once. The innocent
Slim brown-haired girl had picked this serious sir
Because she felt him nobly different.
And he for his part hit upon the slim
And brown – that since had somewhat run to seed.
Surely she never would have given him
Her love, less innocent, for now her need
Was to be loved for qualities as rare
As formerly she thought that she had found.
Thus was the stout grey goddess going bare
Thrown by her protégé upon the ground
To yield not power or wisdom but the old
Brief trivial commerce with the common fold.

She thought with great alarm: what if I die
Before somebody mines the real I?
His sleeping face was visible close by
That masked an intricate interior
Of which she'd long been the interpreter
To ordinary modes of being. Her
Pleasure at having been the choice by which
He proved himself to own a human itch
She'd almost grown out of. Now it was a rich
Vulgarity and thoughtlessness she craved,
Dreaming that even yet might be engraved
Her name upon a simple heart enslaved;
And issuing thence a troop of noble sons
That would return the doting of a dunce.

THOUGHT IN A DRAWING-ROOM

Tea served on satyrs' legs or eagles' claws
And lions carrying handles in their jaws;
A middle-aged suburban fountain-pen
That rhymes carcinogen with magdalen –

Such incongruities amuse: and yet
What measure can the horrifying get
Except against the cosy human heart
Or the ruminant captivity of art?

[245]

SONNET

Sonnet, n. Poem of 14 lines (usu. rhyming thus: pig bat cat
wig jig hat rat fig: lie red sob die bed rod . . .)
– Concise Oxford Dictionary

In fables, day-time evil is the pig,
Replaced at night by the less obvious bat.
And who would think the solemn, lazy cat
In its essential life would wear a wig
And, standing on two legs, perform a jig?
A robin hood or clown's or opera hat
Poorly conceals the nature of the rat.
The lion eats an uncomplaining fig.

Alone the little fable-readers lie:
Clenched eyelids make the darkness almost red
But no less disconcerting. Scarcely a sob
Escapes them as they realize that to die
Is mixed inextricably up with bed;
And sorrow for the love that giants rob.

SONG IN A WOOD

Caught in the branches of a tree
A condom sang: 'I served it well,
But thinking I'd no lasting part
In the involvements of the heart
Love then abandoned me.

'Yet I remain within the grove,
Symbolical of all that passed,
Neighbour of moon and dove,
While those that called themselves in love
Go separate ways and die at last.

'Love's only immortality
I hold: the generations that
Lovers sow carelessly –
Being young and blind, averse
To recognize their happy murderers.'

BY THE LAKE

What bird is that among the branches bare?
It is no bird but a rag blown idly there.
I am afraid because no one is here.
But I am with you, dear.

I am impelled to speak my secret thought:
At first I did not love you as I ought.
I know, and must confess I was the same,
And played a deceitful game.

Oh but you surely love me now, as I
For his sake found that possibility.
Look, dear, the distant currents of the lake
Are coiling like a snake.

You don't reply, and now your eyes explore
The stony litter of the lonely shore.
This winter sun, how bloodshot and discrete!
A plum against a sheet.

I swear he loves me oceans less than you.
To his own flesh, my dear, he must be true.
For him you bear the image of the thing
That I can never bring.

Stepmother, I have watched you bend aside.
Oh and I see what still you try to hide.
Descend, my patient shadow, from your tree:
No longer feed on me.

THE KING AND THE GOOSE-GIRL

Said King to Goose-girl: 'What princess
Once bedded down among the mess
Of goose nests to produce your frail
Wrist and neurotic tiny nail?'

[247]

But she failed almost to remark
The greybeard straying from the park
Of toga'd marble, steed and elm
To this rude portion of the realm
Where multiplied the vermiform
In heaps fraternal, gamy, warm.
So much the exemplar of the race,
His bulk was peasant-like; a face
With bags and snout of tyrant coins;
Dynastic and saddle-apt the loins.
No wonder she gazed past, to where
Shepherds piped in the country air,
Young sires of the anonymous.

'How strange to find it always thus –
Beauty uncaring for her ways;
Destroying the laborious days
That power built his image with.'
So mused the king, that monolith
Whose policies had sunk her cheek
And banned the common to the beak
And clad the tallest swains in red
And let the epoch live in dread
And made the Muse of history blind.

The girl, though belonging to that kind
Whose fate it is to change to hags,
Ported her stick and wore her rags
As though the spring were everlasting,
Resigned to injury and fasting
Like a more brutish order – say,
The fox that in the spinney lay
Panting and rank, its ears at cock
For the loud echelon of her flock.
And in her elevated jaw
And calmly gazing eyes he saw
That aspect, noble and fulfilled,
Of creatures that have whelped or killed.
He could not help but feel disquiet
At sensing a kingdom where his fiat
Could never run; and knew his doom
The unfilial issue of her womb.

Prodigal curiosities
Of nature, girl and coloured geese,
And their machines, that will arrange
A future still more diverse and strange.
From delicate thighs there runs a cord,
Slippery, wrinkled, strong, abhorred,
To putti of marvellous innocence;
And the straw-sullied ovoid hence
Will break a beauty which perhaps
May not entail the tragic lapse
That aged the avian daughter once,
And burned the town and slew the sons.

BRAHMS PERUSES
THE SCORE OF *SIEGFRIED*

The photograph by von Eichholz

Enormous boots, thick-soled, elastic-sided,
Rest on a carpet shaggy as the pelt
    Of a mountain beast – perhaps
    Is precisely a mountain beast.

The chair adjoining, being unoccupied,
Reveals its antimacassar of scalloped lace
    Like the lower half
    Of a bikini of our day.

The frock-coat is disposed in folds as ample
As those of saints' robes in Renaissance painting:
    The pants, large cylinders
    Of a more recent art.

The background is a dark and shining wealth
Of gilt-tooled books, mahogany and frames
    For photographs – for this,
    Eventually, no doubt.

The peering old man holds the little score so close
His white beard sweeps the page; but gives no sign
    That he perceives – or smells –
    Anything untoward.

[249]

He could not be expected to be thinking
That the legend of courage, kiss and sword arose
    From those atrocious Huns
      Who ruined an empire's comfort.

But how can he not be falling back aghast
At the chromatic spectrum of decay,
    Starting to destroy already
      His classical universe?

BROTHER SERENE

The peaks are visible from the verandah
– Baboon, G 26, Bright Nipple.
Someone is bashing with the mallet
That hangs by the dented block at our gates.
One more of the epoch's escapees,
Who certainly will knock in vain;
For the novices are already so many
They have polished all excrescences
Off the gods – though neglecting to ignite
The stove, so that my hands are numb,
Scarcely able to grasp Reminder
As I wait alone for prayers to end
And the hours of meditation to start.
Today it's my office to bear this great staff
And totter between the rows of brothers
Administering first the Tap of Warning
Then the Thwack of Reality.
Odd, that however tactful the first
The second always comes as a shock.

A leaf that spent autumn in a crevice
Scutters across the floor as though
On feet: the significant likes to assume
A foolish or trivial vehicle –
Just as enlightenment arrives
As one bickers about a roster of duties
Or the frequency of getting the chipped bowl.
And indeed, this season past, unwell –
Weeks in the Preparation Room –
For the first time I glimpsed how things wagged.

[250]

Awareness accompanies alarm.
Seeing my robe on mummies' shins,
Mopping my shaven skull, I thought:
No disguise can stop one being human.

And strong little birds, calling at dawn,
Called of their reckless otherness.
In those days I used to look at the swelling,
Stand wrestling with the stricture, feeling
As far from surgeons as from god.
Some talk of cities' unfriendliness,
But we have fled from help, albeit
The hands are prompted by profit or fear.

The sky turns slate, the peaks even whiter,
Then on the vast negative there blinks
A light incongruously golden.
Quickly the verandah is dredged with hailstones
To the sound of thunder and a gong
That calls me to the interior chamber.
Once, I had a name – other than Serene;
And once a body, like a sparrow;
And a life of families, worry and pets.
In fact, despite my hairlessness
And saffron skirts, you'd say, if asked,
That even now I was a man.
The individual nature must
Be evaluated by its secrets.
So I learnt in the world, and because of that
Perhaps gave up the world; and now
May put down my irregular heart
To indigestion as much as fear.

I limp among the squatting Elsewhere,
Passing the grooved or pneumatic napes
Of Vision, Bluebird and Devotion,
Halting at Strongheart. Tap. Thwack.
He will be glad to be reminded:
Even in the ablutions his cloth
Exudes a sanctifying ichor.

[251]

What brought me here? The quest for a father?
My own died in my infancy:
Ever after I was an inchoate rebel.
Suppose when he gabbled the ritual
'What is the clew that runs through it all?'
One answered the Abbot: 'Your nasal cyst.'
The lust for authority presupposes
A perpetual lack of respect for it.
Rather as those who receive the spirit
Seem to be quite unspiritual.
Simpletons of nature, they die as they lived,
Crying unselfconsciously of their joy,
Rich hosts to the parasites of blood.
It is error that leads to metaphor:
The heavens, we murmur, looking above
Bright Nipple's pennant of screaming snow
At invisible dust between incandescent
Sea-slugs, sea-urchins, sea-cucumbers,
Whorls of every irrelevant kind.

ORPHEUS BEHEADED

Even without a body I went on singing –
Though one would think that only those lost swinging
Parts served a bard against the world's hand-wringing.

Like an apple I floated down the Thracian stream,
Across the sea of our democratic dream,
But came to rest in solitude extreme –

An altar on an island in a cave
Where, no longer conscience's or passion's slave,
I was free only to predict or rave.

They asked and I melodiously replied:
'Your monolithic empire will divide
Like a cell, and half will not for long abide –

Rigid, like its gold-illumined cope and page,
And weak as the too-imaginative sage;
Its wealth escaping like an haemorrhage.

Over the other hemisphere will spread
The sackers and the rapers and the dread
Desire to manufacture gold from lead.'

Thus the head's prophecy: its power,
Say, to repel invasion. O lost hour
That shifted cypress and commanded flower –

It was the body's happiness and pain
That practised so on nature she was fain
To shuffle to that diatonic strain.

I never thought to mourn my sordid tripes,
But, ending in a bunch of bleeding pipes,
I found the mind nostalgic for the gripes.

Handless, my lute decays beneath the trees;
Young husbands to the flexed and parted knees
Return, and all organic dancers freeze.

THE TRUTH ABOUT PYGMALION

Do not imagine I was glad she breathed.
My ear was pressed against the ivory:
Suddenly appetite and longing seethed.

Since to an ideal form I had bequeathed
All that ennobled and disquieted me
Do not imagine I was glad she breathed.

It was a trap that I myself had teethed
To find that in my virgin private she
Suddenly appetite and longing seethed.

I took away my arms that had been wreathed
About the flanks of perfect slavery:
Do not imagine I was glad she breathed.

The territory was deeply cleft and heathed
Where, art turned back into reality,
Suddenly appetite and longing seethed.

To sense the puny sword that had been sheathed,
To know the unequal clash that had to be,
Do not imagine I was glad. She breathed.
Suddenly appetite and longing seethed.

LOVE AND MURDER

Strange that in 'crimes of passion' what results
Is women folded into trunks like suits,
Or chopped in handy joints to burn or lose,
Or sallowed with poison, puffed with sea,
Or turned into waistless parcels and bestowed
Under the fuel or the kitchen floor.

Perhaps those ardent murderers so prize
The flesh that it disturbs them not at all
To separate an ankle with an axe,
Or contemplate some leathern lady, long
Of the spare bedroom pungent occupant.
Love, after all, must overcome disgust.

We lesser amorists make do with girls
Prim or unfaithful, loud and ageing wives,
Loving too little to implant them deep
Within our guilty dreams where secretly
They would take off their green and purple clothes
To show the unchanging shamelessness of bone.

THE HISTORIAN

I

The scene my study: Faustian locale!
I speculate on my lack of energy
Before the tempting foolscap, and decide –
My theories staggering, my learning sound –
That I am sickening for a minor ill;
And wonder how in my solitary life,
I caught the bug. Unquestionably I ache.

Two days ago (or was it yesterday?)
I ventured to the city. By the river
The famous towers of our tyrannies
Were half washed out by rain, and I was conscious
Of being part of the infected mass
Hurrying all ways on the ancient bridge.
Even historians catch history.

II

So long sunk in dynastic scholarship,
I look out of the window with surprise
To see bare branches, and the ghostly tits
Ever appear and reappear without
Overt existence in between. The grip
Of winter took my country while the prize
Arcadius to Marcian transmits.
And what the jarred succession was about
Seems, after all, the bearing of the nip
And burning of the planet. That my eyes,
Instead of the world's imperatorial splits,
Now rest upon a rain-debouching spout,
Seems equally irrelevant before
Our curled trajectory from frore to frore.

III

I overlooked your manuscript and saw
(In the quiet room, illuminated by
Culture's immense resources, a candle flame)
'Rescued the world at the brink of the abyss'
And felt a sickly fear. I had not known
That you had also come to this conclusion –
Thinking not of the rescue, the abyss.
I turned away, said nothing, marvelling
At the comparative indifference
Of previous fears. Almost immediately
I realized that *you* meant Diocletian
Or some such name of the unrescued past,
And looked again less guiltily upon
The maelstrom breaking in your youthful nape.

Even more brilliant pupils will possess
Illusions neither reason nor disdain
Eradicate. Astonishing to find
The young full lips, set off by hair and dress
In a bizarre contemporary strain,
Voicing opinions fatuous or blind.
Though even those tender mouths themselves, I guess,
Are put to uses I would think quite vain –
Imprinting merely their own callow kind.
That fear and credulity led to excess
In judging the Vandals' numbers, I explain
Once more. It does not need that to remind
My cultured heart of cracks made by decay
Through which the stunning and uncaring stray.

V

Berengar von Horheim, from the Codex Manesse

What is he doing underneath the rose tree?
The minnesinger crosses fingers with
A long-haired, gold-haired girl who carries a dog:
He bears a sword, and both are ruddy, smiling.
I realize all at once that this took place
At dawn, and that the afternoon it was
That blasted rose and girl. Were poets gay,
Ready for action, courteously in love?
It seems their ladies thought them knights, their hearers
Of similar material to themselves.
Eventually arrived a century
Of mad old age and horrible mulattos.
The railway sidings waited and the lights,
Visible from here, that stain smoke-scribbled skies.

VI

'Almost invariably a eunuch, the
Grand Chamberlain.' No doubt, no doubt, since he
Would be at times unlikely not to see
Augusta in a bath of milk, or hold
The crapulous forehead of a twelve year old
Curopalates. What undevious, bold
Spirits, the ancients – to create a class
So apt for jobs of consequence, but crass.
How unlike us, whose gelding comes to pass
Not with a stroke but over painful years,
And then – why, then are deemed fit engineers
For the great car of state; or, with our sneers
At vulgar speech and realistic line,
Drive art into a consummate decline.

VII

The dread of barbarization in that late
Empire – impossible to grasp entirely,
Since of the nation that they feared so direly
Many were *princeps* in the cultured state:
Besides, that state itself was ferine. Thus
One cannot help but see this paralleled
In age's censure of the lascivious
To which it is by appetite impelled
In vain – its horror of a licence which
Its earlier tolerance handed to its daughters;
And also in the doctrine that negates
The primacy and nurture of the rich,
Instinctive, sensuous poles of man – from quarters
Where members, doubtless, far from match huge pates.

VIII

They see dark skies of unshed snow behind
The snow-sleeved trees like dancers touching hands.
The northern frontier. Vast unfriendly lands
Far from the groves of red and golden rind
Where, in alfresco schools, the cogent mind
Hatched a philosophy that brought these bands
Of civilizing privates – fate none understands.
To think there is another, strange, mankind!

[257]

So nearly indistinguishable from
Barbarians, the inhabitants, that for long
Their masters goggle with inquietude
At women with their hair like pelts, snow-strewed;
Until they are, insidiously as song,
Possessed and haunted by the idiom.

IX

Even the paltry things the unmounted craved
Were wrested from them by the cruel riders.
The tombs of conquerors came to be engraved
With the illegible signatures of spiders.
Dyspepsia and sleeplessness derange,
Instead of opium and octoroons,
The artist's senses. All is senseless change:
History turns to oceans from lagoons,
And from democracy to lethal whims
Of Blues and Greens in violent hippodromes.
And thus the individual life: there brims
A poison of love inside us aged gnomes
That cannot be released; whose citadels
Fall to proliferating barbarous cells.

X

'Names of usurpers in italics' – why
Does putting down this rubric rake my scalp?
For, after all, the catastrophic try
At diarchy (one emperor like an alp
Or jelly) happened to another order.
And when I further muse I feel that these –
That lived along a terrifying border
And wore the clothing of our tragedies –
Though doubtless forked and papped and *sapiens,*
Were not, as we are, man. Hard to conceive
That in the future's culture one will blench
At reading of our state, and not believe
That those who kindled the appalling fires
Were his erect and ordinary sires.

XI

Should the barbarians be not at hand
A dissolute culture will destroy itself.
So it is nothing great that no vile band,
In search of females, stimulants and pelf,
Our frontier happens currently to prowl.
Waking at night, I hear the embouchure
Of locomotive, chimney-pot and owl,
And for our limited and insecure
Kingdom of kindliness and order tremble.
Yes, of that dissoluteness I am part,
But how remarkably can I dissemble
The promethean steadfastness of one whose art
Is doomed to rubble for a thousand years
Before its armless beauty quicken tears.

XII

At least, I tell myself, we do not chuck
Slaves to wild beasts. But still the yearning burns
For springs of culture when the tribe for crowns
Of vegetation raced along the wrack,
And, masked by obvious emotions, played
To sun-lit, wind-swept theatres, in terms
Even more stringent than reality,
That fun or vengeance of the gods, called fate.
Agons not circuses in those far times;
Not sport, gymnastics; not the factory
But lyrics. Though I know my dissident mind
And puny body would have matched as ill
Such innocence and health as these unkind
Years that yield cities to the hawk-nosed will.

XIII

The notion of the Wall and Counter Wall,
For instance, came to them at Syracuse.
The Wall was reared by those who most of all
Were frightened of the unspeakable abuse
Of foreigners transforming Syracuse.
And thus by building this immensely tall
Protection led the investing force to use
The taller cover of a Counter Wall.

I see at every crucial turn of fate
Those soldier-labourers, those citizen-
Victims at their crass, suicidal tricks;
And find, to say the least, inadequate
The rueful groans that rose on all sides when
They turned from love or art to handle bricks.

XIV

You ask me to attend a conference.
The theme: the freedom of the historian.
Venue: a city of ever-changing name.
My hesitation calls to mind our youth,
When we espoused the cause of change, and merely
By adherence hoped to nudge the course of change.
And then I telegraph the message: 'No.'

The journey would involve too much expense.
The congress itself would fall beneath the ban
Of truly free historians. The same
Old points on which I know I have the truth
Will endlessly be brawled. Besides, it's nearly
Time to set out upon a trip more strange
Than ever men as history undergo.

XV

'Zeno was not beloved.' The words promote
At once uneasy stirrings in my soul.
I look up from the text and in a bowl
Of tulips see returned my stringy throat.
Outside, on leafy billows, towers float:
The saint- and beast-carved strongrooms of the whole
Species' achievement. Is my harmless role
Played by permission of the snake and stoat?
Why should I care? The great ones of the realms
Fall soon or late to our recording pens;
Haters of truth, become its stuff at last.
But this is not the dismay that overwhelms:
Youth that brings down or hoists the crown looks past
My work and face with equal indifference.

XVI

Familiar with the Rome of Crassus – that
Famous triumvir and all-powerful
Building-site speculator – I must wonder,
Alive in this metropolis where at
Every street-corner cranes pile cell on cell
To some great lucrative aesthetic blunder,
Why I myself have failed to profit by
The copying in my epoch of the ills
Of history. Impoverished and in lonely
Opposition, even at the stadium I –
Unlike the roaring mass – admire the skills
Impartially. In fact, my hope is only
That blood will not be spilt and that each side
Will with defeat be somehow satisfied.

XVII

The Dead Gate . . . for an instant the adjective
Seems neutral and innocuous as 'West',
Until I go on to read the thing was used
For carrying corpses out; and I must give
A glance at the passage from my room, so blessed
With awkward corners and by gloom suffused.
I now, in all the lodgings where I live,
Have pondered the arrangements for my rest
Eternal more than the springs on which I snoozed
– Rather as cultures through the purposive
Terror of death left slabs still manifest
In water-forsaken regions; or excused
Questions proposed by iron, water, coals,
By tenderness for the escaping souls.

XVIII

Historical, too, this lady I sometimes visit,
I think, as her bosom props my bearded head;
Her shape determined by the progress in
Mechanical engineering, whaling and
The metal industry. O pink-lit room,
What issues your activities must burke!

I hear the horse of Asia's brutal triumphs
Clop in the little street below, conveying
Suburban theatre-goers. Time to leave.
Goodbye, then, to the mammal attributes
That goddesses had no more of. A moon, so high
One does not see it, silvers stones that seem
Already fit to part and show what had
Originally to be vanquished there.

XIX

They journeyed on and met the careless Queen
And learnt from her to loose the sweat-stained leather.
Their tall propitiatory fires green
With coppered logs, they left in fabulous weather
And sailed above the caverns of the god
Whose dripping daughters hauled their breasts in vain
Above the gunwales. Then the period
At last began. They saw through fertile rain
The shore whose name they'd always known; and landed,
And marked the city out between the hills.
Not one for his posterity demanded
The burning essences that time distils,
With which it brutalizes kings, and dooms
Philosophers to mad and futile glooms.

XX

The myth of Paris and the apple never
Impressed my heart with its significance
Until that part grew elderly. Whichever
Queen got the prize seemed of indifference.
I craved no kingdom; military glory
Absurd for my cowardice; while I was dead
Sure charm could manage that part of the story
Which brought the fairest in the world to bed.
But now I see that Juno and Minerva –
Fine figures of women, doubtless – were in fact
Too womanly for that antique observer
In whom (his being a legendary act)
Apple breasts, thin thighs and fur, uncertain voice
Of girlhood were the more appropriate choice.

[262]

XXI

The fleece, the bough, the apple, Persephone,
All things that in the golden age were gold,
We know to have been the images of grain –
The stuff most precious to those men of old,
Which heroes lifted from the dragon's tree,
Which brought the hell-descending husbands pain,
And in pursuit of fleet, breast-trembling girls
Delayed the most eager. Spring revealed the shoot
That summer turned the hue to be desired,
But the same season that they cut the fruit
Held chill disaster. Then the whole race hurls
Itself with weapons on the desolate and mired
Domain. At last reluctantly it yields
The slender queen to sparkling sepia fields.

XXII

It slept: its dreams were powerless to renew
Its former invention, being all of faint
Desires imperfectly recalled on waking.
Its great extremities and capital grew
Withered, incapable of harm. The paint
Peeled from its frescoes and, the gods forsaking,
Column and pediment fell in fields of blue.
And then appeared the mild, self-centred saint
Whose sick environs seemed of his own making,
Who indicated what was good and true
In orders too remote to bear the taint
Of temporal decay. Its heart stopped aching:
Except for crowns the unenlightened hated,
And virgins never to be violated.

XXIII

The Other World's a concept that has seemed
Always far-fetched or puerile to me,
Whether beyond the grave or in what 'gleamed'
Through molecules discrete of alp or sea;
Significance assumed by the unfree,
Appalled by their brief servitude before
Strangler and priest unbolt the prison door.

But see, today I've gazed upon a page
That reproduced a statue's photograph
To show the god of some sand-blotted age.
The head was missing but what held the staff
That ruled the living from the cenotaph
Had fingers each with circumstantial nail.
The long, dark grooves were on another scale.

XXIV

All winter I kept mistaking for a bird
A hanging leaf. And only in old age
Have I admitted it to be absurd
To think Dame Nature not a personage.
So that beyond the window this impassive
Order might hide a pantheon which sighs
For all our woes; or comprehend a massive
Variance in state we can't ourselves surmise
(As though historical process were to end,
Having at last forborne its noblest forces
To corrupt). And imperceptibly will blend
With notions of robot nightingales and horses
Faster than light, the body's ancient skit,
That once seemed destined only for the pit.

XXV

And actually survived. And changed. And made
Them happy with their soil-skinned globe because
The destination of its fruits obeyed
The appetite of reason, weaklings' laws.
Wars ended. No minority of men
Was prejudiced or felt itself to be.
Waking at four, the sensitive had then
Only art, passion or senility
To keep them from the dream-packed rest of slumber.
The planet seemed to spin on such a point
It shocked when summer trembled into umber;
But as the snow enlarged each branch's joint
They lit fires on the river, and befriended
Flocks of strange birds, that fearlessly descended.

OFF COURSE

I

The ageing prowler, envious of his prey,
Each killing as the last must contemplate.
The victim at her lithe and leaping play
Lives always as though she will escape her fate.

II

What's the mysterious lure
Worn specially for me?
Not rare the slenderness
Extreme; incurving hair:
And even I must see
Other children climb
In my remaining time
To disyllabic years.

Nothing less crucial than
The species' posterity
She undertakes to bear –
The enormous spreading fan
That hinges, how well I see,
Upon the repetition
Of the preposterous proposition
That one be thought the most fair.

What catastrophe absurd
When simple biology
Is thwarted by the stricture
Of society's moral word,
Or the sterility
Of an old heart, or just
Within the other bust
An identical ideal picture!

III

Enough to have glimpsed the face
Of the dutiful daughter;
Distantly followed both home
To a strange quarter;

Drawn later a puzzled smile
By confronting her;
Been forced to let her remain
In that dead milieu.

Did you expect, then, not to suffer?
Imagine possession
For hours, even years, would resolve
Your obsession?

Stays in the wound of your mind –
A blade turned to show
Its improbable, dangerous concave,
Her throat and turned jaw.

That image enough, revived
As it is, for ever,
By all other nymphs of choking
Fire, ocean, river.

IV

When the fisher slit the gut
The long-lost ring fell out.
What chose the face to join
The monarch's on the coin?
Only to usual toxins
The wound's renowned indifference.

Benevolent, the grave
Attention that she gave
To opening others' letters
Or more ridiculous matters;
Oneself became the leg
Crossed by its analogue
As, filing a card, she pressed
A drawer to her breast.

On lips in corridors,
Suddenly far off course,
The taste of happiness . . .
A moment later, regress
To the naturalistic part
Of a constricted art.
O elderly visitor
To the house of daughters, pour
Your farewell vodka and
Rejoin the bankrupt land.

That she can never staunch
The welling she will launch
Is quite beyond her knowledge,
And sending her to college
In my particular school
Of introverted rule
Must earlier break the fusion
Of beauty and illusion.
For though romantic, too,
Her simple dreams pursue
Fatuities more apt.
Renounce the naively-wrapped
Neat skull, long limbs, slight bust.
Renounce because you must.

V

How can the freakishness of age possess you?
I see you running always but on feet
Eager to meet life not to get it over;
And your distinguishable traits seem merely
Those of physique. What talons must caress you,
What spell of imprisonment must you complete,
Before you change from loved to hopeless lover
And sign your face and motives insincerely?

Perhaps your impulsive gestures are those same
That will define neurosis with a name –
As now I see my crazy lack of nerve
The caricature of sensitive reserve.
And I, who am part, would history proscribe
That brings the ruin of the happy tribe!

[267]

VI

Never too late, no hurry (idiot notion)
To claim her from inevitable passion,
Sophistication, even spouse – as though
During the next decade and a half she were
To be, as in that just past, inviolate.

Therefore keep mum, continue as *voyeur*,
Her ardour and frivolity ignore –
In the pretence that she will duplicate
In time one's introversion and one's woe.

VII

Strange, it's your ageing that I fear –
Born in my thirty-seventh year.
Even the elapse of days
May deviate your simple ways,
Add contours to fragility –
The more, since I'm not there to see
By watching on its very face
That time lacks mensurable pace.
No use to tell myself I could
Own you at eras of equal good;
That seventeen may find your soul
Still free; eighteen your virtue whole;
And even five more circlings of
The sun lack power to stale the love
The end of childhood brings – and brings
Not just to those in whom it springs
But, like revolution's change,
To a class outside its range.
Dear prey, you must escape – if not
Through the old hunter's hopeless shot
Then down spectacular falls of time,
And only stay the same in rhyme,
Where others may as harmlessly
Enjoy illegal charms as I;
Commune with your unopened mind
As if that bud might comprehend
The rankness of its neighbour weed;
And dream decay can be renewed;
Dream that compassion stirs in youth
And on their muzzle feel your mouth.

VIII

Though he foresaw it all – the halting word,
The assignation, passion's declaration,
The impossible triangle ensuing – yet
He spoke the halting word and, yes, they met.

A windy night, the cars on other business,
Nothing planned except to clutch the still-far hand.
Between the move, the parking, and the move,
He let out nothing of his tender love.

And so all stayed within the possible.
That is to say, she went unschooled away.
And clouds blew from the constellations' law,
And once again his future he foresaw.

IX

How touched he was when those soft wings
Dropped down from dismal skies!
First a mere speck, and then the things
To his surprise
Were vast against his eyes.

How white, how long, how strange the form
Folded on breast austere!
Miraculous it should be warm
And lacking fear,
Though from an alien sphere.

Never, he hoped, would be relaxed
The clenching sense of awe.
Though soon his outstretched arms are taxed,
Wrist cinctured raw
With the dependent claw.

But how can he wish the visitation
Returned this time for ever
To orbits of imagination;
And stilled the fever
Of bird blood, wings' threshing lever?

X

The living rabbit's ear inserted through a fistula
In a dog's stomach was digested by the gastric juice.
That classical experiment was hardly necessary
To prove the lack of magical properties in life itself.

Your youth fills my heart, where it's transformed to gall.
                                              Indeed, what stops
The necrosis of the organ, washed by the poison it secretes?

XI

Equally as astounding
As the safety of your being
In days when we're apart
Is that it was preserved
During the years before we met.

What dangerous epochs must
You live through when I'm gone:
Renewing for others the sense
Of the scarcity of time
While you recklessly expend it.

And the length of your forgetting
Will exceed that of our knowing
By a lifetime, your lifetime –
Of which I shall be even
More ignorant than of your past.

XII

I had a dream of you in which you were another.
How did I recognize you under that disguise,
Since in the dream we were unquestionably together?

Even in sleep it seems there can be no one else –
Where somehow black or red denotes your umber head,
And wishes strive to make joy less improbable.

XIII

He saw the dark king carry off
His fragile love to regions of
Prolonged and sweaty dark.

What matter that it was the phone
And petty cash book she was wrenched from
To the municipal park?

Only by returning to infernal
Fires, test of his ancient vernal
Heroism, could he

Have made the delicately closed
White valve once more push through the frost.
Forgive him, ruined and bloody

Nymph: think that happiness may come
Rather in underworlds of dumb
Gropings, betrayal, hate,

Than through his offering of trees
Obedient to shifting keys;
The flayed nerves of the poet's fate.

XIV

Forked slightness, nylon'd far along the fork –
The fork itself – leave me with a sense
Of a wound, my wound, impossible to heal.
Even this softness in my hands, since it's not yours,
Can't console for your elusiveness.
How can the concept of 'love' attach itself
To nothing possessed, unpossessable, evanescent?

Yet as the scab inevitably forms,
Only inflamed at its edges, over the lesion,
Grows an incongruous joy – at the thought of love,
Of its prolongation and doom in the glands of old men.

O love, be happy in my secret woe,
Exist in your particulars of dark
Transactions to which I cannot be a party;
Exist in my own unfaithfulness even –
In the gross sensation of release, whose thoughts
Are of similar regions, remote from those dense woods,
Where I never went, and now shall never go.

XV

I come across some lines to her, months old,
Unfinished. From which my glance averts in pain.
I much prefer the unyielding of the cold
To this occasional and tepid rain.

PART SIX

New Poems
(1968)

THE PAINTER

You object: the paintings are not for the mass
Though I've chosen for models those exhausted by labour
Or worn out by a life of shame – having at first
Been preoccupied with dancers and thoroughbreds.

Well-taken point: few can stand seeing their arses
From a low, rearward view; or like having fixed
The moment when no amount of scrubbing
Seems to remove the ingrained dirt from the knee-cap.

But one wished to exclude the enviable element
Inherent in horses and girls. And you can't
Have art be about nothing. Hence these saddles
Of fat, these toilets we devote so much time to.

Wouldn't I really have wished my technique
To be put to the service of princes' triumphal entries
Or the death of God? Better still, perhaps,
For it to have accompanied dreadful emotions.

Yet to get down the bowlishness of zinc bowls
And the way the nature of zinc presses against
The nerve-ends of organic life – something,
In these days of bureaucracy and the re-arming Huns.

THE SYMPHONIST

To write just too many symphonies
For the memory easily to
Identify; to have made love to
Her in a variety of strange
Rooms and woods; to dream of clear meanings,
And on waking utterly forget . . .

Is it the Sixth where the initial
Largo is chased by two raspberry-
Blowing rondos? And the Ninth programmed
The withstanding by heroes of the
Siege of the boulevarded city,
Or the gazing at a young harpist.

In some uneasy interlude of
Peace the lake fell. Embedded in its
Strata was her skull, exemplar of
Eye-ridges on their way to thinking.
For 300,000 years or so
The axe-heads scarcely altered their shape.

Then the dream was recalled. It involved
Rolling fire on the far-off plain,
A flight in which she was left behind.
Out of that agony of loss sprang
A score for a thousand voices, and
Seventeen years of complete silence.

Think of quite outrageous conjunctions.
Have the tympani slogged during the
Viola's cadenza. Enfold in
The long hirsute arms two tender breasts
And a white rib-cage unfitted for
A time of ice, of philistine rule.

To make four movements out of four notes;
To end with a transformation of
An early, almost forgotten theme;
To devote a whole life to wordless
Communication . . . Trumpeters, where
Are your ox-horns? Girls, your rouge for bones?

[276]

THE ART OF THE APPLE

The apple, stolid centre of assemblies
Of bottle, napkin, pipe, assumes in autumn
A more active role in art by casting
A pointilliste shadow for its tree, composed of
    Blobs: green, blush-red, rotten-brown.

What forces you, apple-tree, to become a firework,
Throwing up coloured orbs that stay suspended –
The previous shower, not all extinguished,
Still on the ground; is your cylinder hollow,
    In fact, though so gnarled and dense?

'Draw lines; whether from memory or after
Nature. Then you will be a good artist.' Thus
Ingres to Degas. The apple-tree is about
To reveal the rectilinear essence
    Of its vague superstructure.

Confusing conspectus of periods and
Schools, how can we make up our minds about you?
Even plucking the compact heart from your depths
And biting its blend of flesh and sinew, sweet
    And tart, leaves us uncertain.

Some monk in a past century grafted on,
Perhaps, to the original feeble crab
A vision of blossoming stigmata and
Miraculous food. One finds suspiciously
    Romantic the concept now.

SINFONIA A GRAN ORQUESTA

Feeling my heart about to accelerate,
I swallow a pill of phenobarbitone.
Odd how one enjoys the bitterness, knowing
It will fade, as will the cutting edge from the
    World of ludicrous anxieties.

[277]

But not that world only contains the destructive
Bodies, of course: waiting the normal, I play
The Ariaga symphony; the boy dead
Of Koch's bacillus at nineteen, at the door
    Of an epoch of relative calm.

Though how can one measure the effect on the
Metabolism or on the corpuscles'
Resistance of a long campaign of burning
And rape? Staggering indeed that should be shaped
    At all the score's industrious lines.

For the heart's increased action attempts in vain
To keep up with the interpretation to
Itself of an age of nonchalance to art.
    Before we sleep, the throbbing horns underline
    A tune of complete irrelevance.

One wrote to me out of the blue: 'Dear comrade . . . '
Touched at the address, after thirty-five years,
I replied, found he believed in a divine
Intervention in human affairs at this
    Stage of almost complete disaster.

Is it weakness that makes me curiously
Not unsympathetic to the notion that
In a century of culture's sickliness
Something is working on the other side – that its
    Death is a required prelude, in fact?

No, but the goodness of the gods cannot be
Counted on. They came once before, grey-eyed or
Bird-shaped, and through those they were enamoured of
Imparted such secrets as optical columns
    Surrounding an evident justice.

Nevertheless, comrade, one is not compelled
To envisage ruined pantheons stretching
To eternity, agreed. Moreover, one
Can enjoy the bitterness, waiting for the
    Oppressed libido to take over.

CHINOISERIE

I've always been comfortably off.
In my poorer days my desires were modest:
Now I earn more, my previous habits
Circumscribe the area of my extravagance.
I've tried to take care that being a poet
Didn't get in the way of making a living,
And eventually this other occupation
Actually incremented my income
And stopped hurting my respectability.
It's a toss up whether I turn first
To the literary or the financial page,
And I find it just as painful to read
Of a bonus issue of shares I failed to buy
As of the success of a rival writer.
Yet I can seriously assert
That finally money doesn't matter.
It's supported a life I can't approve of:
I've saved it for a life I shall never enjoy.
Like my neatness and punctuality,
My interest in it denotes a fixation
At the irrelevant anal stage of existence.
If I became penniless tomorrow . . .
Still impossible to change to a hero of art!
An incurable lack of high seriousness
Is indicated by concern about cash;
A deficiency in the religious sense;
A fatal practicality for life.
Given this species of character,
My follies have arisen from denying it –
Underestimating the greed of others,
And the longevity of capitalism.
How much happier I'd have been
Had I put my patrimony in low-yielders,
And been less timid and considerate,
And voted Tory, and stuck to prose.

READING *THE BOSTONIANS* IN ALGECIRAS BAY

For Alan Ross

At the next table, on the terrace
(*The Bostonians* open on my
Knee), a pale pumice domineering
Head; in the prosperous buttonhole
An order. Behind the lush hotel,
Folds of burnt-brown, donkey-littered hills,
Beyond which runs the river with the
Battle-name. Old man, did you, thirty
Years ago, fire shots that killed my friend?

'Whatever money was given her
She gave it away to a negro
Or a refugee. No woman could
Be less invidious, but on the
Whole she preferred these two classes of
The human race.' Though even Henry
Found history grave at last; came to
The 'unspeakable give-away of
The whole fool's paradise of our past.'

On the concrete sheds by the quayside:
PESCADOS S.L., dominating
The life of the town, arsehole of Spain.
In this suburb, round the stinking stream,
An African poverty, from which
The boys emerge, asking for 'money',
Threatening with the mock horns of bulls,
Plucking a pack of Marlboro from
The breast pocket of my ink voile shirt.

Despite the cigarette-evidenced
Yankee subventions, only the jail
And the *plaza de toros* look clean
And in the least substantially built.
And to guarantee the lottery's
Success there are inexhaustible
Supplies of the wall-eyed and crippled
To be led to street-corners by boys
And there reassure the unlucky.

[280]

Dear friend, all is still to struggle for.
In our middle-age what engrosses
Is the play of human emotions –
In the hotel today, a wedding:
A girl of eleven perturbed at
Her mother wearing only one glove,
Dusting down her elder sister's dress;
Though herself bustless. Illustrative
The guests, of all stages in love's game.

But in that room of our chance meeting
Over the crumby Piccadilly
Of 1944 – did we think
Then to succumb to slide-rule metrics,
Hear social-democratic England
Object to the roasting merely of
Civilians in yet another
Civil war, and to stay *de luxe* in
The realms of a tyrant of our youth?

It's not enough to have chosen
The figurative (and preferably
Front view) to hang on our walls, alas!
Nor to have laughed over luncheon at
Numerous other *littérateurs*;
Borne the medieval and junkie
Blend of today's medical science;
Nor even, in your case, to have slaved
At friendship, and support of the arts.

What a mess, societies of men!
At first spreading out along these coasts,
Leaving their driftwood and turds afloat,
Amphorae capsized by sand, pillars
Broken, democratic orations
Echoing hollowly to lands of
Fog – where, posed as abstract principles,
The punks of a class's lust gather
A patina of factory grime.

As well as with unrequited love,
Dying, and distaste for our own verse,
Shall we always have to put up with
Delusions induced by the very
Apparatus intended to cure –
Sick doctors, nurses with biceps,
And inside the asylum's high walls
Its own individual banner?
Yes, in our time; and in our sons' time.

ASTAPOVO, 1910

The old man who died at the railway
Station, ready to leave for somewhere
Else, said: 'Whoever is happy is
Right.' The birch groves silvered the land to
Asia, and the peasants were about
To throw in their lot with factory
Hands and the cheesed-off military.

But at the moment he was fleeing
A marital sexuality
Turned grotesque with age. Locomotives
With top-hats for funnels, that had run
Down Anna Karenina, passed to
And fro while he lay dying, dreaming
Of the end of all authority.

His diary was found to observe:
'Only old people and children, free
From sexual lusts, live a true life.'
No doubt he was off to find it. The
Rest of humanity, he believed,
Was merely a factory for the
Continuation of animals.

Utopian textile mills, cigar
Smoking women, students with grenades
Tagged 'Czar', apostles of deep breathing,
Vegetarianism – all these
Had to flourish and then be subsumed
In the amendment of bankers' aims
And an electrical policy.

'Many people think that poetry
May be found only in sexual
Life. All true poetry is always
Outside it.' One sees what he meant, though
Reluctantly disagreeing. Make
Poetry out of this, said the head
Of heavy industry, with reason.

Each generation is unhappy
In its own way; looks on its children
With complacent envy. 'For you we
Expropriated the unjust and
Rich. Why aren't you laughing?' But the young
Feel no more than poets and old men
That matters accord with their vision.

THE MAP

A brilliant conjecture indeed,
Where the very shape of our wishes –
Innocence-smooth belly-curve of coast
And single deep safe inlet for our vessel –
Was adumbrated from mere glimpses
Across impossible seas. Peaks rose
From hinterlands of ignorant white,
Twins dimly familiar from childhood;
And even the capricious climate,
The zinc veins, croppable savannahs,
And fern grottos diamonded by torrents
Were indicated on succeeding
Folios. But what are these added
In the margin? Mere fancies of the
Cartographer or croakings of some
Returned, stick-limbed, insane explorer?
Farting winds from gross cheeks of cherubs
Blow trivial devils to the Poles,
Arses revealed by tattered small-clothes.
Supporting the whole, a recumbent
Skeleton, detached fore index joint
Reflectively along a toothy jaw
From which on a scroll the legend winds:
New Found Land, graveyard of fat monsters –
Anchorage ice-locked at all seasons —
Loud gales, crabs in lichen, smell of fish.

[283]

ON THE RAILWAY PLATFORM

Infant on the railway platform, whose
Head as I pass I dare impress
With a communicating finger,
This Mad Hatter figure scarcely knows
Whether he longs for your innocence
Or the youth of your nearby mother
Or a generalized human love.

Encountering you again in my
Pacings, I quite needlessly enquire
About the cardboard carton you clutch
Of veritable Dolly Mixtures.
A gleam of detached amusement fails
To check your search for the train that you
Conceive will appear close to the ground –

And rightly so, I admit, thinking
The matter over as later I
Repose my bowler upon the rack
And settle to perusing *The Times*.
Beware, child, of your hand in crazy
Crashing doors and of ostensibly
Benevolent, unknown gentlemen.

CREEPER

A tendril's actually entered
The house, and faintly tinted it is
(A sinew or duct from deep inside
Some anatomy) compared to the
Shining magenta leaves on the wall.

These, hung in September stillness, have
Made the yellow brickwork reflect their
Flushing; and at death's approach, lesser
Leaves having fallen, show the tangled
Cordage with which they have been hoisted.

Probing filament, what do you seek
In our affairs? You have waited too
Long to arrive, in any event,
For your pallid reach must fail soon, not
Even leave a dry whisker, perhaps.

What a frail representative of
That serrate, cinquefoil splendour! Yet it
Can be seen that even the foetus
Shapes along your lank length have the same
Strange oneness of contour and number.

Undoubtedly in a season of
Dying the preparation, though much
Of it abortive, is for re-birth;
However perverse the confidence,
And grotesque the sacrifice of flesh.

Doesn't that reassure the body's
House, invaded by extending rods
Of foreign or unruly objects?
Or merely remind our furniture
Of the restless empire of nature?

AMBIGUITIES OF TRAVEL

And will you really wake at the hotel
With the mountain in the garden and the crippled
Gardener? And go to see the wall-paintings
Of the wall-eyed flautists, and the pink sandstone
Water nymph with vulva-exposing embroideries,
And the silk banner (reconstruction) of Lord Kanishka?

Poetry is something between the dream
And its interpretation. Through pleached boughs
Of blossoming, still vivid your pantisocratic
Imaginings, how hurtful to think
Of the past dragging its foot to meet you,
As though a mirror stood at the pathway's end.

[285]

A saying of Kanishka: 'Human love –
So much beauty lavished on so much goodness.'
Dear child, it's only that the colours have flaked
That the musicians are so repulsive;
And the sepulchre of the ruler was long ago
Shat on by pillaging baboons.

What song will your mind rehearse as, shaving,
You see the girl still slumbering in the striped light?
That late sonata movement where, trilling each note,
The performer's hands move farther and farther apart?
Strange, both expounding life in likenesses,
Voyaging through the other's boiling wake.

MY DEAD BROTHERS

When the soothsayer spoke of my three brothers
I smiled in my sleeve, since I had only one –
  Later recalled those two dead
  Babes, their lives measured in days.

Where are you now, you strong men who would have looked
Up to me? The little lives followed so close
  On my own I could well have
  Smothered them in my cradle.

And I can even remember their names, which
They scarcely used. Would they have had my gift for
  Affairs, for art, such as it
  Is; my filbert nails, my moles?

To die before my mother and father was
Your legendary fate, my own to prove so
  Unconsolatory in
  Surviving them one by one.

The tiny internal flaw that destroyed your
Perfect appearances, how could I fail to
  Inherit, since I possess
  Such an assortment myself?

Fifty years in your graves, you rise up in the
Live wax of the hour of your births. Did you
  Sacrifice your kingdom
  For my pre-destined neurosis?

HEREDITY

Mother, it was this, then, you suffered from in
The days of my uncaring adolescence –
This unpleasant and chronic but curable,
It's said, imbalance of metabolism.

How it would have distressed you to discover
That with your timid heart you'd also passed on
A gland too officious, since only the nice
Lessons of life were to be learnt in your school.

You'd have foolishly liked to bear my symptoms
As well, to save me the trouble, just as now
(Though with rather less theoretical risk)
I'd prefer to have been the unlucky one.

Widowed, lacking the consolations of art,
How did you stand the long years of uncertain
Diagnosis, the ineffective drugs, and
Lastly the blundering knife of that epoch?

Well, you survived. And death was still a decade
Away. When it came, I was then fully seised
Of its threat, its grip, its method of bringing
Itself into life, premature grave-breath, bones –

Closer myself to the state of receiving
It. But how far then compared with the present!
Strange we should each get our wish to endure for
The other; or must the same blood expect to?

IN MEMORY OF MY CAT, DOMINO:
1951–66

Rising at dawn to pee, I thought I saw you
Curved in a chair, with head raised to look at me,
As you did at such hours. But the next moment,
More used to the gloom, there was only a jar
And a face-cloth. Time enough, nonetheless,
For love's responsibilities to return
To me.
      The unique character of the dead
Is the source of our sense of mourning and loss;
So, back in bed, I avoided calling up
What I know is intact in my mind, your life,
Entirely possessed as it was by my care.

I could conceive you not as dead but merely
Gone before me to a world that sends to us
Decreasing intimations of its beings –
No doubt because they find us in the end
Pathetic, worthy, but of small importance.

So long had we been together it never
Occurred to me I might fall somewhat behind.
Even when, familiar fur in my hands,
The sickly wave of barbiturate rose up,
I thought it was I who was journeying on –
But looking back there is only emptiness,
Your dusty medicaments and my portrait
Taken with you: sad mode of life you've outpaced.

TO A RECENTLY-ACQUIRED OMEGA

Had we been travelling together
At the limit of velocity
By now we should have made our escape
From the stacked dish-shaped dominions
Of the vassals of the sun, en route
To the nearest star. Several such
Fireballs we'd flash through arm in arm
And then, close companion, you'd soar
Yoked loosely to an archipelago
Of bones until yourself stopped beating,
Long before quitting our galaxy
Let alone reaching the vast Chelsea
Bun in Andromeda – that smear I
Search for in vain with this gun-layer's
Telescope of the last war but one,
Brass white elephant of the junk shops.

Still, even you, viable within
Less frighteningly narrow limits,
Would never survive through such space,
As you now have the chance to, the risks
Of existence and die of worn cogs.
And time is the only measure we'll
Step of any significance. Time
Of the piddling order that prompts me
To come in from the terrace, with its
Awning of myth, to the perception
Of danger to loved organisms.
Death's vacancy unvisited yet;
Unplumbed the possibility of
Resurrection, after two thousand
Million years, on other shores; unknown
The meaning of a cosmos poisoned
By the stale fall-out of explosions
Occurring in actual nature.

But during that fantastic journey
Wouldn't we have seen in retrospect
That our earth was Elysium
After all – dust without parallel,
Miraculously clouded? The dead
Regretting the passing of disease.

[289]

METAMORPHOSES

The girl in trousers wheeling a red baby
Stops to look in the window of a bread-shop.
One wants to tell her that it's all steam-
Baked muck, but really there's no chance
Of stopping her buying a bogus
Farm-house cob. Reassuring to think
That anyway it will be transformed
To wholesome milk, just as somehow she
Has gathered herself together from
The chaos of parturition and
Appears now with a lacquered bouffant
Top-knot and her old wiles unimpaired.
Why should one trouble to disguise the
Origin of the terrifying
Earth-mother, that lies in wait for men
With her odours of bergamot and
Plasma, and her soft rind filled with tripes?

STRANGE CHILD

Couldn't you think, watching the child's grave interest
In behaviour, particularly the bad
Behaviour of her near contemporaries,
That a spirit from elsewhere informed her?

Certainly the erect tower of vertebrae,
The upper lip lifted from really too tiny pearls,
The weeping hair, do not contradict the notion.

Of course, it will leave her, the ghost, to allow her
To divide into the complexities of girlhood.
But for the moment it says: 'Yes, this is what our order
Is like, you imperfect ones, intruders in nature.'
And stretches miraculous young vegetables of fingers.

Some day someone will see again in her
This utter purity, these extensions of mind
In hair, mouth, limbs – himself possessed by a demon
Of most noble generosity, fleeting domain.

ROMANCE

Girl with fat legs, reading Georgette Heyer,
Shall I arrange you in my pantheon?
Only the inspiration may be lacking,
Not your worthiness – for the preponderance
Of evidence favours the viability
Of even chinless countenances,
Just as the mousy day in April counts
In the reckoning of an empire's fall or a life
Consumed by art and syphilitic sores.
Besides, the next moment a shaft of sunlight breaks
Through southering clouds and on your betrothal finger
Illumines the diamond from Saqui & Lawrence.

Absorbed by later variations, we forget
How plain the theme was. Though planned for ultimate
Unhappiness, a world was toyed with once
Of giants mating, dropping their young
After gestations easy and prolonged
As mammoths'.
                   Perhaps the trouble was
That even those sleepers in down-long barrows
Longed for a paradigm of grace,
And artists, chasing the deer's legs of their own
Genes' deviation, sealed the fatal heresy.

But when the Muse of thirteen and a half relented
She proved to be slattern and promiscuous;
And no one would buy her portrait, nude though it was –
Melted chocolate on a couch of boiled-sweet green.

Return, great goddesses, and your society
Where even little girls develop
Strong superegos, and the misfortune
Of woman's weak moral nature is unknown;
And the wars are waged on a lower epicycle
By armour diminutive as stag-beetles;
And poets forbidden to sing of their diseases
Or amatory botherations;
And only with end-stopped irony.

ROAD SAFETY

'Watch my behind not her's.' Yes, I can just read
The insolent and meant to be witty plate
On the car in front – wearing my spectacles,
Of course, and by gum it confirms what I have
Often thought: I shall crash looking at a girl,
Like some mad three-badge stoker choked by his own
Crapulous vomit. But as soon as I vow
To myself to mend my ludicrous habits
The thought arises of inexhaustible
Generations achieving the age of eye-
Catching nubility. Die happy, old boy,
If you can at all contrive to die before
The malignancies of flesh and of the State
Gouge out the gazing and its bonanza mine.

MIND TO BODY

Awake already, can't you sleep again?
Strange body, how you fail to serve the mind
That wishes above all to be the puissant prince
Of sensual indolent extremities!
I see your legs emerging from the rich
Humus of dreams, in some way anxious for
Frustrated action, botched creativity,
In a dawn inhabited only by moths and owls.

At times of physical pain one is convinced
That what is happening is happening to
Another body – that merely passing chance
Has hooked up the throbbing circuit to one's own
Perception. Likely to be a sad affair,
Lean flesh, our final reconciliation.

IN LAMBETH PALACE ROAD

Not far, as the pigeon flies, from Waterloo,
Where droppings are thick under glass awnings,
To the roadway outside St Thomas' Hospital

On which a pigeon is smeared as on a slide,
To patients a supererogatory reminder.
How quickly a habit is established in
A strange parish. Waiting for the gland
To dispose of the radioactive iodine,
And suchlike tediums, I visit a tea-shop
Conveniently under the crude shadow of County Hall,
Close to where Wordsworth found the earth most fair.
Coffee and bun; tea and toast; *The Times* then
The *Evening Standard*, punctuated by
The Freud Journal of Lou Andreas-Salomé.
Already one's actions smack of the legendary,
If only to oneself, since at the moment
The springs of verse are flowing after a long
Spell of being bunged up. It scarcely needed
The slimy tentacles of the cardiograph
Or the sting of the syringe's proboscis to release them.
They would have been satisfied to observe a waitress
Making sure of her lipstick before going off duty,
To mark the desolation here of the new
Concrete, and rudimentary roundabout,
Or just to read how in woman the genital zone
Is merely leased from the anal; and that (in Lou's view)
She is the antithesis of Faustian man –
For why should she pursue the unattainable
Since she herself is the goal?
                                Though immersed in the body –
Its plea to Knife and Drug, ludicrous powers,
To restore the health of youth – my Faustian aim
Is really this faeces-loving, this bourgeois
Collection and comparison of things.
Enough that the pigeon's eye blinks as slowly as
An old-fashioned camera-shutter, and that its closure
Appears to be effected by the same
Adumbrated arrangement of wrinkled stuff.
And yet uneasily I'm reminded that only
By a concession wrested from the gods
In their weak moments as swan-lovers or lyre-fans
Was art accorded the privilege of addressing
A world in which one order felt ill at ease.
Bridge and river, how did you come to be

Such strange companions? Were the grassy banks,
Separated lovers, in need of a restless creation
To mingle their gravels and really enclose the silver
Serpent forever slipping from their grasp?
Unlucky conjunction, that allowed the horsemen
To make the librarians flee, and far products
Feed local manufactories of caste.
But even when the arching stone is broken,
As it will be, and the water divides once more,
And squatting birds, making imperial helmets of boulders,
Are truly the intelligences of the ebb-tide's litter,
The arrangement of molecules will still seem
An utter irrelevance – for what has earth
To do with the purposelessness of divinities?

And yet we imagined them. Found time
From the massing of books and gold, and the mixing of phials
For the elusive elixir of immortality,
To conceive the utterly different giants
In their castle of great fires and freezing corridors.
Is the universal order beneath the poet's
Contempt, then? His sorrow for humanity,
And its complex and pitiful body, too deep
To be comprised in the dust and unneighbourly constellations?
One must think so, submitting to the mercy of hospitals,
Agonized over disaster to birds, and drinking
The real but small comfort of the Indian herb.

PERVERSENESS

A broken pill keeps coming out of
The bottle, almost as though
One didn't want to be cured.
Does the instinctive order life then –
Or is it, as one's assumed,
A matter of calibre,
Chance favouring the forward?

If one meant to take an overdose,
Would you still, misshapen disc,
Keep grinning against my palm?
Rather, you'd be discovered down at
The thick amber foundation
Clutched in a white hand, skulking
Among truly innocent granules.

ORDERS

All through the summer a visiting quartet –
Father and daughter blackbird, pigeon, squirrel.
Soft cluckings in the tree announce the blackbirds:
First it was him, daring the dangerous sill;
Later brought his Cordelia of the brood –
She pouting and shivering, rather remote.
Now in her nature like all other daughters
She drives him off the grapes and bread I scatter.
Slate-flat, slate-blue taffeta tail embraced by
Matronly wings, gray marbled evenly gray,
The pigeon drops draughtsmen on the terrace squares,
Patrolling ceaselessly. And in the mornings,
Anxious at the window, one hand clutched at heart,
My chinless friend, with soil-crumbed neurotic nose,
And tail a brush for cleaning babies' bottles –
Disconcertingly like Sam or Sue Squirrel.

This summer, too, I saw in J.B. Bury
'That mysterious prae-Aryan foreworld' –
Not really understanding the phrase, dimly
Conceiving a life before the oil-nurtured
Legions, before the language of short, hard words,
Before the death ships, the bronze, the chalk horses,
Which now survives only as our consciousness
Of the dotty element in our natures,
Or as a tiny, round, thinly black-haired head
Called to the colours from a cretin valley,

Or as the unmemorialed existence
              To which we may be doomed.
              The quite senseless war
Through summer days will run into winter days,
The war that during my life has scarcely stopped.
And the government that I elected, like
All governments, whether elected by me
Or not, will be powerless or uncaring.
How strange that in this sphere my desire should be
Always so different from the general will!

'There is no bridge between directional time
And timeless eternity,' wrote the gloomy
German; 'between the course of history and
The existence of a divine world order.'
Though far from belief in a divinity,
One sees indeed what he meant (and perhaps there
The translator was gravelled for the right word,
As one is oneself) – for certainly what may
Be conceived to be the principles ruling
The stuff that surrounds us, they have not to do
With bird-song, bird-love, the propulsion of metal
Into men. And what but the material
Can ever confront us, its open constants
Expressed on inevitably baffling clocks?

But I am thankful, on the whole, for this chance
To share in irrelevant events – being
In any case borne on to a species of
Significance by the drives of a motive
(No doubt falling far short of the eternal)
That will change my egotistic young blackbird
Next year to a care-worn mother. Take note, you
Gods, how my boyhood began with my father
Reading the news of the killing of young men;
How my adult body struggled with a mind
At odds with the task an unjust world imposed
And broke out in lesions that the mind despised.
Goethe said: 'The idea always appears
As a strange guest in actuality . . . The
Idea and common actuality
Must be kept strictly separate.' Very well:

[296]

Assign the business of being a poet
To an order of things entirely divine,
And the anguish to its historical material;
And accept the consolation (in Kafka's terms)
Of a wound that precisely fits the arrow.

But suppose the divinities relented,
Said: 'Your existence shall accord with our wills' –
Would our being prove even more frightening?
What would the creatures cry out at our windows,
Dark on a sky of furnace yellows: 'Join us
In the dumbness of utterly pure feeling,
To the forces that stretch you out over time
Surrender, and rejoice in the cellular
Mishaps that must bring about your extinction'?

And what if ourselves became divine, and fell
On the pitiful but attractive human,
Taking the temporary guise of a swan
Or a serpent: could we return to our more
Abstract designs untouched by the temporal;
Would we not afterwards try to get back those
Beautiful offspring, so mortal, so fated?

VARIATION ON A THEME BY SANDARS

'All our birds are capable of flight,'
Said Edmund Sandars in his *Bird Book
For the Pocket*. What a relief to
Think that nowhere on these islands are
Birds with mere elbows, or too stout birds.
It makes one, like some woman poet, want
To clap one's hands so that from grimy
Red chimney-pots, white cliffs, marshlands by
Power stations, mangy-lion moors
Rise up flung lassos, particle clouds,
Turning oscilloscope traces of
Wings; though doubtless superfluous thus
To test our author's observation.

[297]

THE VISITORS

Powers that seem to arrive from elsewhere, I
Bewilderedly open the door to you, though
I sent out the invitations and, indeed,
Recognize the visages from a lifetime's
     Dreaming of dining with gods.

No one could be more suspicious than I of
The sudden appearance of divinities
In middle-aged verse, but how else to describe
The double nature of nature in epochs
     Of creative happiness?

Besides, little use to recall, strolling at
Dusk on the suburban common with my thoughts
And walking-stick, as I stumble over the
Dung of lions, that in fact in this place a
     Circus encamped some days past.

And the tragedies of our infancy, a
Degree more real than the howl of the guilty
King, we rehearse till our death. No wonder They
Visit us sometimes to remind us of our
     Right to be blessed and consoled.

Well, enigmatic beings, though you lurk in
The gloom of book-shelves and vibrate from the grooves
Of whirling discs, I resolve to devote your
Imparting of blinding connections to those
     Who would spurn the locales.

And assert that your order, somewhat concerned
For our world, demands the expropriation
Of all whose motives are ruled by the fetish
Of things and not by the hominids who at
     Times can enchant even you.

I don't suppose you ever try to enter
The chain-hung doors of terrible rooms where the
Plotting of our downfall goes on. No, it's just
Us you can help, and our enemies frighten
     You more than they do ourselves.

[298]

And you never conceived of a species whose
Members could injure each other. In your land
The jealousies and hates cannot matter in
The end because of your immortality.
　　That's what you try to confer.

UNDERGROUND GOD

When the ground was dug for the steel, glass-clad cube,
Turned up a gigantic hand. The workmen,
Mystified, brought it to the foreman; then
Students with tea-spoons unearthed a temple site.

We were amazed to find, not that the city
Had faith once, but owned a choice of deities.
Now in our office, whose casements do not open,
Whose tenants are legal fictions, we ponder such things.

Jill, Carol, Lana, succession of innocents
Straight from school, substitute Muses in
A philistine age, we search your lucid features
For signs of adhesion to one sect or the other.

Sly god of decadent empires, you were here
Already, your altars reeking of blood and semen,
During the rational century and its long
Industrious and continent aftermath –

Unknown to everyone except a few
Bedlam'd nobles, rippers in dark ginnels,
And theorists of nation-outflanking horse.
Under the drains waited your great welcoming grasp.

What forces now can your opponent put
Into the field? The gormless labourers;
Watchers of pulchritude undestined for art;
And, as in nature, autumns strangely prolonged?

DISASTERS

Can they be part of our dreams, so disastrous
They wake us, and stay in our life of waking?
Just as the assassin's shell, pitched from a world
Of black suns, and wireless voices in the head,
Comes to lodge in a situation of blood-
   Stained skirts and hopeless sorrow.

Or is it simply not true, the sense we have
Of a life ruined by us, unprompted by
Pre-existing paradigms? Didn't in fact
Primaeval fluids hold terrors for newly
Created proteins about to find out how
   To perpetuate themselves?

And galaxies move in fear of colliding?
But try to conceive the author of a whole
Hierarchy of unease; ineptness, no,
Nor malevolence could account for the lack
Of allegiance of an entire order
   To the rules that expound it.

One sees how legends came to be invented
Of gods, so to speak, picking their noses while
The dolls they'd made tore off each other's fingers,
Or of an atrocious angel whose revolt
Put the divine omnipotence for ever
   At the issue of gunfire.

But such is the rudimentary prattle
Of those whose very birth implanted a sense
Of disgust for their origin. Protest rises
From sunsets cobbled by exploded islands;
Plumage in children's water-colour oblongs;
   From fountain, doorway, rose.

Early in these November mornings, who'll dare,
Passing by portraits of worried-over love,
To open curtains on a world still dark, still
Doubtful of blackbird chinkings, moon-livid still?
The mildly-drugged with coffee and self-regard,
   Language-infatuated!

[300]

Symbolist Creator, would we have had you
Leave less to chance and speculation? How else
Except through flight along the margin of the
Permanent, heaving thing could its nature have
So imprinted itself in our sternum pulse
 And arches of our insteps?

Nymphs come from goodness knows what shrines, messages
Between their gravity-neutralizing breasts:
What does it matter, even death and failure,
Utter impossibility of knowing
Their god, so long as a lifetime's aperçus
 Are unsafely recorded?

And the fires lick the violas' bellies,
Algebras lost past recall, great men dateless.
In viable atmospheres breathed on rondures
Far off, the same griefs delicately inflate,
Walking hills like mist, fogging the alleyways
 Of heroic city-states.

GODDESS

 Only brown hair, he thought – as though the disguised
 Goddess shouldn't have owned human attributes.
  But what other point, after
  All, had her startling entry?

 It would have been an improbable, not to
 Say undivine idea had she assumed
  Even a golden fleece or
  A bird's total sootiness –

 Let alone masks she was capable of, as
 She looked down and, at the sight of *anthropos*,
  Felt her unapproachable
  And icy nature relent.

 Besides, it was part of the design that he
 Should fail to identify his visitor;
  Though he drew from their fleeting
  Transactions not only luck

[301]

But also a chill sense of the purpose for
Which his lust was being employed, of her mere
  Acting of yielding's part; of
  Luck, yes, but more of mishap.

THOSE OF PURE ORIGIN

Ein Räthsel ist Reinent sprungenes. Auch
Der Gersang kaum darf es enthüllen. Denn
Wie du anfiengst, wirst du bleiben.
  Hölderlin

A mystery are those of pure origin.
Even song may hardly unveil it.
For as you began, so you will remain.
  Translation by Michael Hamburger

After a throbbing night, the house still dark, pull
Back the curtains, see the cherry standing there –
Grain of the paper under wash of rain-clouds.

No, our disguises are not intended to
Deceive. On the contrary. And could you name
Us we shouldn't be compelled to appear so
Confusingly – smothered in white stars, whistling
Hymn tunes, putting out scaly paws to attract
Attention. Under comic aliases –
Even the specific for insomnia:
Peppermint, lime blossom, betony, scullcap –
We entice you into our dissident realms.
The staggering plots you invent in hours
Abbreviated by anxiety are
Hatched by our logic. Just as when you try to
Talk with the girl of fifteen we tilt her shoe
Inward to imply her different order.

For it's *your* world we're expounding. Don't mistake
Our endeavours. We can't tell you where you're from.
Indeed, despite our immanence we're the last
Who could reveal more than is there already.

Let alone where you're going! Darwin's infant
Enquired about his friend's father: 'Where does
He do his barnacles?' – assumption of a
Universal preoccupation no more
Naive than yours, whether of indifference or
Concern. It's quite plausible that the concept
Of outside disappears outside – in that place
Where nebulae no longer have to awake
And pretend to be happy.

                      Our advice is:
Prefer the less likely explanation.
Different evenings, the evening star appearing
In different corners of the pane – conceive
No senseless revolution in the heavens
But a lucky change of erotic fortune;
A goddess steeped not in urine but in love.
And then so often you've been wrong why shouldn't
You be wrong about the extinction of man?

It's true we tend to avoid you, fatal as
You are in general to our fragility.
But sometimes one of us, whom you knew in flight
And particularly admired for his looks,
Lies down and allows the wind to blow the wrong way
His once glossy pinions. Look into his eye.
It regards you still, though fixed as well on worlds
More real than at that moment you can bear.
Of course, you'll soon take your spade and among
Pebbles, lapis worms, inter the eye from sight.

'Considering my present condition,
I can neither concentrate on poetry
Nor enjoy poetry.' That final letter
May seem a defeat after a lifetime of
Assuming the reality of the art.
Not to us, though it's we are the defeated.
For we boast of our patience – coral *croissants*
Anchored at last to just too-heavy hill-tops;
Laboratories of finches; Galapagos
Of revelation awaiting an observer.
And you, even in the children's puzzle, are
You certain you've seen all the hidden objects?

[303]

Yes, there's the extrusion of the wall in
A clawed hump, and a grey frayed rope-end blown round
And round a bough. But what are the abstract shapes
As enigmatic in significance as
Those painters find incised from oceans by arcs
Of a parasol or enclosed from a beach
By the severe bay of a young throat and jaw?

That countenance whose eyes are as pale as if
The flesh had been clipped out to show the ash sky
Behind it . . . The voice that unavailingly
Says: 'Do you remember taking your laundry
To the woman with elephant legs?' . . . The past
As ambiguous as hailstones in the gales
Of Spring: the future certain – the instant when
You stop being convinced of our existence,
And meaningless that blackbirds masquerade as owls,
That also in the dusk, making free of it
For assignations, jealousies (those affairs
Of energy and waiting unwearying,
Of obsession with menstrual blood), occur
The strange pre-marital flights of humans.

What does it matter that the baptistery proves
As dusty and void as bad nuts when its doors
Provide a progression of style, the basher
Of bronze breaking out from pious platitudes
Into arcades of applied geometry,
Thronged with our perfect but realistic forms?

The mad poet called us, untranslatably:
'Those of pure origin' – left you to divine
Whether we rise from phenomena or,
Perhaps more likely, also require your presence,
As the cathedral the plague, pity the war.

But how can we pretend our hemisphere-wide
Lament, the random trickling and joining of tears
On acres of glass, is entirely for your
Predicament – as your lives, borne upon the
More and more dubiously physical, move
To regions of abnegation and concern
Whose angels we are; though, under cruel casques,
Our curls, our thick, parted lips ever youthful,
Complexions marked with still unmalignant moles
Of the actual, scabs on unfolding leaves?

AFTERNOONS

Mothers with taller daughters, shopping
In afternoons, what sustains your lives?
Here's a pair of crimson plastic lips
Left over from a Christmas cracker:
To which generation shall I offer it?

Conceived after the last of wars that surely
Could possibly lead to works of art,
Shall these saplings be hacked down?

Like bluebells in a wood the uniforms
Through the palace railings. Some insane inscription
Cut from a poet's elegy
Identifies the ill-horsed author of carnage.

De-birding jelly, black with grime, on the shaven
Polls of the persians – a savage concept of coiffure –
Has failed to shift the sense of a plaza
Snowing with fragments of brain, the pavement stained;
Debris of an exploded urban dream.

Towers strike out the time for tea,
The time of rehearsals, the time before
The hard liquor of old age. Come in
From your gazing at stockings long as prunus boughs
For almost calfless legs,
And open patterns for knitted bed-jackets
To the jangling of guitars. Poor Gorgons –
Doomed to decapitation in the very
Instant of parturition; the question is
How to prolong your breeding
Of the Muses' continually defeated favourites.

WINDOWS

Easy to tell how habitually I
Look through these great spectacles that enlarge the
Soul's eye – so that sunsets, for instance, of quite
Undifferentiated madder seem to
Possess the glamour of unapproachable
Geniuses, in an existence apart.

Sometimes the sky has a ghostly lampshade or
Countenance watermarked in it, as if it
Were making abundantly plain its divorce
From phenomena; for although the lenses
Intensify perception, to the object
Their attitude is deeply ambiguous.

Should a bird come out of the darkly-banked trees and
Alight on a seat's conveniently bent
Arm, one sees that its pupil (if a pigeon)
Is not, as one thought, the core of a target
But oblate, as though to keep tripping, while it
Revolves, some shaft from a dangerous image.

And one's fingers against the pane are stopped, by
A force that whitens the nails, from seizing the
Dove in their grasp. How tender the world outside
Seems to be, how full of things one could adore –
Were it removed, then, this manner of vision,
Should I fall in the wings of a vast embrace?

Or rather a climate of lunar harshness
Wither my hopes? These tears on the glass are shed
From beings outside with sorrows so huge as
To overwhelm our pity; and not even
Our miniature fires are really printed
On the darkness that incessantly comes down.

DEPARTURES

No, I'll not let you go yet, sweetest
Girl, though you ache to depart from my
Boring house, where you're fed with the crumbs
Of experience, loved with the most
    Perfunctory of kisses.

I've something still to tell, if only,
As to a comfortable old wife,
The trivial news of the day, how
I avoided drowning an insect
    In the lavatory at dawn –

Where cyclamen leaves on the lighter
Tone of the window brought to mind the
Lotus in those banal surroundings
That the hour made mysterious;
    Prince Buddha in the passage.

Or perhaps you'll reveal to me why,
Say, the well-concealed Schoenbergian
Mathematics of art have meaning
In the actual intervals, and
    Tremblings of the finger-pads.

As you make a tough, Guinness-drinking
Quintet aware of an odd man out:
That flautist, is he the emperor
Or even perhaps the composer,
    Playing too many wrong notes?

Unworthy to receive your embrace,
I'm always resolving to do much
Better in future, an eternal
Unsatisfactory boy; somehow
    Believing that I will, too.

Possibly I'll dare to write my last
Songs for soprano. Certainly, you –
Exciting and wholly unexplored
Landscape of secret features – sometimes
    Hold out encouragement.

And even when all else fails, the child
That emerged from my truest because
Uncritically accepting life
Will blessedly know of your demands
    And help warrant the future.

For you can't pass in the street, as though
You didn't know them, quite all my race.
Dear Muse, as I grow older you get
More desirable, and in your youth
    (Theoretically free)

You tantalize with the innocence
Of the unpossessed; even the cross
Between your slight breasts seems to render
The transcendental a prey of the
    Conceivably possible.

Besides, since you represent the whole
Human world, your being continues
Apart from the favours you fail to
Bestow, and it matters not at all
    That your slave weeps in his room.

Yes, it's only the deprived who can
Appreciate the beautiful life
Of the entirely committed to
Providing an area in which
    Wrong proteins can make marvels.

Future readers, whose predecessors
Expectedly neglect me, may find
I spoke truly of our posthumous
Life they are enjoying, because of
    My dull faithfulness to you.

What cosy times we've had together,
Playing the gramophone, sipping scotch
And soda; and I very often
Not even getting as far as the
    Nylon cords behind your knee.

Apples are clinging to yellow boughs,
Fruit that the birds have made
Decayed moons; in the false cover of
Fallen leaves, pink worms: drapes just meeting
    Across the stage of corpses.

We look to you to bring to cities'
Repetitive machinery skies
Of marine splendour behind marble
Porticos where Baudelairean
    Hand-maids are already nude.

But should it be thus that the body,
Otiosely ill and naturally
Deficient, appeals to a goddess
It knows to be a figment of its
    Death or of its thoughts of death?

No, the best should await with humble
And excited awe your routine calls,
And dogged life itself must tempt you
To descend, or whirl to remotest
    Quasars in flurries of apes.

LAST SHEET

. . . Suddenly it's autumn, I think, as I look in the garden –
A gloomy dripping world, tree-tops lost in cloud.
Is it possible that anyone so silly can
Write anything good? I don't hear, like poor Virginia,
The birds outside the window talking Greek. I see
My blackbird visitor and wonder where he sleeps,
As sleep he must. And catch my face in the pane,
Becoming ancestral, a cartoon of the mask
To which I've always been indulgent. And turn
To put a disc of Debussy on the machine:
This is what I'd have written had I had genius.
A pity to have got so far along the road
And then never arrived. Give my regards to the Minister
And tell him I've drafted a comprehensive instrument
For the administration of suburbia.

This is the time the robin starts to sing at dusk,
Like a cog catching on cardboard, but the human throat
Is not subject to seasons except those of the withering heart.
They're trying to cure me of my maladjusted glands –
Amusing; rather like trying to change the art of Sickert:
'I've always been a literary painter,
Thank goodness, like all decent painters,' he said.
One can joke, but nevertheless the situation is tragic –
A human lifetime's limited store of eggs, and then
Their very last descent into the longing womb.
It's certainly on the cards that I shall never write
Another letter. This will have to stand, as usual,
For the prodigies I was about to tell you of,
For the connections I never quite saw, the melodies
Played gently while the beauteous statue reconciled
The jarred generations, and Sicily and Bohemia.

PART SEVEN

Mainly from
Tiny Tears
(1973)

TO AN UNKNOWN READER

You, too, are a poet, I guess, though lacking
Perhaps any public success – or even
The patience or skill to write the notation
Of your song: a private bathroom vocalist.

Have you thought that you may be happier thus?
Woman past youth, pottering in the dead ground
Between lunch and the return of your children,
Boy in the Pentonville of the provinces,

Ageing widow with leisure, friends fallen off –
Aren't your dreams better than syllable-counting,
Than a whole lifetime's remorseful exposure
Of a talent falling short of its vision?

Envious even of the present success,
Your answer will be a denial, I'm sure.
And if so, why then you have entered our ranks
Without need of further proof – timid haters

Of cruelty and hostilities, to whom
All history is the history of pain.
From a sharer in your weakness you'll get small
Reassurance, and pleasure's not my motive.

Yet you read on, having kept, like a junkie,
The text for solitude, though undoubtedly
Turning to far stronger drugs in recurring
Times of less easily relieved unhappiness.

[313]

In chambers of torture, alcoholic cats,
Chain-smoking rabbits, provide the antidotes
For the injuries inflicted by ourselves
And by the societies we have fashioned.

It's part of the character we share to fret
About the animals we've condemned: indeed,
What's worst to contemplate in the forthcoming
Doomsday is the extinction of their courage;

Let alone of the evolution down time
Of sonneteering rats, observant wood-lice,
Comparison-discovering barnacles –
Poets without fatal taint of the human.

Would you want me to end in such a forlorn
Key? I think not, for the poet is disposed
To believe the domestic bell will be rung
At last by the understanding stranger –

Quite against probability. And it's just
That continuing expectation of words,
Of opening portals, to promise more than they
Really signify to which man's hope adheres.

Alternatives to dead-ends of history
Are what's conspiratorially offered;
All verse threatening that, as the Yankee said:
'The astonished Muse finds thousands at her side.'

DEFICIENCIES

They will look up: 'You never really saw
Those objects we placed on earth for men to name.
Even the trivial hours need not have harmed you
Had you acknowledged the divinity
Of all that wasted your life.' No use to claim
How well I visualized the stinking gloom
Of the wharf where just then I'd docked, the stink being me.

THE LAWN, SPRING AND SUMMER

Presumably ejected by the mother,
Three ochre scraps of skin, just avian:
Aborted result of the long and hungry sitting,
Brief tenants of a nest miraculous
As landscapes drawn with toes, the wasted weeks
Of a season crucial and counted out in weeks.
I salute your ruthless clearing of the decks,
Blackbird, for further action. And, dismayed,
Am seized again with Nature's heroic nature,
So different from my own; what's more, see called
In question culture's terminology.
'Nature' – quite ludicrous to subsume in that
The gods' and scavengers' approach to death,
The brusquest concentration of the art
Of the possible – the only art that bridges
Dying and dead societies, those species
Extinct and those that scheme against extinction,
The temperate mantle from its boiling end.

But if confronted by a similar call
To start once more, then wouldn't one contrive
To love afresh survival's ancient means,
And court on the very mattress of the dead?
What else but summoning of feeble power
Distinguishes the organic from the rest?

And isn't one precisely so confronted
This Spring and Summer of one's Autumn life?
The window shut against the noise of brakes,
Ascending gears, and aircraft, nonetheless
Bad dreams remain – made by interior fears,
The penalty of being here at all.
This is our nature, only overcome
By trying to disremember what we love,
The individual life included, grass
Littered with history's debris; and the will
Loud in rosetted branches, master of air,
Preparing generations for the wars
And thwarted happiness. Not bad, old tree-rat,
I think, encountering in the hard, late lawn
A green and reasonably buried walnut.

Anticipate the ice-age as you can,
Anticipate the burning should it come,
Live with your death, your species' death – with craft,
That on this globe, and those unknown and past,
The gases and the carbon spirals clasp
A spirit fearful but immortal somewhere.

ROBINS AND WOODLICE

Since I'm careful not to throw
In the bonfire any wood
Whose wrinkles hold woodlice, why
Do I welcome the robin, descending
For no social purpose,
Let alone love of humans,
Merely for rot's denizens?

Half-baked thoughts of the Great
Chain of Being occur:
Preference for the higher,
For greater beauty, however
Dubious the mode of judgment.
Robins are farther from the earth
Than sparrows, let alone woodlice;
Their legs nearer the spiritual.

The robin's song, though small,
Is not for me, but simply
Establishing its rights
Over the rot uncovered.

Needle beak, wire legs,
Breast-cushion conceived
By Sardanapalian upholsterers –
I acknowledge you and acknowledge
The little, pale, oared barque
Pasted in crevices,
That falls from crevices,
Helplessly overturned.

Our justification is
The destiny we share
And the purity of our sense
Of all that's fitting for
Its reasonable prolongation.

Woodlice, I leave you to your fate,
Adding not too much to your pain.
And, robins, I've extended
Your winter introspections.

Is the god whose function
I usurp my own creation,
Or will his meagre mercy
Be conferred also on me?

FROM A FOREIGN LAND

On the death of John F. Kennedy

Sceptical of the cult, suspicious of the nation,
Nevertheless we had to grant the amelioration
Of the one by the other; and certainly the alternative
Had seemed of depressing threat.

Given this tepid and grudging view, why do we yet
Flinch from the murdered consul's images, remember
(In the far February following the November)
That the spouse still has to live?

It's not that by their taste for intellect disarmed
We were unconsciously adherents all the time,
Nor that strong vulnerable youth unfairly charmed,
But that the senseless crime

Is what for us he had the power to postpone
Who now approach within the assassin's range alone.

THE FINAL WAR

Dreaming that the final war had started
(As it has), I saw once more
Balloons grey-skinned as dusty mercury,
And on the disordered city a colander sky.
A nonentity, some minor office colleague,
Was there encountered, in whose anguished aim
Of catching a train at the scheduled time of leaving
I was involved . . . For me, sufficiently
Alarming, such bodying out of present fear
With dreaming's anachronistic images.

And so my tertiary period
Begins. But where's the devoted daughter-figure
To care for my frailty; the honours, homage?

Those nightmares police my sleep from sounds of harmless
Aircraft, and getaways at traffic lights
Beyond the opposite Augustan houses;
And when I wake break in not only man-made
Disasters but also the major forms of nature –
All, all inimical to organic life.
How fragile, that experiment conducted
Under the heat of stars, in seconds from
Virtual eternity, glued to a globe!

What of the minor poets of Sumer?
What, indeed, of the major? Almost best
To have been the author of 'This stone was laid
By so-and-so on August 3rd.'

Irregular metabolism turns
Even the era's joys to morbid waste.
No one would guess of my cachinnations at noon;
Mockery of Juggins, affection for Ponsonby.
Ambiguous all the more my pains to guard
Against, to conquer natural maladies
And reach the days of general extinction –
As though my affinity were not with that
Basel historian who was prepared
At every moment to exchange his life
For a never-having-been, but rather with his friend
Who threw his arms around the ill-used nag
And collapsed into madness, under off-putting names
Like 'Dionysus' and 'The Crucified'.

To think of seeing through the Little Ice-Age,
Writing from 1300 to the threshold
Of the rational century one's panegyrics
To the Spring in an overcoat!

                Though always sleeping
With it, one's never reconciled to death.
And now to come so late in life to death
By fire, death of the world, death of my art!
I feel the pain of everything assaulted,
Even boughs licked in rubbish-heaps of Autumn:
Their boiling sap's my own. If what we sense
Were so – if from a dream we merely wake
Into another! Thus heroic, atrocious
Nietzsche would have preferred to be a Swiss
Professor rather than God.

               Who's going to
Usher me into any dreamless sleep?

ON THE TELEPHONE

Child of my dead friend: dead friend's voice.
Regret at unexpressed affection,
For trivial joys cut short, is sour
As ballsed-up history against
The sanguine tones that nonetheless
Gravely imply a daughter's loss,
Acknowledge the sadness of a friend.

The contradictory role of art –
To render permanent the loss,
Renew perpetually the sadness,
So that child is always young,
The gone preoccupy the living
And music celebrates the dead
Hands' skill and not its own aesthetic.

Hoping that children down the years
Will read and, reading, read with tears.
For in still latent loss will be
That then antique one – just as music
Sings on through other finger-pads
Because of inorganic signs:
Notes, keys, dynamics, feelings, time.

DINOSAURS

One idly reads: 'Tyrannosaurus rex,
The greatest of carnivorous dinosaurs.'
At once a curious opening of doors;
Both time-scale and the usual scene perplex.
There was a history when I wasn't here,
Perhaps a similar period to come;
But how amazing that the huge and dumb
Could dominate this all-familiar sphere.

My being master of the world's as odd
As having lived a freeish citizen.
Contemporaneous with the louse and cod,
We never count our blessings; now and then
Indeed, hear through the noisy wars of men
Time whisper to the rodent: Be a god.

[320]

DOVES IN A TREE

Beak along feather, beak on beak,
Strike us as not quite adequate
(Though somehow apt) to demonstrate
That love of which the speech-blessed speak.

Still, every species must descend
To plain continuance of its kind
And who can say but what is blind
Proves most expressive in the end?

Certainly compensations shine
Among the blossomed and the boughed,
So near to June's immobile cloud,
So far from where we sprawl supine.

Would angels likewise find our touch
Of palms an enviable thing
While they renounce the brush of wing
That for the wingèd means so much?

FEATHERS

Feathers of cloud move northwards this evening:
Indolent summer weather stretches its wing.

A Bacon-like sense of justness smears a few
Otherwise neat white coverts down the blue.

Flight of reverse migration, all too soon
You'll return with snow-feathers some yellow noon.

No wonder your pattern falters as it goes
And threatening thunder blackens the loosened rose.

ADMISSION OF THE SUMMER

However old the son,
Long dead the mother,
He is liable to cry:

'Mother, remove my sickness.
Comfort me for the hurts
Done by less loving women.'

In the decade of death he pleads
For death to be postponed,
Like a father's punishment.

The admission of the summer
Is that the care is such
That even vestigially

It cannot be absurd.
Bearded with worms, the blackbird
Poises before his staying

Of the species, undeterred
By his own orphanage
Or visions of helpless crying.

APPLE TREE

I puzzle why the flowering tree
Is also in song, until I see
Each flower's stigma is a bee.

Great magnet, drawing from the lawn
The scattered sparrows when I yawn,
I wonder whence your force is drawn –

And then observe the vertical
That sinks into the emerald ball,
Down which the birds would doubtless fall

Were it not full of lymph, transpiring
Through the boughs' dense, right-angled wiring
In scent and incandescent firing.

[322]

Pulling the curtains when I wake
I watch snow tumbling, flake on flake,
From the sky's azure, unisled lake.

It drifts among the buoys of red
At anchor in the tulip bed,
And on the limbs from which it's shed –

Limbs hugely knuckled, crooked, lined,
What ecstasy for you to find
The fair skin brush your old dark rind.

ONE SEGMENT

ONE SEPTEMBER

I

Spider, hanging like a bit of old
Brown leaf beside a bit of old brown leaf –
Millenniums of more disadvantageous courses
Lie back of your scuttling there when I touch your web,
Let alone your choice of that for its suspension.

No wonder the critics of Darwin felt secure.
No wonder my own kind feels insecure –
Comparative newcomers to the world of gods'
Curious fingers, and blundering accidents.
Ancient in wisdom, I see you give a leaf-like
Shake and settle down for another million years.

II

A breakfast apple, wet with dew,
Taken from the marble garden table:
Birds' food, prehistoric food;
Its very bounty chilling, cheeked
With a low sun over plains of snow.

III

Linking the border when I turn the hose on –
Diamonded sudden concentricities.

[323]

A helicopter towards evening
Similarly catches the rays of a hidden sun.

The moon comes up like a near-dissolved
Tablet of alka-seltzer. Time to go in.

Time with my notebook to ponder on
The inscrutable. Why do pigeons frequently limp?

What is that late bird, the blackbird, doing
Chuckling alone in leaves inked on the west?

Their eyes so near the radix of the beak.
I rub my own and feel my nose's bridge.

If strange the physiognomy of birds,
What looks less outré have ourselves to bear?

PRELUDE IN C SHARP MINOR

As children we were told
The music represented
One buried alive,
Beating on the lid of his coffin.

Convincing fancy, in that world
Of prolonged time and rude health,
The non-literal meaning
Beyond us, beyond the teller.

We've grown again to the legend,
Hearing the music with new ears –
Ears of our old age,
Frequencies sliced off, fear added.

And knowing the gift of talent
That's nonetheless never great enough;
The talent that buries us in art
But not far enough.

DIARY ENTRIES

'I'll burn it off now if you like,' said my GP,
Apropos of the papilloma on my thigh,
Bothersome of late. Would that all worries
Disappeared in a whiff of over-done pork!

*

An aircraft's linear trail on the evening sky
From apple bough to pink hibiscus – first
Speculative but bold foundation of a web
That fades as the predator sees no hope of victims.

*

A negative report on the specimen
Of urine. So am I after all to live
Into the epoch of apocalyptic beasts
And utterly depersonalized demise?

*

Giving away old suits – preparation
For a journey. The letting-out of waistbands –
Dicing with the proximity
Of terminal emaciation.

*

Even peeing in the garden, giving moisture
To a shaded plant, organic nurture
To legginess, mad midges presaging heat,
Also brings gloomy thoughts of malignant strictures.

*

Deep in the medicine-chest are remedies
For ills it seems I no longer suffer from.
What forgotten wounds have made me the man I am?
Where's the historical record of my health?

*

Through numbness the arm behind feels amputated;
The arm in front is hovering in the air.
Can it be at the age of fifty-nine
I haven't learnt how to dispose my limbs for sleep?

*

A good thing on waking to drink cold water
Through the nose (I read in some Yogi handbook).
A good thing also to stop writing verses
About one's ailments and daydreams of romance

*

Old theatre programme: against the Second Lord,
Great heroes' name. A file of ancient verse
Above the signature, evidently spurious,
Of a quite accomplished reactionary hermit.

*

Dear life, I struggle awake to greet you again –
Fetching the honeyed hot milk, finding my father's
Cigarette-case among the debris of yesterday's pockets,
Realizing that after all it's not you that frightens us.

READING POEMS BY BRECHT

Looking up, for a moment
I think our dangers over –
What I feel about the age
Having all been said.

With a heavy heart
I return to actuality:
Nothing changed for the better,
Even what's been said
To be said again, certainly worse.

My grandchild's photograph
Confronts my stare,
And I search for a wish,
The best, most practicable –
A moment of happily
Looking up, and then the power
To say what she'll feel
Has to be said once more.

LATE PERIOD

After a few laps my old cat walks away
From the saucer with an irritable jerk of tail:
Five minutes later is back to try the stuff
Again. And well I know the mood myself.

How long shall I settle to these discs of Brahms'
Late keyboard pieces? Yet what else but art
Could I hope now might echo and assuage
The tenderness and sadness of keeping house?

– A fireside slumber broken by restless pacings,
Lift of a head incongruously still noble
That only hears its dreams. The claws retracted,
Murderous tonalities but softly clash.

IN THE RADIOACTIVE ISOTOPE DEPARTMENT

The retreating plunger draws the blood –
So dark, reluctant, alien . . .
'I'll see if I can find a vein,'
She said. With rather false sangfroid,
Offering my etiolated arm,
I answered, something of a card:
'No one has ever found it hard,'
And grinned with boyish fifties' charm.

In their mad scientists' abode
(Part of the path lab, found at last)
These doctors analyse and cast
The awkward sums of ailing blood
And carboys of radioactive pee.
I look at reasonable fate,
And see the chill precipitate
Of two mid-morning cups of tea.

Irrelevant before the dials,
Culture's restrained, facetious tone.
The marrow of eternal bone,
The sluices of the heart, in phials;
And running through my stringy throat
The dangerous secret of the age,
Threatening to char the unwritten page,
Geld and deform the grape and oat.

[327]

Absurd the grey flannel, reassumed;
Absurd the chrome and azure car,
Parked where from art and algebra
Come girls unfarded and ungroomed,
Mysterious and beautiful
In the amazing life before
The dominance of that thick gore,
Long, long before its sickly lull.

Only the covert gland had sinned.
The fibrillations of the heart
Could well have been put down in part
To vain desires, in part to wind.
I look no different outwardly –
The mask that so far has endured
In the disguise of one insured
Against the cost of surgery.

Is this the simple meaning – all
Rehearsal for the moment when
One buttons up one's shirt again
And hears the sentence truly fall;
While the fantastic myth of health
That other organisms keep
Goes on proliferating deep
Philosophy, verse, love and wealth?

HAPPINESS

Some say this is a golden age,
That never again
Will there be such a deal to eat,
Such space between the race of men.

My day's benign routines incline
To such belief
However startling, since it's sure
In time (and more than likely brief)

One will awaken not to eggs,
And isolation
In gardens, but a bed of crowding
Visitors, and emaciation.

[328]

OUTSIDE THE SUPERMARKET

Grasping with opposite hand the side of his pram
As though an idle sceptre or marshal's baton,
A look of serious surveillance on his face,
This infant for an instant restores to me
        The sense of mankind's worth.

No matter that soon he'll be in floods of tears;
Who can blame his frustration at a recalcitrant world?
Thus wept Isaiah over Jerusalem.
Long years must pass before like Caligula
        He weeps for a single neck.

MAGNOLIA

My study has been repainted 'Magnolia'.
Before, it was a sombre reddish brown.
Surely a fresh creative period
Opens, perhaps of spirituality.
Not before time are the dark places lightened:
Surrounded by the colour of a flower,
Ever recalling its name's delicious sound,
One can hardly go on with that depressing work
Which Dr Steiner would label stoical
At best, anomaly of our post-culture –
Assuming he troubled to tie a tag at all.

Though if I'm to start with versicles about
The décor of the womb or tower, what
Increase of range is reasonably in prospect?
The light is now reflected on the volumes
Of those who even as late as Uncle Tom
May be supposed to be part of a tradition.
Can things change in a generation's span
So as to superannuate the whole
Of a poor old talent's toil? Not hard to believe.

Magnolia shows bright enough, if really
Only off-white – yet having been given the clue
Of the name donated to the shrub by Magnol
Its ethereal iridescence can be detected;
Reminding one's verse of nature's cyclical forces
Instead of the constant staleness of human blood.

Besides, it seems that nature – when herself,
Moving without the sense of words – has largely
A catastrophic role: a botany
Professor and the hardening of a g
Prove vital for the bough to fulfil itself.

THE LITERARY LIFE IN LATE
MIDDLE-AGE

Looking up 'love' in Roget's useful charts
(Itself a curious activity),
I find the astounding entry 'nothing'. Why
Should the mind's assent lag behind the heart's?

*

Subscribing to a new press-cuttings agency,
Doubts of extravagance and vanity allayed
By thinking that at least something may be repaid
When one's estate receives the obscure obituary.

MOTHY INVOCATION

Coffin or triangle of moth,
White and motionless as cloth
Outside the dark-backed window-pane,
Misplaced your patient wish to gain
Entry to this cultured room
Whose fleeting light would be your doom.
Fly far into the night of stars
Whose denizen you really are,
Swerving past the open bills
Of random though superior wills
(That in a half-world otherwise
Slumbering send ambiguous cries)
And start again the cycle of
Grub, chrysalis and winging love.

Fly westwards where the Thames divides
And round the tawny city glides
Whose name by luck enlaurelled mine.
Fly on and brush the foreheads fine
Of my three grand-daughters asleep
Under the prehistoric keep
That let its nameless men survey,
Then nameless too, Caernarfon Bay;
And leave an image for my son
So verse of his may also run.
Then fly across the homely ocean
To Ireland's saddening commotion
Where foes will call you by the same
Vulgar and Old English name.

What can save if language fails
(As it might even do in Wales)?
Though possibly that unique gift
It was that made our species' rift,

To heal which special remedies
Must be distilled from the disease.
This fork-tongued nation came together,
To flourish in a various weather,
Each from a less salubrious corner,
And join a largely tiny fauna –
Leaving in turn their floors of flints,
Their fish-bone middens, downland dints,
Great clocks of stones and roofless rooms,
Grassy or ship-configured tombs:
Rich lands an insect almost might
Survey in a single night.

Look, strange but not too alien face,
In all the dwellings of our race;
Teach social order to be pure
And personal frailness to endure.

EDMOND HALLEY

'Dr Halley never eat any Thing
but Fish, for he had no Teeth' – so after
Royal Society meetings dinner
was invariably 'Fish and Pudding'.
As on a silly marriage, he embarked
at sixty-five on a programme of moon
watching planned to last a whole sarotic
period (223
lunations, near enough eighteen years)
and saw to the end his voyeurism through.

In the eyepieces of his telescopes
the cross hairs were dried cobwebs split in half –
to fairy means opened a fairy world.
Despite his long life his greatest triumph
was delayed till after his demise.
In 1758, Christ's season,
(as 55 years before he'd foretold)
the old comet reappeared in the skies,
announcing not the birth of a god but
the temporary triumph of reason.

Observe on a roof in New College Lane
his Oxford observatory, hard by
my son's undergraduate rooms of times
when I little recked that I, too, should be
an Oxford professor, not far now from
the fish and pudding stage. Comet-like ways
of destiny! Quite disproved by Halley,
the notion of human life written out
by the night's constellations returns to
grizzled craniums, in uncertain days.

TO MY GRAND-DAUGHTERS

I shall hope to cheat my own predestined thread
And live to see you weave the fates of young men
    For whom I shan't be sorry
    As they fade down Norham Road.

I visualize your fair hair, small noses,
Prowess on many musical instruments,
    Enticing several years of
    Freshmen: triple Zuleikas.

Your suitors will wait for you uneasily,
Caught in the hall by the expert on Auden
    And invited to join him
    In some devilish word-game –

Vague thoughts of transferring their attention to
Your mother, as a simpler but equally
    Agreeable way out, by
    This meeting nipped in the bud.

But will you stay in your provincial milieu?
Won't you yearn for Moscow and get there at last;
    And bravely take on as well
    The ruin of the dunces?

Powerful goddesses, I prefer the names
That as your friend Father Levi would tell you
    Pausanias averred were
    The ones you really owned:

More apt than those usually conferred on
Deities properly depicted in crowns,
      And white robes spangled with stars –
      Almost truly Friendly Ones.

Eventually you will continue my line –
And for me that will be some consolation,
      Perhaps, for your capture by
      The lucky but unworthy –

And as Venus Urania Robinson,
Fortune Smith and Ilythia Jones descend
      From your thrones or (some will say)
      Your hell's ministry resign.

1965

Asked for a photograph in uniform,
I get the dusty box down from its shelf.
Turns up, a prophetic study of myself
In sailor-suit, but that was in the storm
Before the one in question. Solemn spook
Of fifty years ago, what did you make
Of now familiar collar, lanyard, hook?
The later seaman was an equal fake.

The foolish masks demanded by our time
Make for unconfidence in all one's roles.
Kneeling is bagging-out my dark-grey flannel
And certainly I feel this gloomy rhyme
A parody. Beyond, there twitter scrannel
Threats from a line of cardboard Capitols.

CONFRONTATION OFF KOREA, 1968

      Return our boat that you've
      Pinched from our serious play
      Or with another toy
      We'll roast you alive.
         *

I pray that any nuclear war
Will be deferred till after the
Diminutive requirement for
My coming book of poesy.

*

The captured will confess,
Their captors arraigned. Believe
Me, both will fry unless
Tumour or clot reprieve.

*

The Times like a shameful secret in my case,
I pass a grinning brace
Of nymphets on their way to learning. Are
Then, you Earthman, to endure?

*

I wake at some ungodly hour
And fearfulness floods back. I try
The switch. Surprisingly, the power
Still sends its intricate reply.

*

Old order, twice before this I
Have watched your so-called death-pangs. Why
Can't one or other of us be
Put out of our misery?

*

Civilization has bred
A species absurd – the timid;
Which additionally is at
The terror of not surviving it.

*

Is the crisis to pass, then,
In the anticlimax of relief,
As a nagging pain
Proves an unmalignant spoof?

*

And how to enjoy the luxury
Of reprieve, we essentially
Condemned? Through the jokes of art,
Children's tragedy-shaped start?

SONNET 155

Two loves I have of comfort and despaire

Admit you found at least the lady real.
– No doubt one laid it on a thought too thick
In boasting what a noble limb might feel
And how the life welled from the climber's prick.
But now I must confess that even she
(My black and white cartoon of soul and thighs)
Seemed quite unconscious, at our two or three
Encounters, of my dog's denuding eyes.
The pain went on, but in another place –
Far from the disembodied lust of art –
And all unsung by me; the kitchen face
Crumbling before the bedroom's baser part.
    And, brawling through the house, love never once
    Disturbed the sheaf of sonnets with her glance.

AT T. S. ELIOT'S MEMORIAL SERVICE

A man comes on the stage clad in a robe different from all others, with lute in hand on which he plays, and thus chants the Great Mysteries, not knowing what he says.

        Jessie L. Weston: FROM RITUAL TO ROMANCE

Arches cut across each other, open out within each other, till
Winter sky the shade of old men's hair appears beyond the final
   sill.

Rectangles of iron-tubing for the pensile lamps draw down the
   eye
To the choir-stalls' vandyke timber and their submarine uphol-
   stery.

Here the lights themselves seem gloomy: golden stalks with
   single crimson flowers.
Distant pallid busts the monuments of poets longer dead than
   ours.

In the drama set to show the spirit's primacy and endlessness
Piping choir-boys pustular remind one of its transitory dress.

Revolutionary writer of my youth, how far must it have been
From imagination so to see you to the brink of the unseen;

And in your relating of the myth to find at last that it was thus
Fell the strange and frightening adventure in the Chapel Peri-
  lous –

Which is fraught, we're made to understand, with danger inde-
  finable:
Details vary; sometimes on the altar there is laid a lifeless
  shell . . .

Suddenly I notice that the arms that isolate me in my place
Are the backward-spreading wings of angels each with polished
  plump-cheeked face.

Simple craftsman's image, words and chords by more sophisti-
  cated pens,
Celebrate the sad illusion that the mortal nerves and brain make
  sense.

Tributory bowler on its not entirely unaccustomed head,
Leaving through the great West Door, bells muffled for the now-
  accepted dead,

All is changed until I see that it's Victoria Street and not the
  Square
Lies before me, purgatory-crowded, hideous in the sharpening
  air –

Half expecting one to hail me, marks of mould upon him, grave
  of tone:
'Wounded still the Ruler, waterless the land, omnipotent the
  bone.'

TO A WRITER ON HIS BIRTHDAY

W.H. Auden's sixtieth

Not hard to feel kinship with a quadrimane ancestor,
But to descend from a marine animal
Of the ascidian type! With some such amazement
One acknowledges the influence, the awesome debt.

I mean, think how that pale-blue pamphlet dignified
The banalities of my provincial adolescence,
With scarcely a word unknown to Hengist and Horsa –
Calf-love in sick England from a falcon's height.

Or the Latinities of the enormous vision that discovered
Under the state apparatus of the superego
The libido's proletarian brotherhood, while the
Irretrievable errors led to unforgivable blows.

From exile's magic island you still kept your sway
As the deposed duke of our ill-ruled realm of words.
But soon you'd burrowed too far into the lexicons
For the clumsy native order of the notched to follow.

Perhaps from the alp of your latest domicile you'll alight
Once more to beautify our country dandelions –
Though we give thanks, not advice – for how many other
        sapphires
Have stuck in an early groove, or slid off the song entirely?

Besides, it was Juno devised the storm that drove Aeneas
To Libyan shores; and poets are no less in the hands of a goddess.
Moreover, albeit Pater in time turns elder brother,
One can't ever lose the fear of being biffed by a stronger arm.

HOMAGE TO KAFKA

For Malcolm Pasley

I couldn't sleep, and went at five
Through city streets – a smoked-out hive,
Except for one old pallid face
Behind a drooped eye-lid of lace;
Like natural powers, not watching me
But conscious of my activity.

Great houses of the wealthy where,
Now, seedy civil servants stare
At puzzling files, surround a park –
Its foliage mouldy, tunnels dark,
In the dawn light; and from its birds
Clear, unintelligible words.
Inside the park there is a maze:
Entry is easy. Through the haze
The lines recede: across them run
More avenues. The choices stun
The Theseus with a causeless dread,
But having made the first is led
To where no further choice exists.
Compulsive ways, confusing mists!

At first I wandered with the time
Still in my favour: then the lime
Of nightmare glued my nervous feet.
At last palms sweated, pulses beat.
And for insomnia, the age,
I ached as though they could assuage –
Those ambiguities I'd fled –
My guilt about the age's dead,
And insufficiency of will
In the departments of my skill.
I saw I must rejoin (despite
My fears) all that had prompted flight –
Merely a flight to free a bored
Mind and a tortured body scored
With floggings of its own neglect.

And then my forward pace was checked
By coming on the maze's hub –
A little clearing with a tub
Of evergreens, a noseless bust
And, drawing patterns in the dust
With rolled umbrella, one I knew.
The chance, unreasonable clew
Was strung to him whose smiling beard
My unwished truancy most feared –
Prober of conscience, source of bread,
The gentle comprehending Head
Of the employers of my life.
Out of his breast he forced a knife.
I saw once more the look of pity
For clowns in the eras of the city,
For art and lung that fight in vain
Their lovers, bacillus and pain.
He fell: from crumpled clothes, between
The walls, his blood crept, strangely clean.
The image, the catastrophe,
Lacked (or held) meaning utterly.

So I was left, in ways that must
Point to the murderer and his lust;
And this was not a dream nor art
But the world's working on my heart.

FOUR POEMS IN MEMORY OF MAX BORN

Ob. January 5, 1970

Born's 'observational invariant' –
Flying away, a bird stops looking like
A bird, eventually becomes a point.
And yet one knows one's seeing all the time
     A bird, the same one.

The single life flies away, perspectives changing
As imperceptibly as birds in air;
Though friends may die before you and culture seem
No longer culture, still Born's principle
     Undoubtedly runs.

And only in my sixtieth year, perhaps,
Has the sense come of having myself endured
A period that with astonishment
I see may accurately be conceived
          As historical.

Though going about my life the invariant makes
The thing a homogeneous slow farewell,
Not till long afterwards to be defined
As the degeneration of iambics
          Or surge of Cathay.

                    *

Einstein's objection to the quantum theory:
Using it for the macro-world one would be surprised
If a star or fly seemed even quasi-localized.

Bless the old boy – though the stricture lacks validity.
Indeed it was he who put us first in doubt of what
Light meant in terms of human life, and where to swat.

                    *

So all the labours of the scientists –
Brass cogwheels, Himalayan voltages, bits of string;
Abstruse hypotheses disproved by drolly
Naive experiments – were these designed
Merely to expedite the end of nature?

Unthinkable – yet only too probable.
No use, it seems, for anyone to regard
His work as 'beautiful', let alone as true.
Even investigations into the stuff
We're made of, and galaxies and particles,

Are appropriated by the silly chieftains
Of nation-states and joint stock companies:
Thus, after long searching of their consciences
And subtle evasion of passport barriers,
Traitors find they have simply exchanged asylums.

                    *

I am certain that the human race is doomed, unless
its instinctive detestation of atrocities gains the upper
hand over the artificially constructed judgement
of reason – Max Born

Yes, and our sense of loss at the great man's going
Is tempered by relief that after all
He hadn't to endure the most atrocious
          Times that might have been.

Dresden, the Camps, the two cities of Japan,
He also in a manner of speaking escaped.
Perhaps we reasonably warmed his exile
          In icy Edinburgh.

And one could argue that the peaceful death,
As well as his life, gave hope to the human race.
Though nothing can excuse what made unsafe
          His extended years of safety.

AN ENGLISH SUMMER

Roberto Gerhard watched in his Cambridge garden
The changing evening light; and even called
His wife to observe some conjuror's effect.
Appreciative and patient immigrant!
The English summer passes for the English
In a succession of departing trains –
Attention fixed on the boredom of farewells
Or anguish of far-too-early, just-too-late.

What's rescuable from the wreckage of a year?
Earth-coloured infant blackbirds, wise in choice
Of colour; flower-beds in rainy dawns –
Yellows and mauves of Enna carried off
To the underworld; surviving fingers brown
From unremembered and unmanmade suns.

IN MEMORY OF RANDALL SWINGLER
AND ALAN RAWSTHORNE

Randall, how ill I knew you!
Perhaps the last time we met
Was on Charing Cross station
During the far-off Fifties –
The epoch of your evening
Lectures at Goldsmiths' College,
Occupation not too absurd
For a poet's beggary.
Easily we slipped into
The chaffing of the Forties –
But you already somewhat
Battered, myself still more
With respectability
Veneered, and lacking the secret
Compartment of the Thirties.
I remembered a review
Of your first book, which asserted
You should stick to politics.
Quite wrong. You went on, and fought
In the war foretold and dreaded,
And knowing the arguments
For just hostilities,
Burst out in protest at
The absolute evil of killing.

Now your friend's also dead –
Rawsthorne, who gained rather more
Public recognition
But far far from enough.
A few days from the event
A trivial film revived
On television brings
The unmistakable music –
Angst through an upper lip
Stiff with Lancashire phlegm.
Poet and composer gone,
You can't but be diminished
Though what you stood for will triumph;

And even your works endure,
Temporarily swamped by the mad
And fashionable. When
We hear of any murder
Or the tuneless and disordered
Surrender to the *Zeitgeist*
Our thoughts will spring to you,
Seeking your heart-felt marks.

NO RHYMES

We have no rhymes in English for warmth, month, wolf, gulf, sylph,
breadth, width, depth, scarce, wasp, pint, rhythm, bilge, film.
Swann and Sidgwick: THE MAKING OF VERSE

What first had seemed of manageable width
Opened up now a fanged and slavering gulf
And fastened to itself the name of wolf . . .
Away from that guardian, dragging the weeping sylph,
He fled through all the apple-ripening month
And came at last to seas whose purple breadth
Smudged out the islands. From the fading warmth,
In a small boat, they launched upon the rhythm
Of the unknown. A brown leaf and a wasp
See-sawed across the scud-reflecting film
That dulled the stagnant water in the bilge.
And, after all, her breast was but a pint
Of squid, prawn-topped; her brow of minnow depth.
Had myths of virginity ravished been so scarce?

VERSIONS OF BAUDELAIRE

SPLEEN POEMS

The elements exacerbated by
Life itself, wrap cold and sodden sheets
Round the pale people in the cemetery
And the mortality upon the streets.

Twitching at intervals his scruffy tail,
My cat's uneasy and at pains to show it;
The gutter gargles hollowly – the soul
Of some long-superannuated poet.

The sad falsetto of the smoking sticks
Fills in between the clock's arthritic ticks;
From an old pack, with its stale sweet perfume,

Once used to tell the fate of fat old-maids,
The pretty knave of hearts, and queen of spades,
Discuss their mouldering love in tones of doom.

*

More memories than the fossils of the ages . . .

A chest of drawers stuffed with novels, pages
Of verse, love letters, writs, old balance sheets,
Forgotten curls of hair wrapped in receipts,
Hides fewer secrets than my poignant skull.
That is a pyramid, a massive hull,
Rottener than mass graves of despotic states.
– I am a cemetery moonlight hates,
Where the long worm, remorse, extends its dread
And feeds on the most precious of my dead.
I am a boudoir full of browning blooms
Whose fashions are those of excavated tombs,
Where naive pastels and Boucher's pale style
Exude the faintness of an empty phial.

Nothing as these lame days could go as slow,
When under heavy flakes of years of snow
That offspring of incuriousness, ennui,
Stretches as long as immortality.
– O life, your truthful visage now appears!
A stone reared in the midst of unknown fears,
Sightless, surrounded by a Gobi's patience,
A sphinx left by the world's migrations,
White on the map, whose dotty soul cries out
Only as twilight conjures dread from doubt.

*

[345]

The image is a rich though powerless king
Of a monsoon country, young but doddering,
Despising his bottom-sucking pedagogues,
As bored with boys and girls as with his dogs.
Neither his falcon nor its brilliant prey –
Nor suppliants dying waiting – make him gay.
Unchanged his expression of the chronic sick
At his best jester's filthiest limerick;
His decorated bed's become a grave,
And those who attend it, and consider brave
Even frog-princes, won't find gowns cut deep
Enough to interest this fleshless creep.
The genius who transmogrified his lead
Couldn't distil corruption from his head,
And gory circuses of Roman style
Tyrants think back on fondly in their exile,
Quite fail to reanimate this live cadaver
Sluiced not by blood but Lethe's stagnant river.

*

When, a great manhole lid, the heavy sky
Falls and fits neatly on the horizon's ring
And on the spirit, bored with misery;
The day dark, sadder than an evening;

When earth is changed into an oozing cell
Where, like a bat in daylight, Hope's frail wing
Is bruised against the walls, its little skull
Beating and beating on the leprous ceiling;

When, as the bars of an enormous jail,
Spread and descend the verticals of rain,
And a silent race of noisome spiders trail
Their similar filaments inside one's brain,

A terrible shouting rises to the sky –
The sudden furious clappers of the bells –
Like the beginning of that endless cry
Of souls condemned to temporary hells.

– And long cortèges, with neither drums nor trumpets,
File slowly through my being; beaten Hope
Weeps, and the atrocious tyrant, Anguish, sets
His sable banner on my outstretched nape.

CATS

Lovers and austere dons are equally
(In their maturity) attached to cats –
Cats soft but cruel, emperors of flats,
Touchy like these and like those sedentary.

Friends of the sensual, the cerebral,
They seek the quiet and horror of the dark;
If they had ever bent their pride to work
They might have pulled the funeral cars of hell.

Asleep they take the noble attitude
Of the great sphinxes that appear to brood,
Stretched in the wastes, in dreams that have no end;

Their loins are electric with fecundity,
And particles of gold, like finest sand,
Star vaguely their unfathomable eye.

OWLS

Swaddled in yews as black as ink
The owls sit in a tidy frieze
Like oriental deities,
Unlidding their red eyes. They think.

They will sit on quite motionless
Until that hour, nostalgic, dun,
When, rolling up the slanting sun,
Shadows reoccupy the place.

Their attitude reminds the clever
That in our time and world one never
Ought to seek action, or revolt;

Man shaken by a creeping shade
Bears always in himself the guilt
Of having wished to change his fate.

FRANCIS TO THE BIRDS

O timid new generation,
Descend the hierarchy
Of branches and feed on my bounty.

Rightly suspicious of
The ambiguous evening light
And my well-preserved physique,

You hide behind summer leaves
Commuting from tree to tree –
Light hues, instinctive evasion.

Little you know of my vows
To preserve your innocence,
Of the god that wings my flesh.

SONG CYCLE FROM A RECORD-SLEEVE

I

This Spring, the thrush's song seems more hysterically impassioned than ever before. Do I, because of my advancing years, merely imagine this, or is it that the bird, tabarded like a stout herald, has itself a premonition of impending war?

II

I am at the time of life when I look over my past life.
Now I come to consider it, I am not sure that I have ever been loved in the way I myself conceive of love.

III

I see now the extent of the love that my mother, long dead, had for me. And how bitterly I regret that in her lifetime I failed to respond to it.

Yet even if such days could miraculously come back, that love would be far from the love I long for.

IV

Coming on him suddenly, I say: 'Hello, blackbird' – giving the human name but slightly embarrassed at the poverty of our invention.

I half expect him to recognize it, and my harmlessness, my kinship – which I supremely feel – with all living creation.

And indeed he slantingly looks at me with brimming eye for so long that I imagine a strange contact made. But then after what were really only a few moments he swoops duckingly away with his warning call.

V

Life, quite independently of the ludicrous touch given to it by humans, goes beautifully on.

As in the twig of the apple-tree set trembling by a vanished blue-tit.

A twig whose buds are breaking with the colour, as one conceives it, of the tip of a girl's breast.

VI

Even the brown sparrows inspire it, what I seem to have failed with; the male bird with tail shamelessly uplifted, the female essentially fleeing but apt to be captured.

Neither male nor female the attitude of my life in these matters whose paramountcy I have nonetheless always recognized, revolved.

No one encountered before whom I could be completely shameless, no one capable of catching the elusive. No one like myself, whose deficiencies, however, I could adore.

VII

Yet suppose one had put the case.

Of failing, the doomed to failure.

Because of oneself, one's ancestry.

Wouldn't the human in the other have responded?

Isn't it just this that love is concerned with?

And couldn't the shabby brown feather have been taken in the beak?

And forgiven?

VIII

I wonder whether elsewhere in nature there are examples of the lame or out-of-series being accepted by the fit-for-propagation. I say 'accepted' meaning 'loved'.

But those few birds I recognize year after year and who seem happy enough are after all merely tinged with albinism. Indeed, their deficiency could be taken for a specially fine quality in the wing or tail that catches a dazzling edge of light.

IX

Early in the morning I look in a particular part of the garden for a certain pale scented flower.

When I quite fail to find it I realize that my thinking it there was a poignantly circumstantial dream.

X

Still my imaginings run to the time before self-knowledge – insight of such appalling penetration that naked contact with life was thereby inhibited except in secrecy.

The imaginings are of, say, blades of grass imprinted on tender, faintly amber flesh, cool zephyrs playing over the most shameful areas of the spirit.

XI

On the dark side of the house a morello is in bloom, so white against its boughs and retaining wires that one is reminded of a human body nude among furniture, and apparel just cast aside.

Each flower has five petals – a number that seems as significant as that of the organs or limbs characterizing the human.

And as mutable?

XII

The garden was created from a wilderness and will return to it, hastened by the gardener's death or the disaster among his kind that he predicts. The life of the birds will perhaps be less affected.

It may be wondered whether human intervention in the affairs of other orders wasn't always damaging or, at the least, futile. So that the disappearance of the garden may result in a greater earth.

The memories of future generations of the flighted will nonetheless hold the vision of shorn lawns and edible exotic buds; among which the figure of the gardener used to move with clumsy benevolence.

TINY TEARS

Life is an epiphenomenon of the hydrosphere – J.D. Bernal

Strangest fossil in a place of fossils –
The navel of the barely nubile girl,
Disturbing the disturbing slenderness,
Making the illusive fragility
Plausible, the pâtisseur's final flourish.

Open the great library of the cliffs:
Pressed between stiff blank leaves an ammonite's
Very occasional coiled impression,
Pathetic souvenir of a fatal
Visit, to a world, to the mothering sphere –

Which eternally receives coolly her
Offspring, who to live have enclosed her wet
Saltness in membranes of varied splendour
And complication, truly analogous
To polythene, as one might have expected –

The very material of the doll
Called Tiny Tears, whose ambiguity
Of urination resides less in her
Crude thigh sockets than in her creator's
Modesty. Even her weeping throws doubt

On our sorrow for slightness lost or
Never possessed. Quite otherwise the case
Of the distinguished, unpossessable,
Utterly nude, competitive beauty,
Who sails in streaming from archetypal parts.

How can be questioned the emotions of
The procreant goddess? She at least must
Truly love. Our models, so plausible
In essential apparatus, are doomed
To be dismembered by the shores of their birth.

When the tide goes out, small heads, wristed hands,
Are left in the wrack among the litter
Of tougher experiments – comic-book
Monsters' green hair; pointless ribbons; flora
From prehistory. Somehow reassuring.

THE SCHIZOPHRENICS

Even as children such patients were strange and dreamy.
But then self-love was underwritten by their beauty.
A charming trait, not opening the hands to be washed.
Who would have guessed the irreversibility
Of their complaint, their fate to live the dream out
In asylums for prohibited desires?

Cramped are the margins of history and culture.
Those infants reared by beasts fail to evolve
A normal brain. The founders of our clan,
Wolf-boys – the origin of all our woes?

Regarding the human newly-born, with reason,
As merely an extra-uterine foetus,
The ideal state would make a Caesarian snatch
And raise those upturned beetles to a breed
Of timid heroes, fear of dark postponed
Beyond that guilty month, life's twenty-fifth,
And dread of death confined to natural death,
Aggression to chivalries of beak and horn.

Then, would the mutually unrewarding
Clinical dialogues be otiose?
Or is it the very chemistry of this
Smart animal that makes it set up states
Whose currency is excrement, whose laws
Are nonsense, frontiers ineluctable locks?
Copies, indeed, not much less damaging
Than the real thing. The word associations,
Quoted by Jung, of a catatonic, thus:
'Dark – green; white – brown; black – good-day, Wilhelm;
Red – brown', come to mind as proving all too clearly
The limitations of the power of art
To heal, for its irrationalities
Need ordering by the profoundly rational –
Rare as the pusillanimous controlling peace.

Why else are vast mausoleums even now
Uncovered; why after revolutions do
The revolutionaries still revolve?
Isn't the doom of the species demonstrated
By its continual failures with its cities?
Or is the nature of children to think themselves
Exceptional the proof of some so far
Frustrated adaptation which at last
Will burst from such realities as immured
Hölderlin, and create a slaveless Greece –
Under whatever grizzled skies, with what
Unmarmoreal columns, lame hexameters?

THE UNREMARKABLE YEAR

The great thrushes have not appeared this year,
No more the sickness of excessive
Evacuation. Taking one year
With another the debits and credits seem to cancel out.

When I recall the family
That fell like a camouflaged platoon
On the garden in 'sixty-eight
(Or was it 'sixty-nine?) I can't help feeling regret.

But there is much to be said for a summer
Without alarms. The plum crop is modest,
The monarch has remained unchanged,
Small differences only in one's teeth and hair and verse-forms.

There'll be no memories like the visit
Of the orchestra of *gamelangs* –
Enhanced by the naked mamelons
Of the dancers – influence that goes on reverberating.

So that the year of painting the shed,
Of missing strange calls, deep dappled breasts,
Is also that of harmonies
That have made one's life and art for evermore off-key.

GEORGIC

I

It trickles in my palm like blood, the plum juice,
And on this premonitorily autumnal morning –
Small pebbled windfalls, pyrocanthus berries
Clustered and flushed as from tropical marines –
It comes to me that I'm drinking the elements,
Even the snow-flakes, filtered through and syphoned up
       Out of my freehold wedge.

Retire to your estate, the world commanded,
As though sick of a writer they'd never even read.
Well, what now will emerge can scarcely be
Considered more gripping, a smallholder's journal, spiced
With jottings of a temperate climate's changes.
Back in my study, how can I help but envy
        The tragic, the large editions?

No use to comfort my ordinariness to say:
All's a projection from domesticity –
The incest of the gods, the islands of
Revenge. And even monarchs, did they really
Contrive to elevate their actual murders
And greed to planes above the sordid? No,
        But poets sustained the illusion.

A warning to myself about this book:
Don't sabre the leaves too far ahead – though fear
Or constant anticipation of extinction
Is certainly no decent surrogate
For the sense of ampler life one's deficient in.
A note to take cuttings of hardy shrubs is mingled
        Fatally with apophthegms.

II

Sometimes the young die young, as birds in summer:
A corpse against green, incongruously plump.
A day of trivial labours passed, I think
In the September evening how prolonged
The wait to hear a thrush's evening song.
The losses of a year can't be repaired,
        Even granted another year.

The sun behind a tree, straight lines of light
Arrange themselves around a half-masked face;
Obliging science, each tends towards the centre.
Photography might crudely get the point:
But where are the painters whose technique, their whole
Ambition, will make the marvellous plausible,
        Enamoured of appearance?

[355]

Equally, what words of mine will show that faces
Of horses and men are unchanged through history?
I mean that among the hillside vineyards or
Overcheck hedgerows, in hoods or under caps,
Rope-haltered or caparisoned in scalloped
Scarlet, still wend the terrible masters
        Of a well-meaning earth.

THE CATASTROPHE

The hours that preceded the catastrophe
Partook of the nature of the hours before it loomed.
The earth's triviality and its astonishing
Variety were seen to be related to
Neither catastrophe nor non-catastrophe.

The tulips failed to soak in vivid wave-lengths at
The red end of the spectrum, and their open cups,
Curled by late Spring, shone somewhat lighter at their tips.

The birds went about the various business of birds in Spring.
Their world was Victorian in its multiplication of
Infantile death-beds; and they cared but were enured.

They had a role to play in the catastophe
Which curiously they seemed already conscious of.
It was their destiny to guarantee, perhaps
To man, that after the catastrophe, somehow
There would survive material evidence of Spring.

CIRCUS ZOO

A rather gormless lad, incongruously
Attired in a frogged, vermilion jacket,
Waters the elephants in a long dark tent.

The line of enchained beasts incessantly sways
To a rhythm learned from their ring performance
Or, more likely, captivity's neurosis.

[356]

In the base of each massive head – a boulder
Almost black, and blotched as though with grey lichens –
Is embedded a crude but flashing ruby.

He of the uniform, passing, gives a punch
With the barrack-room's part threat, part affection,
To one head where the trunk starts its wrinkled flow –

A trunk which one later sees, as it probes forward,
Ends like some rippling interior organ
In contrast to the old stucco of the hide.

The jewelled eye certainly recognizes
The visitors from an alien species,
Nominally free – but has stopped beseeching.

To have this virtually on one's doorstep –
Despite the guard's possible humanity,
Haunts a night or two with quite germanic guilt.

APOLLO ON DIONYSUS

For the centenary of Nietzsche's THE BIRTH OF TRAGEDY, 1972

Not only mad himself – drove others mad.
And set demented females on to murder
A rival poet by tearing him to bits –
There, scarcely much encouragement required.

What suffering the sculptures undergo
To be so beautiful! Perhaps it was him
Who on the impressively lucid world
Of classic deities let twilight fall.

Certainly, starting tragedy with that
Unresolved chording made his music burn
An entire people; and even after the fire
The dissonance screams on through wrong machines.

I think with satisfaction that even he
Must use in art my ordering power – pang
Of unease in also having to admit
That in the end one's forced to speak his tongue.

[357]

Whose influence will the race of men inherit?
The portrait in the fairy story could
Roll back its eyeballs and behold itself.
This is the gift to poets of the gods.

Of Dionysus or Apollo? Say:
'It is a dream. And I will go on dreaming.'
Then, human, though the heroic age decay
You will yourself unwittingly be a hero.

My deep belief; that to be beautiful
Everything must be intelligible. O
Opponents of Dionysus, rapidly
Make comprehensible your puzzling lives!

And therefore justified – though understanding
And vindication, both, rise from an art
Riddled with his insanity; as if
There truly were neuroses shaped by health.

HOMAGE TO BALTHUS

What a relief to admit, as Balthus
    with his paintings, that one's poems
are utter failures, without exception.
    Even to have got down, somewhere
along your life, the continuous line
    a girl's hair makes with her arm or
the revealed white band between naked thighs
    – quite pointless in the context of
possibilities. And the small figure
    walking away on the far green
cliff while we ourselves, trivial giants
    in the foreground, watch the artist;
and to light the outflung nude the curtain
    snatched back by a big-headed dwarf;
and in a tinted street the blanched plasterer . . .

Noble artist, it cannot be
the absence of strange intimations
    in wide reality that you
lament but the eternal refusal
    of pigment, canvas, brush to make
a world parallel to blind creation
    and replace that with its order.

PART EIGHT

Mainly from
From the Joke Shop
(1975)

BEFORE

A drift of feathers in my way across
The park made by a rational century
Returns me to the plains of Africa.

The corpse not there, the crime unspeakable –
This is the nature reason mitigates
And yet is helpless when confronted by.

I think about the dying bird brought in –
The neighbour seizing on our catlessness.
By a coincidence, not rare in man's

Affairs, it proved to be the orphaned stare
I'd stood as sentinel and victualler for.
Perhaps some lack in me had then compelled

Its anabasis to another lawn
Where it did battle with a feline foe.
Hope sparked at first, though swiftly doom came down.

I put the bird upon the grass to die
But when it spun on frantic, feeble wings
I snatched it up and held it at my throat.

I might have had it there still (I suppose)
If warmth and anguish could have kept it quick.
Alas, with grace it bowed *its* throat for ever.

I wonder if I smoothed that voyage all
Must take. Or not. Undoubtedly its neck
Was always arched too far. As youthful necks

So nearly are, without the stroke of death.

KANTIAN MATTERS

I.m. Kenneth Allott 1912–73

The years arrive and go and are forgotten.

The tone inevitably elegiac:
As Gilbert Murray said, one cannot write
'And after many a summer dies the duck.'

Drinking the wines of '70 – absurd.
Poet a century hence, to whom your fellow
Bards have been known to appeal, you're almost here!

And we ourselves have doddered on to odd
Times and must try for urban philistines
To make sense out of prosody and dawns.

Yet my contemporaries are dying round me.
Even those silent since their youth seem gagged
Just as their lips were forming some great message.

And more persistent singers by that token
Look to have cheated death, despite our having
To watch them shrink and whiten in their clothes.

After the bird expired between my palms
And I had buried it, I thought: 'You missed
The fireball at nine. And all the ruffling rain.'

Who knows which cataclysm is the worst,
Nature's or history's? I see today
Fasces protruding from a lion's jaw –

Thoughtless baroque idea of decorating
The purlieus of learning and high oratory.
It only means brute's triumph over brute.

[364]

The State sicks up the violent element
That breeds in its craw. 'The old age of certain men
Is like the childhood of immortality.'

– Thus the Goncourts. What change has come to life
In a hundred years! How unserene my soul!
Yet the two Kantian matters still remain

For admiration: first, the moral law
Within us; secondly, the stellar sky
Above us – outside our rooms, our self-regard,

That haunt our years and flick them swiftly through.

CONSOLATIONS OF ART

For Jack Lindsay

J.M.W. Turner on Switzerland:
'The Country on the whole surpasses Wales.'
– As parsimonious with praise as cash.

It was this little down-to-brass-tacks man
Who saw that nature, history and time
Were mostly fields for Cataclysm's advent;

And on his 'waking eye' (he wrote in verse)
'Rushed the still ruins of dejected Rome.'
The exciting revolution also brings

A constant sense of parallel disaster –
As well I know, who followed '17
Like artists who came after '89.

No doubt the dying age, not dying fast;
The new society murdered in its youth;
The need for stoic individuals

Recall the line of empty cities, force
Poets to see in all phenomena
(Even in landscape) culture's coming doom.

[365]

A sky of Turner's, said the critics, is
'A heap of marble mountains.'
The painter himself observed about a salad

(Conversing with his neighbour at a dinner):
'A nice cool green that lettuce, isn't it?
The beetroot pretty red though not quite strong enough.

Add mustard and you've got an oil of mine!'
Despairing of the State, Euripides
Became a quietist. Thus creators end.

INSOMNIA

A memory of some preposterous
Experience makes me realize that at last
I must have dozed; and getting up to shut

The window on an aircraft's whinny, note
The curtain's crack still sabled by the night.
What cries and danger do I also damp?

And all in vain, since worse are in my head.
At eighty-five Stravinsky saw his birth
Certificate ('very yellow') in a dream.

I start myself towards historic age,
Shocked by obituaries of contemporaries,
Thinking that I'm becoming odd enough

Myself to tempt a spare biographer;
The habit of friendship, as of life itself,
Turned to a whim of waking up or not.

Then, after more of Robert Craft, cold drinks,
Hot drinks and pees have somehow doodled in
The cipher hours of insomnia,

I see from my study, in the morning sun,
That what were formerly judged a dirty brown –
Cock sparrows' periwigs – are really auburn.

To understand the brute: not difficult
In view of all the sensitivity
Engendered by the night. More speculative:

Having to live with humankind. That bird
Only when dying would allow itself
To be embraced. Quite other with most men –

Demanding to be loved for qualities
Unlovable. . . And so the pen runs on,
Trying to bring together what it knows

To be least trivial: not rhetoric, facts;
And failing. For in art I'm timid as
In life. The summer burns the best away;

Umbrellas flying to the fists of clerks,
Leaving the operating-table bare –
At least, save for the suffering aptly there.

DEAD POET

Going across the piebald summer green,
By the glass pond, the willow's waterfall,
I wonder suddenly if I shall see you

In one of your familiar emanations –
With walking-stick, perhaps, or musing on
A bench of the municipality.

At once I remember you are dead. A step
More on the slippery beige and then the thought:
But shan't we soon be meeting, after all?

Fanciful concept, since I disbelieve
In after-life. Nor shall I join you in
Some notional pantheon of immortal bards –

Part of the irony of coming death
Is just its confirmation one's to be,
Despite a life of trying otherwise,

A nonentity. No doubt too late I note
That people usually choose as favourites,
Out of my poems, pieces (all too few)

On the demise of cats, or filial guilt.
It seems I rarely found the common touch,
Though my emotions common as they come.

Drawn to a tapping stick run creviced ants,
More than a hundred times as old as man.
The heart being recently invented, they

Own just a cardiac vessel. Poets sunk
Within their art ostensibly possess
Such myrmecoid heartlessness in life itself,

Yet, as one's circle, like a dish of cherries,
Gradually decreases to the tough
Or the deformed, how copious the tears!

The chairs stay out all night. Shall I get through
The shortening days to laze in them again,
And say once more: I'll savour these at least –

Make them go slowly as the gnomon's shade,
Or even stop, like green nasturtium wheels;
Spending more time out in the hedgehog's moon?

August itself has undertones of Fall,
Some inexplicable, imperial,
Elgarian sadness. Don't we long to assume,

As simply as the starling, winter plumage,
See off our final brood in mellow days,
Die stoically, and carefully out of sight?

Licking each other and exchanging food –
Is how ants spend their lives. So far as men
Swerve from that model is the measure of

Unhappiness, what makes precisely for
The human: culture of neurosis – cities
Ant-riddled from scratch, chronicled by the sky.

CHANCE

At lunch I mention one who was a child –
Of brains – I knew twelve years ago. That night
I dream I take the hand of such a child.

Profound beyond her years, she then remarks
My tender interest is erotic; and
Indeed I see her breast is slightly curved.

I say I'll keep that element remote;
And really that is what I would prefer.
She smiles. Is not convinced. Then I awake.

The reason I let fall the name was that
I'd seen her husband lunching in the place,
With a blonde girl I thought at first the wife.

No dark affair was thrown up by this chance
So far as I'm aware – no more than life's
Normal coincidence and consequence.

Though, as I write that, I'm appalled at what
May possibly ensue. So I cut short
My workings-out, both real and in the mind

In case they can be used to alter fate
Or that my phantasies may hurt too much
A fair girl's selfless care for deepest themes . . .

I glimpsed a flourished hand splash out some wine.
How different from my own bibacious rites!
Life, in a dozen years, transformed to dreams.

IN PRAISE OF WAKEFULNESS

Theatre light draws me out upon the lawn.
The middle of the night: two garden-chairs
Under the yellow moon and Jupiter.

Both empty: somehow I expected them
(Or one, more likely) to be occupied.
It is as though we'd left the house for good –

That curious epoch, sometimes talked about,
When others' furniture is in our rooms
And strange flowers in the new-shaped borders blow.

I read Craft on Stravinsky, back in bed.
In retrospect it's just those moments when
He's pissed that make his life for him worth while.

One must enjoy the migraine blur of moons
In the binoculars' image of the orb,
Unsatisfactory as it is; enjoy

The prospect of recovery in that chair,
In sunlight, from a night of sleeplessness;
And, more than that, enjoy the actual,

The bothersome nights themselves, which after all
Are ludicrously shorter than the night
Through which one's sleep will be without a flaw.

After my death may well turn up that file
Recording jests for use when speechifying.
What extra wry banality revealed!

How, Beachcomber enquired, to cure a red
Nose? Answer: go on drinking till it turns
Purple. Here's to insomnia, the worse the better!

VARIATIONS

For John Lehmann

According to a *TLS* review
Franck 'led an uneventful life . . . was not . . .
Prolific'. Might have been describing me.

The window frames a leggy yellow rose.
I hurry out to rescue drowning bees.
The bedside notebook yields its gibberish.

Franck: many boring bars; a schmaltzy tune;
Arguably, wit and singularity
Confined to the *Variations symphoniques*.

[370]

Not bad to be remembered even thus.
Each decade trendy geniuses arise;
Non-geniuses nearer to oblivion.

Ancients on benches, crumbling bread for birds –
It's they I should be with! Don't mind the young
Doing what's daring: I just want to think it.

The games of human love are infantile,
Admittedly: my tragi-comedy
Is seeing them as puerile as well.

Making the relative allowances,
You're not, dear friend, as antique as your dog.
I can't yet pity you for walking slow

Or coughing when you rise to welcome me.
As for your fifty years' affair with iambs,
I envy it. No cause for faithlessness.

Creation seems continuous, looking back;
Yet we both know how random and how frail
The hours that make the opus numbers up.

I wish your study windows *cloches* for flowers . . .
More and more sweetness in your neighbours' hives . . .
Dreaming recalled and always metrical!

READING IN THE NIGHT

In the Stravinsky book by Lillian Libman:
The old idea that this very hour
(Because the sun lies farthest off from man)

Is the worst hour of the twenty-four.
Initially surprised we still depend
On that outmoded god, that dying fire,

One soon is reconciled – for, after all,
The star had grandeur and is ours alone.
Besides, far back it gave us life, although

We now may look askance at the donation.
The ambiguities of day return.
Light enough to discover with a pang

A spider drowned, like scribble, in a bucket.
Yet seeing that emblematic, as if art
Had vanquished superstition, even death;

As if one didn't know the final plight –
For it to be beyond our human powers
Even to orchestrate another's fugue.

ORPHANS

Product of pigeon love – pale legs and beak,
Dark plumage ruffled in a boyish way,
Behaviour vulnerable and innocent.

Who would have thought the conscientiousness
Events built into me in youth would be
One day directed to concern about

A fledgling pigeon extant suddenly
In the once carefree garden; parentless,
It seems, unwanted (least of all by me);

And helpless, more or less; and probably
A hopeless case? It's in my character
To feed, and guard it from the cats all day . . .

Wake to a dawn of worry . . . till at last,
Searching the spider-scuttling shrubbery's depths,
I have to admit the coming of its fate.

Strange that my poetry isn't taken up
(I mean by an audience more numerous)
Since cosiness seems my overwhelming wish.

Perhaps what jars – the echoes of remorse.
If I had only persevered I might
Have caged the fledgling safe from wandering.

[372]

Practice has let me almost overcome
The fear and repugnance that my fingers feel
For fluttering, and another's alien softness;

But what deterred me here I know of old –
A sense of not presuming to impose
My will, existence, ineffectual love.

Flaws of the mould on every replica
Made by a life – and to repeat itself
Is how life comes to be, alas, designed.

Calamitous, a bird's abandonment:
But what about my own young orphancy?
The unreachable corner where I hid or died?

THE CARD-TABLE

Today it spends its life against a wall:
Facilities inside quite unemployed.
Its top can be unfolded and a leg

Swung round to make a battlefield of baize
With shallow cups to hold one's cash or chips
And zinc-based corner circlets for the drinks.

It comes down from my father and my youth.
Round it sat Issy Gotcliffe and the Weinbergs,
Powers in the textile trade in Manchester.

There I first stole an aromatic sip
Of scotch, midst laughs at my precocity:
Could be the last year of the First World War.

World vanished, almost in the mind as well –
Too young, my brother, to remember it.
All, save we supernumeraries, dead.

What point or virtue in remembering it?
Except to make it stand for everyone's
Possession of such a world – and of their loss.

The bearded faces carved upon the table's
Thighs (so to speak) will quite soon start to mean
Part of his childhood to another child.

His father will have had the enterprise
To lay out cash for art – extravagance
Condoned by delight and use, as ought to be.

My album of those days reveals that Issy
Served in the infantry – maybe in fact
He perished there, for all is speculative

In my recall, I'm sure; as history is.
At any rate, perhaps he never knew
How fascists tried to exterminate his kind.

Even in '18 he of course looked back
To times astoundingly myself had glimpsed –
A general peace, long days, illusive art.

'*Komm in den kleinen Pavillon,*' they sang –
Of *décor* amateurs would now reject:
Their heroes walrused; stout *grisettes*; and gay

Ill-fitting uniforms, to be exchanged
In a few years for real ones of field-grey.
Ah, music, not made cynical by Weill;

Love innocent in art and so in life;
Empires not cruel save through carelessness;
Summers of mere manoeuvres, courts of cards!

LUDICROUS REFLECTIONS

Sunning myself (high summer in the garden),
My fingers brush against my solid thigh.
I think: quite good material for compost.

The unity of all organic stuff –
Some rationale behind that simple notion,
Although precisely what is hard to say.

If life were atomized, I mean, no chance
Of pre-lapsarian, spontaneous
Regeneration in the ensuing sludge.

In any case, what ludicrous reflections!
Even a friendly critic would pronounce
Such lines self-parody. Still more to come!

I raise my book and read that 'in the age
Of the Antonines we meet a surprising number
Of florid valetudinarians'.

No need to travel so far back in time,
No need to go to Rome to find the type
That takes the empire's sickness for his own.

I don't recall the gay, rich days – though born
In '12, my earliest memories include
Wondering what the Press would do in peace.

Maybe the sorrows of my infancy
Somehow foretold the sorrows of the times.
Even the sibling who survived with me

Was born the very day of deaths by sea
And claims of so-called victory off Jutland
By admirals on either archaic side.

Do bees go home? It's half-past six and yet
They water, still as cattle, at the bowl
Provided specially for such as they;

But where they sometimes drown or, frantic, must
Be rescued by a great and godlike index:
As we ourselves in this ambiguous world.

SHAKESPEARE AND CO

'Tis strange that death should sing – King John

Late Beethoven quartets: Stravinsky, old,
Murmuring 'Wonderful! Incredible!'
– Which leads the memoirist to name a third

'Who might have joined them', he who 'out of some
Terrible suffering' wrote *Macbeth* and *Lear*,   .
Then in his final years emerged to give

'Supreme expression' of the sense of life,
To wit *The Tempest* and *The Winter's Tale*.
One's touched, in the context, by this corny view,

Though sure that suffering's what we all can share
With genius and it needn't be top-notch.
The Victorian painter, Richard Dadd, who stabbed,

He said, 'an individual who called
Himself my father', made for forty years
In Broadmoor wonderful, incredible fairy worlds.

The difference is the hand's resource and craft
That turn the cloudy visions of the mind
Into a change of key, a pacifist isle.

Still, strange enough that autumn period:
The fruit so easily could be detached
But nature through its thread hangs on to add

Colour to seeds, a variegated cheek,
Flesh ready for consuming. Chaos persists –
The troublesome reign, false friends' conspiracies –

Though far from the ailments and obituaries
That almost daily plague old age, but yet
Can't spoil (that, rather, must enhance) the sense

Only possessed by age – that, when all's said
And done, life isn't death, however frail
The finger following the heavenly score.

[376]

ELEPHANTS, ANTS, DOVES

801 – an elephant in Gaul!
They speak about the stagnant Middle Ages,
Of Islam cutting off the Middle Sea,

And yet the monster enterprisingly
Shuffled from Indian jungle to the Rhône.
Puzzling to tell one's place in history.

What lies before us now – a 'dark age' or
An all too necessary rebirth? A worse
Election looms because of man's new power

To liquidate not merely heretics
And enemies of state but life itself:
Life only geared to nature's cataclysms –

These ants that put their winged friends on their feet,
Like aircraft handlers, and those pigeons which,
From mutual nibbling at the exiguous face

And thrusting a bill far down the other's throat,
Take their respective postures in a sketchy
Rehearsal for prolonging pigeon life.

Social and private failure and success –
How like the human! But without its guilt
And its articulate recrimination.

Yes, I would sacrifice mankind if that
Could save the six-legged and the avian.
Though who's to say the formic city less

Unjust than ours, and that the dove, evolved,
Wouldn't impose tyrannical modes of love?
Let's pension off the soldiers, see what comes.

FAMILY MATTERS

I.m. John Broadbent: ob. September 3, 1973

One of my mother's younger brothers dies:
My mother dead, my own age sixty-one.
The news originates in my native north.

Widowered, living in a small hotel,
He failed to wake today. He might have thought,
Going to bed, to amend some work of art –

Too late. Though I believe he'd not kept up
His talent as a water-colourist –
Making his mark as spare-time Thespian.

A mile from here one might, if one so wished,
Into the urban Thames expectorate.
It strikes me that I'm very far from home;

Yet this is where I've lived most of my life.
A sorrowing infant on the Pennine moors,
The borderer became a natural exile.

Or is it class that makes me sceptical:
Descendant of bloody-minded NCOs,
And probably reluctant patriots

Even in the Wars of the Roses? Yet from you –
Ironic, emotion-hiding distaff side –
Comes the true joy of life, creativeness.

Mysterious paternal ancestors,
I have to put you second in my life
To those who must have engineered my soul –

Soloists in *Elijah*, councillors
In local government, heroes of the sub-plot,
Parodists and analysts of tragic life.

How dark the trees grow when, the sun gone down,
I sit on in the young September's dusk
Until invisible against the west

The tiny flies, until a late bird soars
Too swiftly past to be identified,
Until the owl's repeated painful creak

Replaces all day's noises, and I can't
Quite see to write. One only has to choose
A different milieu for one's garden chair

Or just stay till an unfamiliar hour,
And life seems changed somehow – 'prolonged' would be
The word had not the thought come to me now

That last night, too, my uncle might have seen
Clouds first illumined by an orange light
Then disappear, the sky turn oyster grey;

The acacia leaves suspend themselves in black
And graduated brushstrokes either side
Of stems so slender as to be invisible.

DREAMS SACRED AND PROFANE

Our petrified existence with the dead
Haunts wakeful nights like cocktail memories
Sour with the senseless things we did or said.

'What is the *Lear*,' wrote Coleridge, 'the *Othello*
But a divine dream?' – thinking poetry
To be a dream the dreamer rationalized.

But to the author it's no thing of art,
The dream in which he always plays a part:
Merely a run of boobs he can't expunge.

Why should he make the dead come back in dreams;
And re-enact their hurt and his neglect?
Slumbering or not, unsatisfactory nights!

Between the boiler-house and garden shed
September mornings trail a filament
Across my brow: this year a prelude to

[379]

Uncanny subsequence of cloudless dusks –
No more to do with troubled early hours
Than evolution's ingenuity

With man's quite likely self-willed holocaust.
Indeed, perhaps life's something up its sleeve:
Seeds of the arctic lupin can survive

Ten thousand years in frozen soil, it seems.
Possibly there will be at least an earth
That blossoms suddenly in snow-veined wastes.

Ten thousand years! With little chance the seed
Even of sawn-off wrens will have endured.
Let's find some solace in those legends where

Vegetables shriek. And, after all, such lack
Of men is only like one's own old age.
Besides, diviner dreams may yet be dreamed.

GOETHE'S POODLE

Goethe's pet dog, if he had one, must have grinned
During his master's talks with Eckermann;
Both so high-minded, the disciple prim.

Before the soup, a servant brings them in
A tome of topographical engravings
Or crate of tedious antiquities.

Goethe remembers Mozart as a child
But salon-pieces tinkle just ahead.
Goethe's mad science occupies their brains.

18th September, 1823:
'All my poems are occasioned poems . . .
My boy, let none say that reality

Is lacking in poetic interest.'
How much of this the younger comprehends?
How much brings sentimentally up to date?

[380]

To follow, '48. And '71.
But Eckermann by then is dead. Likewise
The putative dog, unpenned his puncturing memoirs.

Eventually Weimar stood again,
But far more sinisterly, for the deluge
Let in by classicism holed by the romantic.

As in a dream, to Eckermann appeared
That ancient, brittle, blue frock-coated legend,
Its parts composed of the Collected Works.

'Mankind is strange: as soon as a lake is frozen
Over they flock to it in hundreds, but
Who thinks how deep it is, what's in its depths?'

'True, Excellency. And the themes of *Faust*,
Right well you balanced them. And how to show
The test-tube Homunculus upon a stage?'

For what naive knowledge did that Faust give up
His soul! A fallacious theory of optics.
Quite puzzling to conceive the need to flesh

The Faustian myth when history scarcely seemed
Set on the downward path; remote, dogs roasted
Alive in millions, even devoured with relish.

F. W. MAITLAND'S DOG

The photograph can't be assigned a date –
The one that suggests the magic of his eyes;
Liked best by Mrs M, who kept it by her.

However, his daughter in old age recalled
The dog as a childhood friend of hers, and thus
The epoch must have been the 1890s.

The dog is sitting on a table-top
Next to the eminent historian:
Its white tail trespasses upon his lap.

It, too, might well have had attractive eyes.
Both pairs have lines drawn slanting from the corner,
Making the man seem thoughtful as the dog.

MR MACMILLAN'S CAT

No marvel I'm conversing with a cat:

The curious thing is it's Macmillan's pet.
(I'm sitting by the former Premier's fire.)
It tells me its master is ignoring it.

I say: 'Why don't you jump upon his knee?
I'm sure the action wouldn't be *de trop.*'
However, the cat replies that it prefers

To wait until the guests go then come up,
From bidding them farewell, alone with Mac.
I think before I wake

How wise the cat is in the ways of love.

YOUTH AND AGE

Pureness of feeling surely ought to go
With youth's inimitably shining hair.
And mostly does. Or so I must believe.

I mourn the tiny spider drowned inside
Your eye. Be careful, turning your bright head
These arachnean mornings of September.

Though empty of event, the days seem short
In middle-age. I marvel you'll have time
To play the discs that will define your past.

And evenings I imagined thieved by beaux
May well be given to Holmes and Monte Cristo,
Or smothering that halo with shampoo.

O years when coarseness merely made more safe
The underground ideal, how swiftly gone!
Strange the ideal should come back when we're old.

THIRTY YEARS ON

I take from the shelves a book of '42
And blow the dust out of the upper edge
And open at the flyleaf quite by chance

And see my mother's love and Christmas wish
In her distinctive hand, addressed to me.
Blindingly, more than half my life comes back.

Obviously she was prompted in the choice –
The book being Francis Scarfe's on '30s poets!
Where was I then? In darkest Africa?

Her writing's vivid still because the pen
Was held between her first and second fingers.
She could be still alive, at 84.

The reason for my getting down the book
Is to see what it says of Kenneth Allott,
Just dead, born in my year of 1912.

My mother was no older when she died
Than he was, or I am. Good God, the years
Spell irony however they're cast up!

How tickled she'd have been at honours since
Acquired – the trivia of longevity
Made worthwhile for her sake.

Thinking of Allott, he by '42
Had uttered what the grudging genius
Of verse was to permit;

Though there is consolation for all those
Who loved him – as Sibelius said: 'Preserve
The themes of your youth: the best you will invent.'

I was too immature to write or care
Effectively by 1942:
The speech choked back, frustrated audience gone.

Faint memory of Christmas of that year:
A Whitmanesque night-passage through the camp;
Ratings with branches, bottles; all dead drunk.

It's certain that I never sent my thanks
So as to touch my mother's worried heart;
And now, in Allott's words, 'Too late. Too late.'

My father, before his youthful death, would find
Because of fingers-slotted pen, his bride
Of twenty-one a fascinating scribe.

Strangely, the feeling is alive today;
And his undoubted thankfulness for life,
And creativity.

THE VOYAGE

Suppose yourself alone upon a ship;
The ocean bare, the vessel under way.
Suppose a hand emerges from the deep

To grasp yours and you take it, not afraid,
But kneeling on the hard deck, welcoming
Its pull to an element inimical . . .

CITIES AND GARDENS

Let the herbaceous border run to seed
And blow the consequent untidiness!
Eventually our birds will find the food.

One frets about the plot's economy,
The subsidies of bread and even cheese:
Suburbia surely should be self-subsisting.

Sustaining an inflated population
Mainly, it seems, of sparrows – is this right?
Here's a strange answer: they're the birds of Venus.

Tails cocked, the plumage markings point towards
The orifice of love – much patronized.
No doubt that faculty amused the goddess

And, though unlikely hauliers, won for them
The job of teaming her triumphal car.
What point have cities or their gardens if

They fail the Cyprian Queen's absurd demands?

OVATE DREAMS

Birds dream in the egg, Professor Jouvet says.
Dreams stranger than those dreamt as, sleeping on
The wing, they change the Fall for Africa.

All's preparation for cold dwarfish days.
Who'll see them out have speckled pinafores
Or yellow sabled with a careful brush.

Dream on, in tramontana or in snow!
The exiles dream of home, the rest of song,
Of eggs and of their former ovate dreams.

Why is the soul united to the flesh?
Ancient Plotinus thrashed the matter out:
No wonder he appears in Yeats's verse.

Cold-blooded creatures, such as fish or frogs,
Don't dream, the bold professor further says.
But how's the flesh sent up the unsaline falls

And the sun prince released from clammy skin?

ELEGIES

Had these been written from a castle on
The Adriatic, all (in Kai Lung's words)
Might have been 'permeated with the odour

Of joss-sticks, and honourable high-mindedness'.
As it is, I note a rain-drop either end
The garden-roller's horizontal bar.

What depth of art is this that seizes on
The peradventures of the weather for
Its inspirational materials?

– Though poets in such swarms admittedly
Could scarcely be thematically sustained
Save by the moods and flowers of temperate zones.

In fact the days were philosophical;
And then the classic sun and sky were blown
To smithereens one dusk of indigo.

But how did you expect the season's end
If not in heavenly artillery
And vulgar yellow switchings on and off?

The curious thing is that such days return –
Though mornings weepier, evenings heavier-browed;
Yet calm and warm the afternoons once more.

And the long year has still the days in store
When from the elms fall slanting showers of gold
And crisp as snow rasp at the lingering shoe,

Before the tan is muddied on the tar.
Times like the world of late antiquity
Amazingly enjoyed in its decline –

Tenth century pagan country gentlemen
Who thought that Christianity implied
The end of science; Greeks in deepest Turkey!

The lenient summer's nearly made us feel
Guests of an elegy-bewitched princess,
Hosts to enfolding unbedraggled wings.

HEART DISEASE

Pain at my heart now, rather a relief,
Since twinges in most other parts denote
A lingering death, in my mythology.

One's sixties find the body's provinces
Needlessly dissident, for they enjoy
Already an unwilled autonomy

Disturbing to the so-called government.
Neither night's gears nor hootings bring a sense
Of reassuring common fate. Then I

Get up and see the rotten windfalls sipped
By butterflies. The dictionary says
The reason of the name's unknown – although

Early Dutch, *boterschijte*, alluded to
The baby's yellow of its excrement.
And I'm once more caught up by art and life!

Risking what Mrs Browning called its 'red
Embers' against pale blue, a specimen
Indulgently lights upon my sweatered heart.

More pain (a tender one!) to note that where
Two hinges, seemingly well-oiled, are set
To slam the enigmatic Rorschach shut

The wings themselves shade down to duskiness –
Mysterious colour of the body, furred,
Lanky and waisted as an odalisque;

Enviably palpitating only for a day.

READING AT NIGHT
ABOUT MARCUS AURELIUS

'The gods are always there to show their power.
They help us humans in their marvellous ways:
They send us dreams; and they it is provide

The oracles for our uncertainties
And remedies for our ill-health. In fact,
They care for us and for our metropoles.'

Too *outré* even for an emperor,
Such words, we think, who've never felt at home
(Nor ever will do) in the universe.

I hope the sparrows roosting in the shrub
Above my window (presences only leaked
By droppings on the sill) sleep more than I.

They may include the hen I saw today
Pick up a small white feather in her bill
And make herself look like an elderly

Colonel, no doubt retired – as now I am.
Perhaps the sparrow did it to amuse.
Perhaps some bird-god does look after us

In such things of no consequence – though I'm
The last to under-rate the trivial
Or comic. 'Like an ill-roasted egg,' I say,

Shifting the ovoid in the simmering pan
As I prepare an early breakfast, struck
With the Swan's penchant for the homely trope.

This is the dismal week when Auden died.
He certainly was hooked up to the gods
As far as we're concerned. Though he himself –

Needing a decent drink, then off to what
More usually was maybe uncertain sleep –
I daresay felt mortal like the rest of us.

And really more than holiness, it's booze
And cigarettes make bearable our lives.
Then cut them short; and leave us to the gods.

ESSENTIAL MEMORY

Fourth of October 1973:
I pick the date to form a line of these
Iambics that keep falling in in threes.

Future historians, and epistolists
On cyclic weather patterns to *The Times*,
May note that I still wore a summer suit.

The bloody oblong that the creeper seems
Beyond the lavatory's striated pane
Astonishes the calls of nature still.

Its life, however, must be told in days.
And even Auden, unforgettable
Because of his creativeness, begins

To fade as what he was: the body – loved,
Or awesome but indifferent natural object –
Breaks up beneath the top-soil of Kirchstetten.

The tractor crawls along – is making! – that
Curved difference between the green and brown
Upon the tilted upland. Here is what

Essential memory depends upon.
For if the plough should fail, the superstructure
Collapses. Howard Newby tells me that

The night of Auden's death he was himself
In Vienna, near that fatal-roomed hotel,
Not knowing Auden there, still less his end.

As what he was. In spite of Howard's health,
Comparative youth, quite soon none will recall
What Auden's 'world' was like when first created.

Autumn: the leaf more insecurely hangs
Than hung the fruit. Nights longer. Weather worse.
Noise of the rain brings other noises near.

Can we love retrospectively the dead
We never really knew? I start to think so;
Especially since there is no question of

Unwished for or unrequited love. And now
The blood's all trickled to the ground; the voice
Only on tape; speculatively warm the clasp.

JOWETT'S NOTEBOOK

Benjamin Jowett's notebook thoughts strike home:
A man of sixty should collect the young
About him, and lead quiet *al fresco* days . . .

'My life has been a waste of vanity
And egoism.' And:
'I ought to rid myself of shyness which

Has detracted from my life at least a third.'
While reading his biography in bed
I rise to get an apple from the shed

And find myself at five
Under skies mythical, euclidean . . .
The Master's gospel of hard, unselfish work,

How much it now appeals – alas, too late!
How curious that today
The virtuous has become unfashionable!

Autumn takes hold. A garden chair must be
Conveyed to eccentric sites to catch the sun,
Which indoors fingers long-neglected books.

Those greying heavens just before the dawn
More or less feebly lit with yellow points:
Diagrams of tremendous destiny

I was too nervous ever to embrace!

LATE OCTOBER

As crossly as a child
I stared out at the rain.
Then summer came again.

The miracle, however,
Was one of resurrection
In death-bed frailty.

The sunlight warm enough
To live in gay as beasts
Must now be told in hours –

Although this wasp seems quite
Nonchalant, washing its face,
Anchored on four still legs.

SOLDIER'S MOON

So, you are shining still, as bright at two
As evening. Now you print the window's bar
On my abandoned page, when earlier

You chalked the city roofs' alternate slopes.
How long and patiently you shine for night's
Infrequent wayfarers!

Your orb reminds me of the bladder's shape
On x-ray negatives – as firm and white.
Strange reassurance of good health down there.

But do I really want to live into
A world of hook-nosed Arab fighting Jew,
The puny sides sustained by evil States?

Still later, heating milk, I see you cast
Darkness the other way – the chimney's shaft
On the pale eastern wall.

My nights are as disturbed as soldiers' are:
Perhaps as dangerous! Our little lives
Are bad enough without the man-made risk.

Dead world, shine on! What interrupts your glare
Can only be of fleeting consequence:
Scorpions and rocks, tall miles of precious air.

THE VERDICT

The verdict has already been arrived
At. But the foreman of the jury still
Must write the record down laboriously;

And others of the panel go and pee
Or phone to say they will be home for tea,
Before all shamble back into the Court

And the judge summoned from his crossword puzzle.
So that some time goes by before his fate
Can possibly be learnt by the accused.

And more: this was arrived at earlier still –
Before the charge was laid, the jury called,
The trial started. To the prisoner

It comes as no surprise to find himself
Condemned to death. The circumstances merely
(Though often attempted to be conjured up)

Strike him as somewhat odd or poignant. Who
Could have foretold that he would be cut off
During a visit from his fleeting Muse;

Or that he'd be less anguished than embarrassed;
Feel more for his survivors than himself;
Making some verses out of hopeless dread

Of rather more than average tedium?

DEATH OF HENRY JAMES

I read while walking (*à la* Gide) beneath
Continuously leaf-releasing trees.
It's the well-known but always gripping tale

Of James struck down upon the bedroom floor.
'So here it is at last, the distinguished thing.'
Genius in threatened death as in his art:

Discrimination, interest and *sang-froid*
Instead of lesser talents' vulgar dread.
Dread at not being stoical enough,

At proving not to have worked hard enough,
Simply at not being good enough, when faced
With the unpleasant parting from one's works.

Why does one skate so near oblivion's hole?
Of course, the poetry it wants to write
Flows rarely from the third or fourth rate nib.

This metre almost that of *Feversham*,
Oozing with *River Duddon* sentiments:
An awkward play, a sequence of decline –

Although not quite desired and in a sense
Unwilled, the words must by and large be right;
For other words belong to better men.

Fourth of November: wasps still crawling on
The ivy flowers, mere withered spheres. And yet
The skies are huge from half-gone foliage.

'Farewell, the latter spring!
Farewell, All Hallown summer!' Not for long,
Surely, can winter's couriers be delayed.

But James got well. His actual death, though made
Bizarre with Bonapartist fantasies,
Perhaps was liker to our conjectured own.

Quaffing the frightful draught, named in *Macbeth*,
Precursor to the following day's x-rays,
I dimly sense the distinguished heritage –

And suck the lingering sweetness from the globe.

MEMORIES OF WAR

Tonight dreams may be had
(To take an instance of my own conceits)
About the one-legged dancers of the Chad.

But now the unromantic dominates.
From the long ward beyond my little room
Come uninhibited sounds, among them groans.

As well as farting, men could be dying there.
The feeling of a war-time mess returns
So strongly as to occasion more alarm

Than that tomorrow's probing will reveal
Malignancy implanted deep within.
Even the music in the ear-phones tritely

Augments the sense of thirty years ago.
Dear comrades, now we well may have to die,
Our span being up or proximately up.

But youth can be kept from the conscripted ranks
That trail the alleyways between the beds
And lie awake or half-asleep on beds

At doom's grossly lessened odds.

THE OTHER SIDE

'You've had your operation, Mrs Brown.
Wake up!' The cry undoubtedly recurs
(It seems to me, who's also lying there,

Scarcely more wide awake than Mrs Brown)
In some congested docking-station for
The dead. The utter strangers strewn about,

The sexes intermingled sexlessly;
The far-off burning of an ancient pain
In my prone, sheeted figure; busy, white

Androgynous attendants; and the lack
Of memory of things before, confirm
After-life's ludicrous reality.

POST-OPERATIVE

Since one's dead drunk or, rather,
Just through dead drunkenness –
Not yet hung over, though –

One wonders why the fun
Of getting drunk somehow
Has skipped the memory.

I expound this to a sprite
In perfect white, but she
Ignores the snail's slurred speech.

Later, I see I never
Made clear I really knew
I was sloshed on pentathol.

Such missing links in their chain
Of discourse is what makes
Drunks so terribly boring.

For them existence tends
To the incorporeal –
Cherubim, proneness, quibble.

HEILIGER DANKGESANG

Sunset: the balding tree
Filters a sudden flight of darkling birds,
Seeming to gain a leaf or two thereby.

Why don't I, lying here,
Give joyous thanks my life is still preserved?
Perhaps I do so, in my grudging way.

Succeeding salmon clouds,
Untidy smoky clouds come swiftly on,
As though cranked by the deviser of a masque.

The unlikely blue of sky
Fades soon, as well it might. But isn't there
Even more virtue in the commonplace?

If one can call it such:
Baroque but normal flutings of the pipes;
Thorndyke, the doctor on the bedside chair;

The aircraft, winking now
Across the gold half-moon, about to drop
Merely a load unseasonably tanned.

A STRANGE DEVICE

I see an advert for the Spatter Guard –
Device for keeping fat confined when frying.
Though we already own two Spatter Guards

I tear the coupon from the newspaper,
Thinking I ought to guard against the day
When we might be without a Spatter Guard.

Rather presuming on longevity –
Possession of three sturdy Spatter Guards;
And that digestion will not even falter

In modest toleration of the fried.
But let us order one more Spatter Guard
(Or even two) and demonstrate our faith.

Moreover, does it matter at the close
That we have unused ingenuity
To leave our heirs – who may not know that grease

Is kept from elsewhere by the Spatter Guard,
Or that it shields mankind from boiling oil,
Or of its emblematic qualities?

THE WINDOW-CLEANERS

Today was overheard
Our old censorious window-cleaner say
'The garden is the proper place for birds.'

Terrace and even sills
Are on their way to being as wholly iced
As some mid-ocean-beaten, igneous perch.

No wonder that he feels
Constrained to excuse the milieu to his mate,
Newly acquired, unused to a poet's panes.

Good job he doesn't come
Inside the house, where moralists might trace
The evidence of parson's noses still.

Yes, lured by kindness, birds
In summer ventured here and then took fright:
Innocent Choctaws brought to the *faubourgs*.

Too easy synonym,
'Kindness', for stale soaked bread and pity spent
On lives at present sterner than our own . . .

We hop quite boldly in
Then panic at the strangeness caging us,
Find windows only feigning liberty.

Our aim is for the soul
To enter on the earth and be sustained;
Then without hindrance whirr into the skies.

Ambiguous the role
That such as window-cleaners play: deceit
With crystal but dissevering barricades.

STILL AT LARGE

I could be so immersed, like Gibbon, 'in
The passage of the Goths over the Danube'
As to miss dinner time.

The difference is he wouldn't have envisaged
Barbarians as threatening his age
Or coming from his set.

And similarly when old Jowett said
That medieval folk were like ourselves
But 'dirtier in their habits'

He'd not in mind the return of maniacs
As heads of state or even torturers
As minor civil servants.

So how have I been able all through life
To write and utter rather more than less
Of what I wanted to?

By helping philistines control the land;
By getting nothing for my work in art;
By squandering priceless time.

To let me stay at large is their award
For service; or the evidence, more like,
Of my art's impotence.

NOTES ON ART

For Huw Wheldon

O 'green-eyed dumplings with an astral stare' –
Thus Schoenberg's paintings, rather well described.
Those who've contrived to cover up in art

Their turgid rhetoric or romantic souls
Should keep from practising another art,
Where dim technique may give the game away.

Now Wilfrid Mellers admitted when he heard
The Elgar symphony of 1910
After 'experimental' works, it made

The events of sixty years astonishing –
The melancholy and heroic changed
To mutterings that dehumanize; and yet

Still didn't call the latter green-eyed balls.
Critics make each successive *Zeitgeist* more
Patently turnip-headed than before.

Surely I've bored the world with this already,
Just as I must have more than once observed
That every pigeon wears pale riding-breeches.

Even technique can't hide that art's about
What moves non-artists. TV (as you said)
Is telling stories, like George Eliot.

Astute of Anthony Powell to extirpate
The story-teller's soft interior,
Not least to leave more room for irony.

The astral stare: yes, that we must admit
(For who denies the rumminess of life?)
But flashed from Mrs Erdleigh, not the hero.

If the poetic vision is considered –
Sharper perception, most things slotting in,
Amused affection, even for ugliness –

[399]

Isn't the poem's importance obvious,
Since this is just what all would wish to feel?
Unless reared on a diet of mad dumplings.

FATHERS

My father may be often in my dreams
Yet (since he died when I was young) play parts –
Or be himself – and stay unrecognized.

In any case dreaming often modifies
The features of the characters we know,
Though usually telling us who's really meant,

Like useful footnotes to an allegory.
This morning speckled foam fell in the basin:
Watching my father shave came flooding back

From over fifty years. His cut-throat razor,
Black beard, seemed things of fascinated love –
And now replace the visage and his speech.

Did he imagine (as I sometimes do)
His son would one day reach the age of sixty,
Himself being almost *ipso facto* dead?

Worse, in his final illness did he think
How he would leave a foolish child of eight,
Himself being hardly out of folly's years?

LATE NOVEMBER

Even at two light's slow decline begins:
Hardly worth starting more affairs of day.
Let's doze, then drink some tea and watch the clouds . . .

Moon in the west sky, ready to be gilt:
Just time before the scotch and poetry
To go and get my shoes – soled, quarter-heeled.

A lady with a pug-dog on a lead
Is saying at the counter how he's been
Attacked by un-led dogs upon his way.

I ask her why I haven't seen of late
The dog at large in our secluded lane.
Reply: 'I never let him off the lead.'

It turns out there's a *doppelgänger* pug.
Do all pugs look alike? It may be so.
Perhaps the freely wandering pug is dead.

Yes, the route home's illumined by the bright
Sliver of moon. The frosty air compels
Breathing as noisy as the squash-nosed pug's.

The curtains drawn, loudspeakers speaking Kern,
I start to wonder what should body out
Astounding images and silvery words –

Canine personae, moon-glow, comic life?

CULTURAL HISTORY

The suburb's life: I've only to go out
To find it subtly changing, like a sky.
The little grocer's now sells 'Pork Farms' pies.

Gombrich maintains it's an elusive thing,
The mentality of people in the street;
Can't be retrieved or even be described.

Eight p, a patron of the baker's shop
Argues is still the price of sandwich loaves,
What she's been asked for at her usual branch.

'The small tin's eight, the sandwich loaf is nine' –
The assistant's borne out by a printed list;
Advises adherence to the other branch!

The almost metaphysical dispute
Obscures what was behind the original point:
Nine new pence for a stunted staff of life.

[401]

Or one-and-nine in ancient cash. I see
The note-book given me some years ago
By Georg Rapp cost only two-and-two

And still serves to record my night-time thoughts –
Which share, as may be seen, the fugitive
Preoccupations of suburbanites.

Nice if they knew the rest of my concerns:
But possibly their children will come round
To Marx's theory of the price of bread

And all myth's golden emblems for the grain.

END OF THE CHEAP FOOD ERA

I check my meagre purchases to see
How the enormous total has been reached.
The culprit is a pound of sausages.

Admittedly, they're Marks and Spencer's best,
Said to be 'over 90% pure pork':
Still, they're a somewhat novel luxury.

We always vowed the revolution would
Arrive when life became intolerable –
Which term we might well have envisaged as

The prospect of not affording sausages.

THE APPROACH OF THE COMET

A human of androgynous *tournure*
Opens the shutter of 'The Topless Bar',
A bookshop on the fringes of Soho.

Kohoutek draws inexorably near.
One's been on the look out for the death of kings
And for the first glimpse of the hairy star.

When did it visit us before? Perhaps
Prehistory saw it under bony brows;
Or farther back its long ellipse corralled

An earth as loose and formless as itself –
Refrigerated nothingness and dust.
Pre-dawns of sleeplessness, I rise and hurry

To the paved garden, shivering in my gown,
And scan with binoculars
The offered range of light: from yellow lamps

In newly-naked boughs along the lane
To the gigantic hunter's outlined frame.
What do I so absorbedly search for? Doom?

I found, some weeks ago, through illness, that
I should be far from glad to say farewell –
Denying a lifetime's pessimistic vein.

I visualize the possibility
Of non-doom, which almost jealously I see
You may enjoy, darling posterity.

So far the comet fails to catch my eye.
The monarch seems to be in perfect health.
The shutter rattles up 'The Topless Bar'.

WAITING FOR THE BARBARIANS

The pay-off of Cavafy's famous poem:
The let-down that the vandals never came.
My modest *aperçu* is that they're here.

Like androids, or beings from another world,
They take the shape of ordinary men,
Even the Jones or Robinson we know.

Then when they form a huge majority
They will reveal their ghastly taste, their lust
For violence, and indifference to death.

What am I thinking? 'Will reveal'? All bosh.
Impatient with slow progress here and there,
Most have declared themselves and taken over.

Too late to sway the president with art;
Mere plastic pumps, the hearts that might be moved;
The brain a convoluted programmed tape.

'I celebrate the instinct's primacy.
To cast my verses into metric shape
Would be betrayal of their heaven-sent form.'

Thus the one voice of multiplying bards
Who claim to be inheritors of the past
Though hairy, barefoot, clad in smelly skins.

STRANGE MEETING

In Boots the Chemists an oldish fellow bars my way –
An eye to eye encounter as I try to pass
Into another part of the emporium.

He wears a sober navy overcoat. His hair's
Indubitably salt and pepper. His regard
Is one of semi-recognition, tinged with alarm.

As may already have been guessed, I've misconceived
A mirrored wall as a communicating door.
I turn with a muttered oath: the old boy disappears.

The young boy still continues on his foolish course.

GUILTY

I know that some must surely think of me
As of potential criminality.
I grin at children, actually converse

With lolling babes in prams by banks and shops
And go along the supermarket shelves
Without the prescribed receptacle of wire.

Also, already I've an old man's laugh:
I wonder how soon the speaking voice will follow –
Sounding like some droll actor playing Shallow.

When they arrest me I'll have no defence.
Useless to say I wanted to express
My solidarity with those who grapple

With tricycles and pups; or sympathize
With tears at neglect, wet nappies and the cold;
Or put the butter where it shouldn't go

Quite inadvertently. 'You planned to make
Contact with little boys and, more so, girls.
You'd have ripped infants from their mothers' care.'

The quavering plea of guilty comes. But wait
A bit. For this I always meant to pay.
There's nothing Freudian in theft. Oh yeah?

Again, a bird-lover stroking cats for pity?
Clearly the man's a member of the gang
That goes round nicking moggies for their fur;

Named in the *South East London Mercury*,
It may be for the surreptitious stowing
Of beans, or Persians with pavement-sweeping hair;

Certainly not for fame in poetry.

ASTRONOMY

No wonder society is in a mess.
The trousers tweedy, very wide, with cuffs;
The shoes have soles four inches thick and tops

Brown plastic, trimmed with lemon. What on earth
Provokes man to discomfort and grotesque
Appearance (I say nothing of his mug)?

No wonder the individual's in a mess.
Terrible forces work to ruin taste –
Unless the ruination is innate.

[405]

And as to that, I see a survey showed
That classical music positively hurt
The tenants on some working-class estate.

All tends to make reactionary chumps
As well as fashionably comic youth.
Is no one to be taken seriously?

Three planets shining in the southern sky
Before star-shine (unusual, I should think)
Prove winter may be enjoyed not merely borne.

Should one ignore boneheaded fashion's rule,
The oil sheiks buying guns, the philistines
Training as fodder for the demagogues,

Content that this temporary observation-post,
Even when burnt-out as its satellite
(Now climbing to outshine its fellow discs)

Will rise with others in December skies?
It was when winter first was loved by man
He saw the patterns of a frosty night

Made scientific sense not destiny.
Brief epoch: following his nakedness;
Before voluminous pants and shitty shoes.

FROM THE JOKE SHOP

'Why doesn't somebody buy *me* false ears?'
I can't help remarking as I pack the same,
Plus a few boils and scars, in Christmas paper.

Returning from a stroll some hours later,
I see my ears are big and red enough.
Even a scar may be discerned. Life-long

Ambition to amuse fulfilled, it seems,
Without adventitious aid. Although some boils,
God-given, might more surely make for laughs.

WATCHING TV

I brush my tickling cheeks and find them wet.
How silly to sit here alone and weep;
Moreover, at vicarious events.

And yet I recognize the attitude
As demonstrating the essential man –
Only required is, after switching off,

To dance before my wife like Jack Buchanan,
Breathing a song of seaside infancy;
Or warble Tosti in the lavatory:

Attention to the tears diverted thus.
What curious masks I've worn all through my life!
And yet how can I call them masks that hid

From time to time in private that fair face
Of reason, not to mention compromise?
There's been one mask and several characters.

I thought for forty years the bourgeoisie
When it took arms would have to be fought back.
And now with Lewis, Owen and Sassoon

(And hairy purchasers of stone-ground flour)
Perhaps what I believe is that it's wrong
In any circumstance to take a life.

Not that the bourgeoisie has changed its spots,
As proved once more by Chile's recent times,
Yet here's a foolish Cambridge English don

Imputing in *Encounter* magazine
Pardon or love of violence in the '30s
To the intelligentsia of the left.

As though it wasn't war they tried to scotch,
As though they gained by moving from their class,
As though the age allowed mild remedies.

No doubt our academic might conjoin
This view with sniffling in one's sixties at
Schoolmasters refereeing football games.

But since I'm part of what's to be replaced
I give away the secret of my rheum
And of my comic or ironic turns;

For surely in the new society
Such matters must survive – and grow. That's why
We bothered with those selfless chores of youth.

DEBUSSY, WALTON, KYUNG-WHA CHUNG

Why don't I play the record more of these
Douze études by Debussy, since their beauty
Differs so little from titles less austere?

Why don't I stand and see the sunset out
More nights than this? Admittedly, the trees
And chimneys coal a sky of fiercest fire

That makes one think December's turning point
More than theoretical. Why don't I haunt
Museums of fine art and schools for girls?

Man can bear only so much pulchritude.
Upon another record-sleeve I see,
With quite offhand benevolence, the old

Composer clasping a fiddler in his arms.

WINTER SOLSTICE

December's early-ending but forbearant days
Produce long bands of bird-egg blue or primrose skies
Divided by angry greys

That threaten to annex the total heavens – though
Rather surprisingly time's left for birds to fly
And even in a tree

Linger and if they're blackbirds play their xylophones.
Premature duskiness makes sparrows sharp as wrens.
Then when the day looks gone

The robin's rattle sounds from seeming birdless boughs.
What am I doing in this world of Georgian verse,
That carries sanguine news?

LOVE

Give me back my life.
Come back to Sorrento.

What words! Dare hardly use them, even for
An epigraph. They wring me like the tale
By Chekhov, 'The Lady With the Little Dog'.

– Poignant enough before the Heifits film
Transformed it into silvery images,
Backed by an unknown's harrowing melody.

Oh yes, it's true that lives can be carved up
By forfeiting the only one they love.
The contrary appears not to apply:

Having achieved content, we seek in vain
In Yalta or elsewhere the bliss of how
It was in the beginning. As in youth.

RHETORIC AND MELODY

Christmas away: returning find *Bleak House*
Unshifted from my bedside chair. What's more,
Still lurking in familiar haunts, the Muse –

The Jamesian benediction part somehow
Conferred on, part self-generated by
Ageing creators; which they're coy about

Since if she goes their lives will lack all point.
And what have they to offer her to stay?
Strolling round my estate, I see through nude

Branches the pallid moon of afternoon
Now shrunken to a bracket. Days stretch out
Of trying to boil existence down to words.

The Boodles and the Buffys still hold power;
The cog-wheels of society don't engage;
The Dedlocks well could last in Lincolnshire.

One has to come back home to gauge the size
And possibly the nature of one's love –
Although I see quite clearly that my life's

Been pauperized by a shyness to confess.
For hardly recompense to show in art
The things one should have influenced in fact.

Dear child, who lives unknowingly those last
Few months or even weeks of childhood, what
Embrace or reassurance could I give?

I play my Christmas-present records, green
With envy at Ravel's command of tart
Rhetoric and memorable melody.

The play of *Cinderella* that we saw
Confirms above all else the everyday
Lust for the triumph of the beautiful –

Though you'll find adulthood is otherwise.
'What the poor are to the poor is little known . . .'
'A certain Jarndyce in an evil hour . . .'

But who would wish to multiply the moon;
Change the well-tempered scale (and yet they do)?
I hope the slipper fits. I know it will.

AGES IN THE MAKING

To W.M. Balch

I'm glad you sent a copy of this work –
A history of Great and Little Waltham.
Over the years you've almost made me, too,

An Essex man! The gift arrived in days
Of strikes, go-slows, and strictured Arab oil:
Some are prognosticating England's doom.

I leaf the photographic section over:
Here, the almshouses at Scrapfaggots Green;
The girls at the Girls' School all in pinafores;

The Boy's School as it was in 1900
('Several boys . . . later killed in World War I');
Ladies (with hats) cocking barley in that war;

George Marshall carting mangel-wurzels; Fred
Johnson, corn-dolly maker; and the sun-burnt
Founders of the Waltham WI;

The band on Pleasant Sunday Afternoons –
Strings, clarinet and what seems penny whistle.
And is the legacy of this to end?

Have we let down these men of numerous skills,
Respectable women, knickerbockered boys
Who leap-frogged in the carless village street;

And farther back in time – the Iron Age
And Domesday Walthamers, who must have felt,
Like sparrows, their generations guaranteed?

As I grow crustier, ideology
Seems less and less to matter. One hangs on
To judging whether colleagues would stand up

Against the intrusion of a Roman nose,
A sovereign who thought himself too too divine,
Or anyone who tried to twist the law.

[411]

Perhaps I always was a patriot;
Or predisposed, at any rate, to craft,
Hard work, jaw-breaking Anglo-Saxon names,

An island life, anachronistic, taciturn!

EXCHANGE OF NEWS

For Jabez

Mysterious cobalt droppings in North Wales!
It seems mice ate a *papier-mâché* bowl
During your absence since the summer days.

We've no news so spectacular in exchange.
Our substitute for nature, Greenwich Park
('Not equal,' Boswell said, 'to Fleet Street'), strewn

Derangedly through its vistas though it is,
After the gales, with antlers from great trees,
Can't match your rodents, patriots and steeps.

Obsessions of romanticism: falls
And fanfares. You may have the former; we
Just hear the young Saint-Saëns on radio.

The Gallic sensibility in art
That even saved Saint-Saëns in his excesses
(But not precluding pathos) we both admire;

And yet it comes that all unconsciously
I've taken as the model for this work
The *Night Thoughts* of the pompous Edward Young.

The stiff iambics and insomnia,
The moralizing tone – the very same.
Thank God (thank God!) I'm not devout as well.

You tell me what I know I ought to do –
More of the anecdotal; but not much
Happens to ruminants like the Reverend Young . . .

Travis and Emery's shop in Cecil Court:
I riffle through the music stacked outside.
I think I shan't be buying *How To Master*

The Tenor Banjo. Curious, writing this,
I momentarily can't place the ictus on
'Banjo' and have to get the dictionary.

All the more strange when later I recall
My long ago unfinished – hardly started –
Verse on a paradigm of Wittgenstein's:

'Asked to select a banjo from some things,
He merely picked an instrument with strings.'
The word proves to be a corruption of 'bandore',

A kind of lute the Elizabethans knew;
As 'What's her haire? faith two Bandora wiars.'
Unlikely story on the face of it –

Resembling, somewhat, mouse shit of bright blue.

VARIATION ON CAVAFY

You will not meet the Laestrygonians,
The Cyclops, furious Poseidon (wrote
Cavafy) unless you have them in your soul.

I wish that I myself could be so sure
Either of coming history or my soul.
Where are the huge Sicilian cannibals –

In healing art or in reality?
Who knows if horror of the smothering god
Isn't one's own suppressed desire to kill?

Burn the ghost apples of the previous summer,
The gardening notes command. Already shoots
Appear under naked trees. What presences

Shall we require to exorcise next year?

[413]

THE FUTURE

It's early February. Snowdrops crowd
As close and with as coy dropped heads as some
Green-leotarded, white-capped *corps de ballet.*

Dusk; and a robin sings in actual moonlight.
Ambiguous time; my birthday time. One year,
A frozen waste; another, song and dance.

Rhubarb's sore fingers peep already after
'The mildest January since '32' –
Year of my twentieth; month, no doubt (I don't

Recall!), of bonus kisses out of doors.
What wretched verse I surely then produced
(All luckily destroyed or in a trunk).

But then I apply the epithet to that
Produced in '42, *et cetera.*
I come indoors and play my latest discs.

There seems to be a basic mode of art
To aim for in this troubled epoch yet,
As well as did the eight-years-old Mozart:

Below a melody *cantabile,*
A busy figuration; what the sleeve-
Note calls the *singenden Allegro-stil.*

However, useless envying those who wrote
In more auspicious periods for taste –
No part of artistry is automatic;

Artists' self-betterment the least of all.
This other sleeve-note's wet but right: Poulenc
'Listened to the little song he had within.'

A third pronounces that 'The *guzlas* dream
As they accompany the serenades' –
Phrase from an unknown Wallace Stevens poem!

Better than I, birds sense the future's here
And even in the sudden creamy snow,
Cow-clapped next morning from a false-ceilinged sky

(Making the ballet's *décor* Muscovite),
Still swear to take the decades on and on.
Somehow they hear the *guzlas* dream: as ever,

Their love *alfresco* and their singing spry.

TWENTY YEARS OF
THE POETRY BOOK SOCIETY

New Zealand House, Haymarket. Sixteenth floor.
The city's white and greys and sudden green
Fill all the vista to the arching blue.

Cruelly level at this chopper's height,
The February sun. It shines on poets
Invited for an anniversary drink

And makes the party like the last in Proust.
To see bent veins, thin hair, large corporations,
Almost cheers one about one's own decay.

Dear co-slaves of the Muse, I might, if pressed
(The mid-day boozing clearly starts to work),
Approve your various poetries *en bloc*.

Such funny shapes to seek the beautiful,
Such feeble minds to make a cogent form,
Such egotists to interpret life and nature!

Are all we present mutual friends – or foes?
And does the rest of England, in the end,
Not require beauty, shape or explication?

Doubtless some fellow poets eyeing my
Trousers of daring check, plus clipped moustache
(With other curious traits that I don't see),

Are thereby confirmed in their low estimate
Of what I write – being less full of scotch
And sentiment and years than now I am.

I can't help thinking how in each crazed head
This narrow craftsmen's world is broadened out –
Beyond the urban concrete to the fields;

Into the empyrean; and the past.

THE SAME AFTER TWENTY-FIVE YEARS

I.m. James Reeves 1909–78

That was the party, hearing a crash, I thought
Some awful bard (even a name occurred)
Was testing Martini's generosity

With over-zealousness. One later heard
Old purblind Reeves had blundered soberly
Among the empty glasses. We talked anon –

Strangely enough had never met before –
He kindly, and I'd always written well
(For once) of him. So on the cruel sea

Two rusty vessels passed. And now it's gone,
That power – to enchant the child and say
Neat forms – that wished to be immortal; may

Prove so, for in the end posterity
Seems to like quite as much as death and passion
Mild loves and mishaps in its forebears' art.

As they move clear of back-scratching and fashion,
Some even on Martini's sixteenth floor,
Share the few victories of the human heart.

[416]

ABERDEEN REVISITED

The gulls laugh madly in the rainy dawn.
Smell of stale fish pervades the railway station –
Indeed, the quays and cobbles and my heart.

Thirty and three years past I sojourned here –
Staggeringly lucky hide-out from the War –
Learning how square waves were to guard old England.

I turn left, have to ask my way: it seems
My *alma mater*'s to the theatre's left.
My tear-filled eyes gaze down a viaduct.

How sad it is about a life that's gone –
Whether about its passing or its mode
Or abdicated ecstasies, who knows?

Yes, I was young and happy here, though bothered
By fate in ways that now seem ludicrous,
And would have guiltily felt blessed to think

More than three decades on I should be searching
For where the Andrew let me live in digs,
And sending postcards to my grand-daughters.

Orderly streets of brownish, greyish stone!
Two drunks – flushed, agitated – stagger past: they were
A little boy and girl in those far days –

Days of impossibly idyllic health;
Days when bad states were doomed, when only guns
Could kill; days that will never come again.

OLD POETS

When Sydney Cockerell told Sassoon how he'd
Told Hardy to give up waxing his moustache,
He laughed his characteristic barking laugh.

[417]

I've often thought I ought to shave mine off,
Albeit unwaxed. But plainly I possess
Absurder, more old-fashioned traits my friends

Don't tell me of, though laugh like dogs about.

THE LIFE OF THE BEE

To Allen Tate on his seventy-fifth birthday

Solved: the enigma of the royal egg.
Man has become the master of the bees!
– Though furtively, without their cognizance.

Beyond the wishes of this deity
(Too big to be seen, too alien to be known)
The bees pursue the duty of their race.

– Enact the great mysterious episodes:
The perilous departure of the swarm,
Foundation of the new metropolis,

The nuptial flight, the massacre of males;
And finally return of winter's sleep.
Doesn't it argue an intelligence,

The mere fact bees accept a common life
Yet do their fellow bees the smallest harm
That's possible? They take as some caprice

Of nature events decided by the 'god'.
They are in hands, in fact, quite capable
Of cancelling their race. And yet give us

Advice: 'Watch closely and courageously
Your terrible sorrows, studying them as joys.'
No doubt at all the false god is the human.

The only true divinity is what
We label 'future society'; which bees
Appear to regard more seriously than we.

[418]

September going, and my neighbour's bees
Have swapped my desiccated lavender
For the more blushing sedum, where they crawl

Appropriately and yet incongruously
As aircraft landed on the tops of trees.
Their cities – even ours – are still intact,

But only human presidents are mad,
Or murdered by chicanery and cash.
All are born Yankees of the race of men.

Where's our god who will rise above himself?

LAST DREAMS

I.m. Bonamy Dobrée 1891–1974

Sagacious Ella Freeman Sharpe says dreams
Are typical of the human mind and adds:
'The only dreamless state is death.' I note

The place. Again some pages later: 'Our
Essential life knows no mortality.'
The obvious poignard strikes home to the heart.

When I release the walnuts' brainy shells
The husks' insides are as vein-netted as
Our human embryos. And gardening late

(The robin's song like snapping twigs or garden
Chairs being shut, the low sky jaundiced through
The trees), I see such things' nobility.

Each species has its general character –
The dunnock's patient pecking, say, at nothing;
Or human dreams – that conquers special marks.

The father, in the manner of all fathers,
Once brushed the daughter's hair. Time has reversed
The roles. To mark my visit, silver silk

[419]

Above the mortal face. I wish I'd said:
'How beautiful you look!' Now it's too late.
In any case, would you have deigned to care?

In those last weeks we used to talk of Tom
And Herbert, best remembered of your friends:
Demotic names, high poets. Gone before you.

'How old am I?' you questioned more than once.
'You're eighty-three,' I said, 'I looked you up.'
You liked it not those months without your wife.

Your life at last seemed almost wholly dreams.
I chose for your committal lines those friends
Would have been sad though scarcely shocked to find

Apt for the grim but not ignoble rite:
'From an island of calm a limpid source of love'
And 'Old men ought to be explorers.' It's

The final folding of the summer chair
The robin mimics. Now you can never know
The meaning of the strange recurring dream

In each man's life – one's reason to believe
It's always about some move into a great
And ruined house. Or have you fathomed it?

DEVILISH TIMES

Just bearable, existence for humankind;
And merely by courtesy of the state of play
Between Old Nick and an all too sporting god . . .

The Antagonist was given leave to biff
Everything Job possessed, although discouraged
From destroying the boily patriarch himself . . .

The October evening's almost yellow west.
Black boughs. Black leaves – comparatively few.
A planet's sparkle on the deepening blue.

The last of the watery constellations climbs
Up eastern skies. No wonder we love our verse
Since it's as near our taste as we can make it.

Satan asleep or occupied elsewhere –
For who'd believe that God these devilish times
Tonight was reasserting his rule of good?

The whole cartload of culture starts to jack-knife.
It's the old story. 'So be it,' said the Lord.
'He's in your hands. Though try to spare his life.'

O cosmos, perhaps as beauteous to the mute
As to us vocalists, I dare say you'll
Survive that theological dispute!

– One trusts not too intolerably for ants
Quick under concrete floors; or elephants
Munching across some far away champaign;

Or any creature whose innocence might well
Exempt it from schematic hell – blest state
Both God and poets hope man will attain.

A QUESTION OF UPBRINGING

For John Lehmann at seventy

Puzzling what now to put upon one's head.
Even my caps, neat variations on
A workers' theme, seem only right for girls.

Modest-brimmed trilbies also are quite dead:
Mere relics of Cagney and Ralph Richardson.
Revived, the enormous gangster model, but

For me the hour is plainly far too late
To look like early snaps of Allen Tate;
In any case, it goes with beards and curls:

There is a kind of vizored Dutchman's hat,
Leisure-wear for the trendy obsolete –
With whom I hope I never shall be classed.

[421]

For business in the City bowlers still
Are just *de rigueur* – though get rum glances till
One's safely on the train to Cannon Street.

So must I, hair disordered, even wet,
Or sprinkled otiosely o'er with snow,
Through life's fag-end resign myself at last

To being open to all things that blow?
Yet, as I've long observed, these cares beset
Only the unconfident in larger ways.

No doubt, dear friend, it was your topper'd days
Prepared you for a life of hatlessness;
And somehow kept you natty nonetheless.

TO GEORGE WOODCOCK, IN HIS AND THE
AUTHOR'S SIXTY-FIFTH YEAR

What Marxian spectre lays its beard on the evening?

Lettere dal carcere: yes, but all
Our letters come from prison. In latter days
I'm reading this book by Gramsci, not for ways

To overthrow the wicked bourgeoisie,
Merely to pick up hints for comprehending
Life from a locked-up hunchback's ponderings.

Long since, in war-time, you opposed the war-god –
A stance not quite uncomical. Though now
I might well think: how right! But then it seemed

Evil would only go through evil done.
Besides, the issued arms might in the end
Save us from right-wing maniacs of our own.

As for the past (ongoing!) life of art,
We surely would have never disagreed
On Seneca's epistolary advice:

.

[422]

'Avoid shabby attire, long hair, an unkempt beard;
A known antipathy to knives and forks;
Sleeping on floors; and other misguided means

Of self-advertisement.' I move from book
To tape, the longest trek that, ageing, I want
To take (and you yourself have somewhat cut

Your literally Pacific voyagings);
Hear music that recalls a time before
You and I'd even met: green then my age!

The pianist of that date a friend whose death
Alone proved he'd become more dear: the fiddler,
Widowered, gassed himself at once – odd fate

For someone utterly *moyen sensuel*,
Although response to Bruch's *schmalz* (our own
Not least) must always put us on our guard.

I tie together time and death and art;
Marvel how close to sentimentality
Is art's essential – lasting melody.

O fiddler, dead in what we'd now regard
As youth! O friend, whose age at death we've passed!
In our last decade what fresh insights grow!

From the jail I, and even you, escaped,
Gramsci (about the parcels sent from home)
Complained he didn't get the Cirio

('A brand of marmalade' explains the note).
The nearer we come to losing them, the more
Precious and meaningful the trivia,

So called, of life. The more prolonged the span
Of consciousness the greater homage due
Its fragile vehicle: to cheer the one

Who's lived so long – still more, his friends – by marking
Odd-numbered lustra, wishing him enough
(And lasting) liberty and marmalade;

[423]

Fighting to get them if we're also tough.
Gramsci in jail's like us at sixty-five.
'No point in having a new suit made for Court.

'After I'm sentenced I'll be issued with
A proper prisoner's outfit – tunic below
Shaved head. But I agree that folk might say

'My ancient jacket at the trial was
For demogogic show, and so I'll wear
The decent suit I'd kept "for best".' The suit

You and I keep for death and anniversaries.

BEING

The dead of night. Strange sound. Unknown
Its origin. Perhaps it's in my head –
Some tumour starting to batten on my brain,

The hissing inviolate and continuous.
The February moon is full and almost
Bright enough, it seems, for me to tell

The colours so far showing round the lawn:
The six-rayed open yellow crocus suns;
Quite blue emerging leaves of daffodils.

The latter's gold I'll hope also to see,
Noise from the growth inside my cranium
Being assigned now to a fizzing gram

(See-sawing in my bedside tumbler) of
Ascorbic acid, prophylactic for
The winter's microbes (soon to disappear).

Pauling's authority in science made
Respectable this surely occult faith,
And so converted me a second time!

The hypochondriac will war against
The common cold but has to leave his guard
Wide open to the wrongly-turning cell.

[424]

Non-being wasn't in the least unpleasant:
Why should we worry at returning there?
Clearly because of this magnesium moon;

Flowers lancing through what's sepia and rotten;
Affection and respect. O months just past
Of lenient nature, ruthless human loss!

Our years arrive and go, not all forgotten.

AFTER

Some slightly swollen daffodil leaves bend over,
Choosing to flower; though days go by before
The part turned down suggests a citrine trumpet.

Wings, throats, vibrate against the murrey sky:
What bird that cataclysm destines for
My bungled care arranges to be laid?

Tea by the barely-budded almond shows
How ludicrously lenient the season.
An actual bee drinks from the man-hole cover.

If lesser natural orders undertake
To see things through, then surely so must I;
Maybe in worsening times and certainly

In worsening shape. It seems to me that after
Sixty-odd Springs I'm still an amateur
Not just of gardens and wild birds but of

Lived history as well. For don't I see
The coming revolution needed merely
To usher in a rather safer life?

For families in hives, of shoots, of starlings, too.

PART NINE

Mainly from
The Reign of Sparrows
(1980)

SNAPSHOT

I pass a playground where
   girls are playing the game
I seem to think's aptly
   called Grandmother's Footsteps.
Those creeping up are still,
   for she who's 'it' has turned
Her brown but gold-shot head
   in order to detect
Some decrepit motion;
   and all grandmothers grin,
Wrongly young and happy
   for ever and ever.

THE OLD KENT ROAD

Cats peeping from beneath corroding cars;
Baskerville dogs on fire-escapes of pubs,
Tongues out like customers' at opening-time.

Graffiti over-estimate the power
In life of Millwall, and exaggerate
The endurance of the love of Fred and Lee.

Can these old battered men who, motionless,
Gaze out near newsagents be merely waiting
For noonday forecasts of equine destiny?

[429]

Do they not rather, having prophesied
A universal doom, stand wondering
Which shall come first, their death or Bermondsey's?

IN GREENWICH PARK: WHIT MONDAY, 1972

I.m. C. Day Lewis

The wallflowers really done for, but still vent
Vanilla where you often used to walk;
Like the lisped brogue that lingered in your talk,
Now faint, now pungent. Yesterday, descent
Of tongues: today, dumb the magniloquent,
Once daring the cruel image of the hawk.
Time crumbles poets' first incisive chalk,
As with these jet-trails in the firmament.

Who except one who shared your age could see
It was no fashion or conspiracy
Lent all your talents to the dispossessed;
That love which (as the dream of change withdrew)
Had to pour out its bounty on the few,
Never gave up its yearning for the rest?

STRANGERS AND BROTHERS

An unknown boy came to us, streaming red.
A bottle (one later guesses thrown by him)
Had burst on a bonfire in the lane. My prim
Arm went around him, some endearment said.

Discovering strange blood later on my shirt,
I marvelled that emotion still could start
Spontaneously from one's self-centred heart
And find a surgeon's attitude to hurt.

So even had the wound, as seemed at first,
Proved to be in the tender mouth, I would
Apparently have faced up to the worst.

Quite sexless, this essential human good:
Leaving my dying friend, I find, unknown,
His ancient hand enclosed by both my own.

DIGGING IN AUTUMN

Robin

A leaf I took it for,
Then saw it was a robin
That fell. So light its soar,
A leaf I took it for.
It rested on the floor
As vivid as a bobbin.
A leaf I took it for
Then saw it was a robin.

Vitreous Floater

I thought a robin flew.
When a spot went twirling by,
Just in my field of view,
I thought a robin flew;
Then saw it was this new
Defect of my ageing eye.
I thought a robin flew
When a spot went twirling by.

DOGS IN THE 1970s

Dogs seem unaffected by the recent
changes in manners; nothing indecent
to be observed in their behaviour,
save, as of old, the random randy cur.

They move, on leads, with alternating paws,
Heinz or the *Telegraph* between their jaws;
or nobly couched outside a garden gate
wait for Daddy's coming, however late.

Perhaps canine culture will carry on
whatever in the human world has gone,
unless the last pair, outlasting our fights,
find we bred them too breathless, the wrong heights.

EINSTEIN'S DESTINY

1

Excitedly I solve equations which
Bear out a theory accounting for
The universe, and hence man's being in it:
So simple that the deity could scarcely
        Have passed it up!

Next day, it's plain the hierograms would never
Have managed to animate the physical.
Yet I continue writing down Greek letters
And scraping with Germanic sentiment
        On the violin.

2

Forgive me, Newton. But undoubtedly
The universe turns out to be
More difficult than you imagined. The
Prism has gone: still stays
Someone's or, rather, some thing's silent face.

3

The Death of Vergil, novel by Herman Broch,
Reminds me what I ran away from when
I sold myself in youth
To scientific truth –
That lonely flight
From I and We to It. And then
I had continually to fight
A Faustian going-back.

Destiny, thanks – for having made
My life seem to exhibit meaning.
Admittedly, other creation owes
Such gratitude. I'd even add
(As, strangely, deep-browed science shows)
That our most beautiful experiences
Are the mysterious-seeming.

Karl Popper tries to persuade me to renounce
Determinism, argues that if men
Experience change in time then time is real,
And not explicable by a theory
That into consciousness, successively,
Time-slices rise, which somehow co-exist.

He says: 'How can you seriously maintain
We men inhabit a four-dimensional
Parmenidean block universe in which
Change is a human illusion?' Even calls me
'Parmenides'! I look up when he's gone
The puzzling word of evident reproach

And grin to find the ancient Greek believed
The Earth was hanging in the centre of
The cosmos, bathed in a fluid weighing less
Than air – so that free bodies all fell on
Its surface. Our ideas will seem as daft
Before two and a half millennia have passed!

Popper went on to say God seems to have thought
A universe with happenings unexpected
Even by Himself would be more interesting
Than one predestined from creation – knowing
My taste for bogus religious paradigms.
Ironically, my work's made them more plausible.

In Hoffman's biography is reproduced
What jealous destiny made the final page
Of a whole life's casting up of the elusive –
Indented and linear as a poet's page;
Also corrected, unfinished, inconclusive.

TWO MUSES

Just as I thought that death could never end
Evenings of aqua-vitae, writing verse,
So I ignored the Spartan lust to lead
The League – and found myself in Spartan jails.

Or, rather, only too keenly felt the threat
Of that displeasing ideology!
It haunted my quiet felicity as much
As expectation of a drawn-out death.

Sunsets were never smug: witness my odes.
The life not uniformly contemplative:
See, in my souvenirs, the years when I
Was quartermaster to the Seventh Horse.

And yet the element of self-delusion
Asserted itself so often one might think
It was in human nature to be calm;
To be united, human destiny.

Who could have summoned up his naked child
Running along some road, her back on fire?
He would have surely told himself: 'Before
That stage the rules of folly will have changed.'

A memory rises of the former war:
One of our stallions, upper lip retracted,
Its somewhat rubbery implement unsheathed,
Alarmingly trumpeting with so-called love.

Awed by the frenzied drive yet pitying
The creature in its toils, I wondered if
The joined and slanting teeth were pincering
The filly's neck in rage or tenderness.

And wondered whether to be safe from force
Would have to be installed a matriarchy.
Now in my less erotic years I see
Fathers are selfless, too. And mothers . . . well.

Touching that jailors sometimes still appear
To belong to the human species: though who can tell
The significance of that? Conviction veers
Between condemning Nature and the State.

Thrusting tin plates of beans before your nose,
They say: 'We sang your songs on windy plains.'
Doubtful. They say that slumber is forbidden –
Rather more like the men of will they are.

That women can be aggressive, too, is known
By comics and benedicts. Children grow to hate
Or ridicule the customs of the nest,
Even the clever artifact itself.

Still, they must improvise their own in time.
Still, we've no hope but that of creature love –
Which the deformed give most, the very ones
Sparta leaves out to perish on its hills.

They said: 'You're an early number in our book.
We took you over from your own lot's list.'
Precisely: were they wise, states and their brass
Need only murder us and not each other.

Artists imagine that they serve the nation –
Mostly against its will. My case: preventing
A few from being shot. The relevant
Passages weren't made much of by my class.

It little matters I remain obscure;
I've had so much from poetry and life.
Can't even care about posterity's
Possible benison. Dear jailors, go

[435]

Off duty to live those lives you think secure;
Torture your children mildly and your wives
And get what comfort comes from leisure time
And being for a little while top dogs.

The plate, once symbol of advancing culture –
Ore that drew travellers to dusty lands:
I dream of making arms of it again,
As though its limpness might defeat the bronze.

As though such counter-violence, being weak,
Could be excused. As though the chanting Muse
Were forced to bear the obnoxious duties of
Her suffering eldest sister, History.

GHOST VOICE

I

We're in the second phase
Of my truancy. At first
Your grief seemed merely designed
To prove my virtue: for me
The greatest sacrifice
Giving up the everyday.
But now I almost enjoy
This liberty bizarre:
Responsibilities gone
I'd forgotten were tyrannies;
Even no need to fret
About your diurnal tears.
And I see you too have changed
Your habits: freedom has come
To draw on my estate,
To let out a social sob,
To sketch another life –
Effaced, the desire at my death
To be absent for ever yourself.

Like you, we absentees with certainty
Can't meet the lost ones of our former lives.
And yet we see more clearly that they form,
With us, a whole confederacy of truth.
For in our novel state they'll never be
Forgotten, as they are in your sad world –
Often by dwindling agents of remembrance.
Scarcely-named siblings, dead in babyhood,
Are here recalled, with visionary force
Now the design's last curlicue is traced.
And, our disguises left behind (spies' hats,
Executive flannel and retired man's slacks,
Each offering a problem of disposal),
Play-acting is no longer possible.
But we suppose you well aware of that
Since our rhetorical gestures of farewell –
Odes, epitaphs, that moved you, though drawn up
By the still-alive – have now been really made.

III

I seem to hear you say
'Don't make too strenuous
An effort to return.'
Are you afraid to have
To live with terminal
Disease a second time
Or that you envisage
The graveyard's further ravage
Of the slight thickness on
The bone, that held your love?

Or has your loss already
Changed to a kind of art
Where the obtrusion of
A hasty scribbled note
(Its source) would give away
The immortality
Your life's emotions claim?

[437]

To your notion, whatever the cause,
Belongs an essential truth:
Humankind's recognition
Of time outside human scale –
Even the deathbed blaze
Of once beneficent suns.

IV

Why do we return? Not in the darkened rooms
Of rattling tambourines and butter muslin;
But as you boil an egg or make the bed
   You hear us and answer: 'Darling?'

Yes, that's our wish, after all, whatever ancient
Boredom or intervening cause of unwelcome
Would face us, for our presence once again
   To be taken all for granted.

We don't come in actuality, alas!
For we're in a place that even cosmologists,
Speculating on collapsed stars and anti-matter,
   Couldn't find more alien.

SAINTS AND STOICS

To P.H. Newby

Forced down the wild peninsula, the saints
Crossed to the island craved by no one else.
Beyond that, only Atlantis, paradise.
Pathetic the resting places on the way:
This mousy church, in size a mere waiting-room
(As earth for human life, so some assert) –
A native font; decaying mural daubs;
Thatched roof; three-letter date cut in the wall.
By the remains of the ash-grove, hop vines
And fruit trees that sustained the bygone fathers.
And round the churchyard, egg-shaped in the custom
Of long ago, the danesberry flourishes still,
Imagined by the one-track-minded troops
To have an aphrodisiac effect.

Mavises litter the horizontal tombs
With broken snail-shells. Under the altar rests
A seven-foot saint who may have named the church.

They say completion of the Parthenon
Left so many marble-carvers on the market
Even the country gods began to get
Marmoreal dedications. Quite unlike
The parsimonious art-work here. There are
Only three windows. Being illiterate
The congregations needed little light;
Two would have served, but lepers had a hole
Through which to see, as from cheap theatre places,
The Abbot raise the Blessed Sacrament.

Shrimps and their shadows on the contoured sand
Of the shallows: oddly, the shadows more apparent.
Today the tide had white-trimmed waves and so
The air to the arching sky seemed full of sound.
Late afternoon, the sea turned a bluer blue:
Orange-burned bathers, distant reds and yellows
Of parasols, and clouts for modesty,
Were clustered as by a water-colourist.

Appearance of the second crop of teeth:
The change from prettiness to embryo
Femme fatale. And the continual rise
Of capable, strong, industrious characters –
Sure to prolong the *patria's* repute –
Detected first in beauteous or precocious
Children. Such things almost relied upon
To cheer up later years, when bodily ills
Of old seem benign compared with new arrivals,
So that one comes to yearn for them as for
Even unsatisfactory former loves.

Yes, then the world was ready to be saved
But somehow the opportunity was missed.
Grass grew up through the long straight street designed
To hold the border city. Since myself
Had gone back home from years of consular exile,
The letters from my stoic mentor ceased.
And time elapsed before the waves began
Of other, more barbarous, infidel invaders:
Yet somehow the opportunity was missed.

Sea winds at night still peal the ghostly bell.
Sleepless, I hear it, back on the frontiers of
The empire. But who else is there to hear;
The congregation shrivelled, lepers cured?
And somehow I've become as old as he
Who sent those epistles in former years and briefly
(It seems) preceded me in saying goodbye
To a strange world. Act of no significance:
For men of science the difference between
Past, present and future is a mere illusion,
Granted a stubborn one. My teacher wrote:
'The queer thing is, about our growing old,
We slowly lose our sense of being with
The here and now: one's as it were transposed
Into infinity, more or less alone,
No longer with hopes or fears, only observing.'
That's how I feel, though much less stoical!

Camomile on the dunes, astounding flowers –
Gold, white and tough as those recurring children.
And half sunk by sand, a hulk as sparely ribbed
As if the remains of one that brought the pirates.
An oar-winged wasp probed each of them in turn;
And peering in the rotten, sea-blanched timber
I made out the entrance to a nest – what dim,
Romantic, ingenious columns stretched beyond,
Home for the insect, gothic galleries!
The triumph of instinct there as ours is
The triumph – I was going to say 'of thought'
Then thought of what goes on in man below.

Answering questions in my seminars
Put by the most assiduous attenders
(Neurotics, provincial boys, unwashed old girls),
I say: 'Don't fret. Most humans contemplate
With terror the end of life. But that's a way
Nature conserves the species: rationally
The fear's unjustified. There's no more risk
Of disaster to the dead than to those unborn.'

Possibly swallows were nesting in the barn
Even in saints' times, feigning mere delight
In air, or aerial insect-gobbling, then
Swooping in at the broken door. Unlike the saints
They know from fate how vain it is to pray
For the coming of God's kingdom on this earth.

When, as it will, the empire shrinks and again
I'm ordered home, who will recall the days
When saints were giant, smelly, island men?

THE SLOTH MOTH

One of life's riddles solved, at least! The moth
That seems to spend its existence on the sloth
(Feeding perhaps on fur or sweat or spit)
Fell under suspicion when no trace of it
In either egg or larval form could be
Descried in the fur. From a sloth in captivity
Moths were removed, their eggs were hatched, and lo!
The larvae would not feed upon the slow
Animal's hide, nor even upon leaves from trees
That sloths inhabit. The only food to please
Was sloth dung. With that clue, biologists
Soon found (through half-obscuring brush and mists)
Among the pellets on the forest floor
Silk tubes that larvae spin! They, when mature,
Pupate in the dung pile, then the fresh-hatched moths
Fly up (to seek and settle on new sloths)
Towards the sun-coined forest canopy.
Thus it turns out the parasite must see
Its host as little more than one providing
Convenient dung and only riding, riding,
So as to be at hand when (sluggish in these
As all their motions) weekly the sloths descend the trees.

MUSICAL OFFERING

Composers and Executants

Required: some daring emendation to life,
A real 'I think thee Ariel';
And thorough heroism and cosiness,
As in Debussy's ballet 'the wounded soldier
Is tended by the affectionate doll.'

The thirty-eight works for girl bassoonists
Studying in the musical orphanage:
What dedication to female youth, and art!
Moreover, the carroty composer, in celibate orders,
Must be absolved from ambiguous intent.

[442]

Actual smiles at Mimi's coughs and sobbing –
For the consummate reprise they punctuate –
Shakings benign of heads, as though the composer
Were not with Edward VII or the dead Infanta
But knew how the years approved his slowish tunes.

The western sky is pale as a complexion;
Passes like drying blood from red to dark.
Under the planets, long-legged spiders sleep
Close to earth. All species aspire to comfort –
'The wedding will be fun. Bears are good dancers.'

Evenings of playing Schumann rather badly
Must yield, as time moves on, to worse affairs –
The sparkling girlish mane next to a madman;
From filial love and intellectual accord
Depart the proud Oistrakh and Shostakovitch fathers.

Broadcast Concert

The Strauss last songs. The solo violin,
Perhaps through too much feeling, makes a boner.
Forgiven! Tears merely run
For human frailty the sooner.

Granados: Escenas Poeticas *and* Libro de Horas

Third-rate, one thinks, but truly meditative:
Perhaps as poets' Muzak it may live.

And then some harrowing melody comes out
Of the turning disc and half removes the doubt.

Besides, since youth, age or bizarre disaster
Tends somehow to confirm the rank of master,

Behind the notes one hears 1916 –
The fatal tin-fish from the Boche submarine.

Quartets

'A willow or acacia over my brother's grave'
– Beethoven's epigraph for that *adagio*
Ceases to shock or puzzle (his brothers then alive!)
    As soon as we come to know

His elder brother had expired in infancy,
Relinquishing the name of Ludwig. Shakespearean
(As might have been prognosticated), the family
    Bed-life that formed the man.

Like all our worlds, mysterious but commonplace
Geniuses' worlds: how else could mortals contemplate
Quartets whose prolongations are designed to face
    With thanks the fangs of fate?

What different pain, nocturnal memories of things
Limping about the house we failed to see or bless,
From the great grief of varying keys and time that brings
    Mercy and happiness!

Opera

A sky, a westering August sun. But all at once
I realize the season of avian opera's over;
So not so perfect as I thought, this ambience
Of warmth, of dusk and colour – lasting, it seemed, for ever.

Musical History

Need Mahler's melodramatic protestation
Have been succeeded by the twelve-tone scale?
Mahler could well have been an aberration;
Schoenberg a later Brahms – or small-town nut.
Would then some saner, blither song have cut
Two wars and Jewry's woe out of life's tale?

[444]

Satie's Jack in the Box

The score turned up quite grizzled with neglect.
He thought he'd left it on an omnibus,
And died. But when they shifted his effects
The score turned up, quite grizzled with neglect,
Back of the antediluvian, erect
Piano. Though alive he'd made no fuss,
The score turned up. Quite grizzled with neglect,
He thought he'd left it on an omnibus.

Concerto

Will my great-grandchildren play
The first Max Bruch?
I mean, in that shrouded day
Will tunes still uncannily hook
The cynical clay?

Ricercar

'A fine sensibility to Music: does
Himself, with thrilling *adagios* on the flute,
Join in these harmonious acts' – and that's about
The only allusion to the Emperor's art
In the whole octave of volumes: even here
We may suspect was meant '*arpeggios*'!
Most pages body out the maps of men
In blocks, by streams, woods, soaking Europe's plains.

A wonder there isn't somewhere the anecdote
That Frederick's love of music failed to survive
Edentulousness and so the power to play –
His passion proving merely self-regard.
Quite absent from the index either Bach;
Also (it follows) the theme *recht Königlich*
Which to unwarlike persons such as I
Is Frederick's claim upon posterity.

Frederick the Great's long-winded pregnancy
Made Jane's valetudinarianism grow
More founded. Finally, the brougham's driver
Saw as they bowled along near Stanhope Gate
The still, tiered hands were dead. The widower
Recalled her overseeing the making of
A writing-room more apt for *Frederick*'s girth:
The attic at Cheyne Row – continental climate!

A rotten architect and 'Irish hodmen',
Bad workmanship ('mendacity of hand'),
Bloomers like Arnott's Grate, self-styled 'Improved',
Made the whole project one more in the line
Of the Carlyles' unprussianlike campaigns
Against such foes as hens, for allies like sleep.
O 'Demon-Fowls' next door; night vigils; heartburn:
Ongoing years of all neurotic souls!

Remembrance after the once-beloved's death
Inspires a new, a tear-inducing style:
Conjugal love, notoriously awkward
Ever to paint with verisimilitude.
Rational art is equally half-willed –
Canons' sequential volleys in the mind:
Acrostics: 'Gentlemen, old Bach is here.'
Rising of tough musicians, no doubt, in homage.

HEDGE-SPARROWS
AND HOUSE-SPARROWS

Our medieval fathers simply named
All small birds sparrows. Hence the absurdity
Of calling these March strangers to the garden
Hedge-sparrows. Bills not the pyramids required
For seed-cracking, chassis altogether longer,
More Italianate, and striped along the back,
This couple trill as constantly as late
Beethoven, restless in trees, and skimming to the border.

I read, you nest in April. Stay till then
And populate our homely area
With dashing aviators, tireless songsters.
But how will you survive the silent hedge-cats
Consoling, too, mankind's suburban life;
Find nourishment, in face of chemical
Warfare against our little green invaders?
I hope my welcome's not as treacherous as Cawdor's.

No wonder that the name's a term of endearment –
'Let me but kiss your eyes, my sweet, my sparrow.'
Even the man-sized ostrich some will know
As the sparrow-camel. Sparrowcide denotes
Destruction of sparrows. Preserve us from that crime.
Instead, let there be sparrowdom, the reign
Of sparrows, for sustaining your kin in name
At least suggests some worth in human habitations.

ON HIS SIXTIETH BIRTHDAY

Fathers must tell their children of injustice
And cruelty, between the rewarding toil
Of lessons on the bassethorn and readings
Aloud of Arthur Conan Doyle.

Some of life's sense, I think, if sense at all,
Resides in the minor artist's artifact:
The variations on a small perception
Heroically destined for neglect;

That anguished harmony, those chiming stanzas,
Whiskers and twigs set down painstakingly –
Left for improbable future recognition
Like girls grown up from storm-launched infancy.

Curious that the robin was observed
By villein, monarch, merchant, factory-hand.
But if I look behind me to the fork,
Oblique in the garden, my particular friend

(Warily glancing back on straddled pins)
Has extra white along his foggy wings.
There are as many different birds as poets;
One bird despite man's botched imaginings.

Wrong, wrong to say that February's mild,
Equally that the Sabine month's severe.
In age we come to welcome February
For what he is, of arbitrary power.

The stares' preliminary coughing: will
Fate let me see them through to actual lieder?
Already I'm consoled by tiny green
Arches that gothicize the frosty border.

Yet, glimpsed below disordered grasses, man's
All-muddled footfalls printed in the mud
Remind us awesomely that still to come
Is the atrocious murder of the god.

So often art's devices are naive:
The watchman's horn after the fugal flurry
Sounding again, a true goodnight; the axe
Struck in the flies on anything but cherry –

Paralleled by the care of man for men:
Such private trouble as is taken by
Schoolmaster referees and wholesome nurses –
The other love that makes us want to cry.

Now oceanographers believe that oceans
Are transient, that even Asias move
Around, like sandwiches, on rocky salvers.
Thus the blue swellings of the globe may prove

To mask calamities far worse than they
Create. Small wonder then that life's a mess,
Its very scenery not yet arranged
To satisfy the director's finickiness.

And can the state of art surprise us when
We contemplate the diathesis of the State –
Though half expecting artists' very weakness
Will somehow make mankind inviolate?

So, sneezing in this cold, bare kingdom, one
Dreams wildly: yes, I may be there for Spring –
Meaning, say, for the end of tyranny,
Meaning the start of some great profluent thing.

And almost one feels sorry, finally,
For February, its lugubrious
Austerity so threatened by renewal.
Threatened, one says, but knowing that the tree

Can't help the shuddering rising of the sap,
Descent of blushing tassels, sparkling stars –
That even now one's faith makes out in those
Nailed branches black against the sunset's bars.

DREAMLESS NIGHT

To Anthony Thwaite

Long night of dreamless sleep!
The problem's how to enjoy it,
Since there's no wakening –
And perhaps no premonition
Of that untypical
Turn to a conscientious
Life of insomnia.

Essential to say farewell
To unsleeping's very pleasures;
And to guarantee the gifts
Of a sanguine testament –
Puzzling strategy for
A being so thoroughly
Secular and not top-notch.

Why days must end in sleep –
The natural contraption –
Is what's in question here:
Uneasy resting-place
In the botheration between
One's fundamental states
Of molecular endurance.

[449]

The status of a world
Of deep ties and fascination
Made by mere butterflies,
Itself an eternal sliver,
Falls for evaluation
Also, but surely not
By its partial citizen.

On August's setting sun
The air is seen to be full
Of tiny creatures: so
Who says there won't at night,
In the dark above our bed,
Be wings, the unsuspected
Guardians of quitted dreams?

Some liken the process to
A voyage, the traveller only
Slowly aware of his port.
Rather, one's packaged under
Hatches and scarcely conscious
Even of the throb of going,
The susurration of seas.

Is it all voyaging then?
I suppose we'd hope at last
To land on a marvellous
But ill-governed coast, as before;
And try with our weak equipment
Its order to amend,
Leave it with words to ponder.

VISITING THE GREAT

One hears of visitors finding a caramel
Adhering to their pants after visiting
The great man, or a tale about his farting
In unreceptive company, or less
Dramatic turns of art or statesmanship
  In the realms of the all-too-human.

Those even of the slightest fame to prompt
Strangers to call will scarcely be surprised.
Our wonder is the chronic expectation
That flawless marble, perfect tailoring,
And flow of wisdom should be available
    Some dozy afternoon.

The elevation of the treaty or
Sonnet above our everyday concerns
Always gives ground for marvel or suspicion –
The authors, unless quite grossly self-deluding,
Only too conscious of the secret clause
    Blurred with their tears or snot.

Yet something in the famous corresponds
To the devoutness of the common herd.
The small-talk of the gods, their dirty deeds
With wine-waiters or river nymphs, detract
Not at all from moments when the thunder barks
    And flora shifts its roots.

While being catechized, the subject broods
On matters that preoccupy his hours:
How could men weld the special instruments
Designed to scald the feet or crack the skull;
Arrange in advance, like dining-rooms, the neat
    Areas of torture.

Gloomily thinking: yet it still goes on –
Craftsmen replaced by great production lines.
What is the human? Difficult to say.
Back in a place of more mundane endeavour,
The hairy sweetmeat is detached and pondered
    But no conclusion reached.

CINQUAINS

April.
The chestnut lifts
White tapered hands from which
Have naturally fallen back
Green cuffs.

Sparrow!
I see why you
Find the invisible:
Your eyes are suitably so near
The floor.

Glitter
Of leaves in clear
And steady moonlight means
No more than that they just were rinsed
By rain.

Midnight.
A moidered mind –
Yet sensing all that may
Go wrong in what it must drag out
Of bed.

I have
To pause and think:
Did she live long enough,
My mother, to know my grandchild's
Mother?

Shaving,
I see between
My lower teeth spaces
Typical of the jaw of some
Old skull.

After
The washing-up,
Two objects by the sink,
Left perhaps by Ancient Britons:
Blue hands.

[452]

NO MILK –
The message blurs
As days go by and rain
Falls in the lane upon the blown
Paper.

Sequel
To death: a life's
Collection of pictures
Sold by one's executors for
Peanuts.

You tell
A brief, chill tale
Of childless friends of old:
You know they had a baby-girl
That died?

Spiders,
With all their legs,
Over irregular
Terrain step lightly as well-bred
Horses.

Bright eyes
Of otters, seen
In some TV programme;
Of female blackbirds in April;
And girls.

Humans
Each possessing
Eyes *sui generis* –
Unlike these brown-beaded begging
Sparrows.

Gentle,
Sad – gorillas.
So observation proves.
As Rochester turned out as soft
As Jane.

Blossom
In May, scattered
As profusely as snow;
Lilac indoors smelling nearly
Rotten.

Touch-down.
But only quite
Long after does the world
Of sound with suddenness remove
Its mute.

Planting
Hyacinths, I
Think: I'll see them again –
So many poets dead this year,
I'm safe.

Strange bird,
You follow me
Round the garden, calling
Most when I pause . . .My secateurs'
Squeaking!

A thrush –
Even before
The end of the old year –
On the bare damson tree, fluting
In rain.

Bonfires.
White smoke pouring
Through the unsunlit air;
Leaving grey craters in the piles
Of bronze.

It is –
It has to be –
The living who provide
Comfort for the dying, such as
It is.

SCHOOL TIME, WORK TIME

From the car's back seat he looks on
Legs long enough for a swan's dance;
Perhaps white-stockinged, like horses'.
Any such young girls, by wild chance
Glancing inside, see papers spread
Apropos some cool million.
Grave nonsense of bonds and bourses:
Glass case of the mummified dead.

OXFORD ALBUM

My footfalls faintly sag the eroded stair.
Through a strait gate the garden of the Fellows.
The awesome line of tenants of the Chair.
March's male sparrows black-faced as Othellos.

The coloured scutcheons of the founding earls
Dim libraries of brown or golden hair.
The dreams of dons are dwarfs and little girls.
My breath augments the whited valley air.

Should time condemn the passionate to be
Oblates of culture in culture's disrepair,
Here will they raise the mocking effigy
Of emperors who deployed the ironware.

If lions may be said to live in yellows
That hue pervades the fenestrated twirls.
Youth pulses through the strangled artery
And knowledge tries to fascinate the fair.

NOTEBOOK

A seven-spotted ladybird
Toddles across the sheet
To which I feel I can't add a word.
Then opening like some cute
Trinket by Fabergé,
It flies with angelic suddenness away.

The book seems dead with things
I've left behind. I want
As ever to start again – on wings
Instead of feet. Yet aren't
To this new world the keys
Pedestrian particularities?

TWO BLOND FLAUTISTS

Bath-water still and tinted as lagoons;
Animal Farm turned back behind the taps;
Shampoo uncapped; all towels on the floor –
The child's abandoned these for rather more
Fruitful and interesting turns of life.
I fondly sigh and dive to shift the plug;
Tidy up book and bottle; make the fold
Follow the stripe, as favoured by the old.
I'm not the last who's going to be her mug,
I think, as Poulenc rises from beneath,
Temperate and punctual as her propelling breath.

A goldcrest probes the wall time has de-mortared.
So rare a creature in the suburbs! I
Daren't stir till its acrobatics end – at first
Puzzled to name a blond streak on a midget.
Later, as stuttery as a flute, the fidget
Sings self-betrayingly. How blest are those
Destiny has engardened and grand-daughtered!
How forceful the flitting shape, green-toned like flesh
Yet actually brown! They merely prove,
The growing days, the truism that all life,
The frailest even, *ipso facto* means to live.

140 YEARS ON

Green leaves with deepening edge of fawn,
  With web of brilliants panoplied,
  And as upon a coffin lid
The thud of apples on the lawn.

That of his own estate he's lord
  Is bruited by the robin's song:
  Now the domain of human wrong
He comes to cock an eye toward.

I take my book beyond the shade
  And open it and read those great
  Lines measured with the rule of eight;
The roman titles time has made

Seem less inscrutable; and see,
  As though the tears were still undried,
  A note that Arthur Hallam died
This day in 1833.

Friendship divorced from flesh – how right
  And precious in our youth! And yet
  If age regrets, it will regret
Loss of youth's other appetite.

Seasons revolve; thought on its stair
  Toils up, and so men deem it odd
  That once geology and God
Combined to bring them to despair.

What point in nature having been
  So careful of the species, should
  Her highest instrument for good
(As a coarse gardener's thumb wipes clean

The aphis from a budded rose)
  Cancel the living from the sphere,
  Pursuing the insane idea
That creatures like themselves are foes?

Blood starting from the creeper nailed
　　On the crossed wood somehow confirms
　　It's not the derms and ectoderms
But man's response to myth that's failed.

Evening: the robin silent; trees
　　Dark on a cloudless, still-bright sky –
　　The near trees calm, but modestly
The far stirred by a transient breeze.

The scene so beautiful perhaps
　　Because unhaltable the hour –
　　As though the extent of summer's power
Were reckoned by the day's collapse.

Comes home to me Vienna's fate
　　After that time-bomb vessel near
　　The brain burst in the former clear
And sanguine days of bourgeois state –

Fate the more bleak through history's blur,
　　Seen from an epoch still ill-tuned:
　　He who dressed our unhealing wound,
Ex-doctor of the Berggasse;

Or the triumphal entry of
　　The maniac's blond automata . . .
　　We lucky old, who seem so far
Beyond the worst of war and love,

What ships may yet sail in our heart
　　With those who died outside our care,
　　And lodge their cargoes ice-bound there,
Through winters of solitary art!

ON BIRKETT MARSHALL'S
RARE POEMS OF THE SEVENTEENTH CENTURY

Coppinger, Pordage, Collop, Fayne,
Fettiplace, Farley, Chamberlain –

They could be the darling poets of my youth:
I almost search among the names for mine.

All have remunerative occupations –
Physician, milliner, playwright, baronet!

Some are locked in a single year – 'alive'
In '62 or 'floruit' '39.

Nothing is known of Pick or Prestwich. Still,
Small wonder what's behind the poetry fades.

Three hundred years ago they were consoled
For lack of genius and fame by some

Astonishing trope or stanza's tailoring.
Strange that the consolation still should work

– Prujean, 'Ephelia', Cutts, Cockayne,
Cameron, Allott, Fuller, Raine.

1935–75

The toothless men of Sind; a faceless lamb;
Hairless mutations of the Norway rat;
The Ishmaels and the Roosevelts; the big
Robertson strain of the Washington navel orange;
Three kinds of triplets; silver guinea-pigs;
The giant salivary chromosomes;
A year of sterilization in Germany;
And polydactyly in swine, in humans –
Having conveyed it home, I wonder how
I could initially have baulked (through sheer
Meanness) at buying from the outside stall
The gathered issues of *The Journal of
Heredity* for 1935.

[459]

For all seems poetry – and largely in
Blank verse! – and pregnant with the innocence
(As of great tribal bards) of scientists.
And all put forth when I was twenty-two
And twenty-three. The binding's been in some
Storm – more than showers on the fivepence box;
Say, hoses playing over fires begun
By sterilizing Germans, who in fact
Were helped appropriately from the eugenics scene
By one of the 'superior' Roosevelts.

This summer of '75 I bedded out
Blossoms striped red and white like footballers,
The end result of doings reported here,
No doubt: that is, the x-irradiation
Of relatively plain petunia stocks.

What Faustian knowledge that in youth could daunt
Beyond my previous ideas of doom!
We saw the photographs of buttocks beaten
Perhaps by six-fingered hands; great oranges
Left to decay remote from hungry lands:
Yet watching Madame Butterfly look over
La rada, il porto, la città di Nagasaki.
Our tears were still for dirty tricks done to
A single member of the nation-state.

AUTUMNAL METAMORPHOSES

A rather untidy bird soars up – a leaf!
Southward, a slanting light from pie-crust cloud.
Trees ginger as a cat. Long shadows cast
At noon. Your breath condenses or will soon
Condense on your moustache. The creeper's changed
Into a red disease of walls. To catch
The post that goes at seven you skim through near
Dark, sanguine flies, invisible filaments.

In houses chequered with yellow windows children
Already hear that gormless sons of kings
Do better than their cunning brothers; that
Small toads turn to lovely girls if put inside
Hollowed-out carrots. Soon, whole families
Will dream of their extraordinary desires.

CRISIS

O courteous ladies of the West Countree!
Visiting Plymouth for the BBC,
I saw in Debenham & Freebody

'Trousers reduced'. And marched into the store –
Trousers sardined in stands upon the floor,
Trousers that won the West, that Oxford wore.

Wanting a pair to work in in the garden,
Before inflating prices further harden,
I laughingly begged the shop assistant's pardon

And asked her if among the azure jeans –
Although a style intended for the teens
Or certainly especially for the lean –

Something might fit one rather broadly-based,
An ageing man, a man without much waist.
'I'm sure there is,' she said, quite poker-faced.

And added: 'Do you know his measurements?'
Dear lady, how experienced with gents!
I meant myself. You twigged. And so I went

Smugly across the Hoe to my hotel,
Pants in a carrier. Against the hell
Of sunset the statue of the admiral

Looked out to Cadiz or the Spanish Main.
On seas courageous and in shops urbane,
Surely our England must be great again.

THE OLD TOY

Bits of me keep falling off;
bits don't work properly;
and other bits are broken
by the girl who owns me.

O vanishing teeth that crunch
things I still love; O part
I know can't now be mended;
O miniature heart!

IN HIS SIXTY-FIFTH YEAR

The October of His Sixty-fifth Year

With beak about as long and hinged as chopsticks,
The starling stabbing among the chocolate whorls
Is speckled like a specimen of quartz,
Except the slanted settings for the eyes
Which are as dark as those of belly-dancers.

Strange that obsessive observation seems
To be an overture to verse – as strange
As wriggling food preceding avian art.

Should old age act as though its missing teeth
And fading sight were mere stage properties
Irrelevant to its response to life –
Which ought to be as though demise were still
As lightly contemplated as in youth?

Ideal arrangement; rarely met, however –
Like that prescription of the Danish sage:
'It's a good thing for monarchs to be ugly.'

Bird-brains somewhat exaggeratedly
Counter the seasons' revolutions: man's
Presumably perturb them not at all.

Not for them huge errors of intelligence
Like Sorel's, who before the First World War
Tried to ennoble violence, which he thought
Was on the downgrade – to the detriment
Of efficacious social struggle – though
In fact a Time of Troubles loomed. Still here!

Maniacs salute annihilating missiles,
And English-beetle nourished nightingales
Winter among the zebras of Zaire.

Getting His Daimler Out at Night

In 1912 Rachmaninov complained
About his motor's poor acceleration. . .
Just such a desultory joky start
I'd deprecate in other poets' art.

Beyond the dark garden, garaged, is my own –
Almost, it seems, as ancient as Sergei
Vasilyevich's – waiting doggedly,
Like some old patient on the National Health,

For rare spares that will staunch her bleeding gears.
The scuffed blue leather hugs my funny-bone;
Her ton and a half through nearly fourteen years
Has been a purring, savage part of me.

I wonder if I'll scrap the rusting monster
Before I die, and buy an automobile
More suited to my later modest style.
Who cares? How right Karl Popper was to say:

'What makes a work of art significant
Is something quite different from self-expression.'
I can't take in the early winter sky,
Seen as I go to unstable those yoked mares:

Too much of it, too complex, too bizarre.
Besides, one's mind is fixed on earthly things;
Flesh shivering. The artist still concerned
About the acceleration of his car!

'It's hard to write a melody,' announced
A critic in *The Times* the other day:
Rather belated witness in our age.
The engine of Rachmaninov, for long

Imagined by others, too, to be a crock
Still eats the years, not far behind the leaders.
Is it the Way, that milky arch of lace,
My dim eyes (born in 1912) enquire;

Or a still cloud against the gulfs of space?

Childhood In the Early Twentieth Century

Even in careless hours
Death's served up with our life:
The memory of friends
Now dead, and of their ends.
– Except in our infancy,
I was about to qualify,
Then thought of former days
When early death was rife.
– Days of my own, indeed.
So did I never play
In perfect happiness,
But set out my regiments
Knowing their bloody fate;
And kissed my widowed mother,
Teased my surviving brother,
Scared of some ghastly face
Upstairs, on sheets of joy?

1976 Draws To a Close

Youth happens only once. I mean, my dreams
Were of us kissing; but being sixty-four –
The age I really am – she as she was
When first we met and fell in love – the world,
I knew, would be censorious to see
A young girl wasted in an old man's arms.

They seek a mate for George and if in vain
He well may be the last one of his kind –
Sub-species of the weird Galapagos
Tortoise, already sixty years of age.
(Though reading on I'm reassured to find
He's likely to clock up a hundred more).

In the same issue of *The Times* I see
That dead at eighty-five, in Munich, on
Tuesday, November thirtieth, is Rasp –
Sinister villain of the cinema
Of Lang. I guess it was 1931
In a flea-pit that still clung to silent films,

On the back row, I watched *Die Frau im Mond*
And through her hair Fritz Rasp, abrasive as
His name. The passion of specific years –
Never repeated – unrepeatable. . .
Yet strangely I class myself with George, as did
No doubt old Rasp, in Germany, last week.

December 2, 1976

Who knows or, if they knew, would care
That Phyllis Monkman, dead today
At eighty-four, a 'dancer and light
Comedienne', was a favourite
Of my mother's and, sedate yet gay,
The name beguiled my infant ear?

Probably even then my love
Of withers-wringing tunes was there,
For don't I still a chorus croak
From my first concept of a work
Of art: that show *Bing Boys Are Here*?
– Where 'the idol of the troops on leave'

Réchauffé what the Somme had chilled.
I do a sum and with surprise
See she was four years younger than
My mother – who might still have been
The survivor. Strange, in such a case
To have found ourselves today both old.

[465]

Singing, 1977

For most of my life, no need to wear specs.
Now I look over them at meetings
With the aplomb of a rotten actor,
Push them around my bumf when spouting,
Needlessly checking the earpieces' hinges.
Of all my portraits I say: poor likeness.
'Colonel (Retired)' or 'Disgusted' stares out,
Doomed to expire of apoplexy;
Whitening moustache, jaw-line sagging.
Like a woman, I think: I've lost my looks.
Reactionary views, advanced mostly
To raise a laugh – taken as gospel!

I've bought these discs of piano music
By Granados – largely unexplored;
And if asked who I'd take to a desert island,
Him or who'd be just as novel, Schoenberg,
Who doubts an elderly buffer would choose
The melodious Debussyan Spaniard?

As a matter of fact I'd not mind taking
The words and music of Johnny Mercer,
Even discounting what really biffs me –
That after the euphemistic 'long illness'
He died in a year of his seventh decade
(Strange years, and each year seeming more strange),
The departed gold summer of '76.
Only the weather will return in the vintage,
Perhaps a corked bottle or two recalling
How bitter some days were to swallow,
Prompting thanks for more commonplace years.

Mercer's pushing the case, of course;
As we do in Cheltenham or Tunbridge Wells.
My life's been a story of ignorance.
I never even used to know
How spiders adhered to walls in winter
(Like blots that need blowing up to be decoded),
Challenging man to accept hibernation;
That wind keeps old folk, like babies, wakeful.
No record made: passion undeclared.

At the junketings for my son's sixty-fifth
I'll be pinching his thunder by nearing
My ninetieth. Not that he'll mind.
Jerome Kern's 'They'll never believe me'
(Pre-dating the torpedoing of Granados!)
And that mysterious Mercer line,
As though from an Edwardian operetta:
'There's a dance pavilion in the rain' –
Things I so often sing, by then
Mad time will have made even quainter.

But could I possibly still own a voice?
Curious enough at sixty-five –
A blessing, too; that sons may note at forty –
Even though one messes about perversely,
Trying, say, four-beat unrhymed lines
Which no decent poet, except Arthur Waley,
Has ever managed to get off the ground.

And why so ego-centred the content?
Emblematic, I try to persuade myself,
Of the entire human condition –
Composers who die in usual pain,
Who drown, meaning to rescue their wives,
Regular soldiers, rain-moulded dancers,
Work of joy and disappointment,
Life of creativeness and bereavement. . .
Peering at some enigmatic blot,
Groping for my glasses in the night-time.

VOLUMINOUS ART, SHORT LIFE

Wordsworth's poems arrive, in chronological order;
Hardy and Auden entire already on the table.
Friends and strange poetasters send me volumes much
Slimmer but somehow taking equally long to read.

I've decided at last to look into Hartley Coleridge;
And perhaps expose the myth that Hopkins's poetry
Had something to do with speech. What time for murder
    stories?
Even in the early nineteenth century (or so

[467]

I glean from Thomas Moore's journal) *Paradise Regained*
Was seen to have more supernumerary syllables
Than its predecessor. Should I check this allegation?
A great sense of the potty, Moore: must *his* verse be ploughed
  through?

As is my habit I stick up on the kitchen wall
The cutting from *The Times* about the mensual sky.
It seems only yesterday that Venus was too near the sun
To be seen; and now she's showy in the early night.

Thus July merges into February for the old.
I glance with most curiosity at the end of Wordsworth.
Lord Lyttelton, kicked downstairs for calling Lady Archer
A drunken peacock on account of her dress and rainbow
  feathers,

Had also rolled a piece of blancmange into a ball
And covering it with 'variegated comfits' pronounced:
'This is the sort of egg a drunken peacock would lay.'
But not long from Tom Moore's youth to Daddy Wordsworth's
  decay.

SHOP TALK

'We have the mauve or the cerise,
And of course the peach.'

'I think that striped is gorgeous.'

'Can these be repaired again?'
'I'm afraid it's your welt that's gone.'

'Four packets of Player's, please.'
'These ones?' 'Those ones.'

'Have you got the *I, Claudius?*'

'Is it real cream in them buns?'

[468]

Poor voices, calling each to each,
In a strange but transparent idiom
(So I think, the ageing bard, all-knowing).

'Hi, dad, you're forgetting your stamps!' So I am.
Another world is also going.

QUATRAINS OF AN ELDERLY MAN

Summer's End

A wasp starts burrowing in my naked toe,
No doubt preparatory to laying eggs.
Does it imagine I'm already dead
Or is it one that dooms a living host?

In the Night

I wake up, vaguely terrified, at three
And switch the light on, reach out for my book,
And slip inside the life of sanity
Of Wopsle, Gargery and Pumblechook.

South-East London

I witnessed the disappearance of the tram,
The trolley-buses' rise and fall, but who'd
Have thought to see a change of climate come –
Hefty black schoolgirls in the Old Kent Road?

Low Tide at Greenwich

BEWARE OF CRANES (it says) but all I see
Are swans at the river's edge, past rusty wrecks
Of piles and barges, preening on polished mud
Their dazzling hulls with dislocated necks.

Listening

I still can tell from high fidelity,
Thank God, low ditto: yet who cares how thin,
When certain cadences get under way,
The fossil baritone or violin?

Writing

What verses, even now, I judge I write!
– Almost as decent as I hope they'll be.
These are the verses I compose at night
When booze suspends my judging faculty.

Poetry and Whist

How enviable Herrick's
Fourteen hundred lyrics!
– Though, as the Scot complained when they dealt him all
The trumps, a lot of them were small.

Robbed

Somewhere along the way I changed my person
With an old man. Where is he now, that thief?
Perhaps enjoying in my flesh exertion
Only a criminal could carry off.

Late-born Infants

His last few cycles for piano Brahms
Described as lullabies of his own sadness.
What marvellous things old men hold in their arms,
That sleep and wake and bring them fleeting gladness!

The Metaphysical

Donne took his propositions much as tricks
To induce belief in something really true.
Strange world, where legs are merely two straight sticks,
Yet flesh turns into spirit at their screw.

Poet's Thought

The baby sparrow eyes a tiny crumb
Like Nicklaus's final addressing of the ball.
Tennysonwise, I think: whence do they come,
The instinct and the near-religious call?

[470]

Dreams

It's dreams of jealousy that now give pain,
Not jealousy itself. The feeling's gone
In actual life – as well as the beauteous, vain
Possession it spied and grew viridian on.

Time

It seems, because of inactivity,
That sombre suits, black shoes and motor-cars
Last longer. But meantime across my eye
Flickers the yearly shifting of the stars.

Ordinary Seaman

The 143ft mast of HMS *Ganges* at Shotley, Suffolk, has been
listed as a monument by the Department of the Environment –
news item, 1976

Inscribe thereon that in 1941
I climbed it twice in fright.
Once as routine but also (to make sure
I dared) the previous night.

Winter

I step from the house at nightfall, thereby knowing
How startlingly life continues in the wild –
Far traffic's pedal, trees very quietly growing,
The air as cool as kisses of a child.

Pacifism

Utterly strange babies offer sucks of lollies,
Like ants to aggressor ants: propitiation
Needless for me. But what more venal follies
Will they commit when *they* form the invasion?

High Up

Pruning an apple-tree among the birds –
Each keeping nonetheless its self-judged distance –
I marvel at the spate of avian words
Through January's still unthawed resistance.

January 1977

New Moon near Venus on the twenty-third.
The satellite's rondure underlined in fire;
Its face ambiguous in the brownish shade:
Love's tiny planet blurred as through a tear.

Kissing on the Bus

Surely I'd be as concerned about other lives
As about my own had I the entrée to them.
As it is, I sneer at these public youthful loves
And smugly read the obituary column.

Accident

My briefcase falls open in the street. Displayed:
Aspirins for migraine, chocolates for my wife.
Despite my 'Oh bugger', strangers come to aid
The old boy picking up his bits of life.

Winter's End

Match-heads of white and ochre on the jade
Match-sticks of snowdrop and crocus; almost pink
Warty excrescences on the peach's twig:
And suddenly birds have time to sing and chase.

Laziness

In the June garden, as supine I lie,
An aircraft's great white loosening cable of exhaust
Blows over. Then the flawless heavens defy
The finding of emblems for a future holocaust.

ON HIS SIXTY-FIFTH BIRTHDAY

Went to the Mini-Town Hall
(So-called) to claim my free
Pass for the off-peak bus.
No one expressed surprise
That I was sixty-five –
Stunned at my sprightly gait
And thick if frosted hair.
The ladies around were concerned
With reduced-price Ovaltine
And other baksheesh of the State,
Befitting unamorous age.

The tawdry building was set
In bogland off the A2:
Blown paper white as the gulls
On the stud-dented fields of play
Deserted now in the sun-
Shot end of a winter day
By home-wending girls and boys.

O feet-distorting shoes,
Lung-changing cigarettes,
How necessary to youth
And painful to contemplate
For the busy-bodying old!
With desperation – or so
Sometimes it seems to me –
I hang on to what they waste
As once I wasted it.

Somewhere I read – what confirms
My sentient life of late –
'Old men cry easily.'
Who would have thought I should mourn
The future of healthy louts,
The bunions of pretty girls?
The heavens sufficiently ope
To show the worn gold ring
Of the moon's beginning light.

Such mild observations fall
In the 'pindarics' used
By Arnold for his laments
Over his father, dead;
Wordsworth; the Kraut who took
So long to die in France;
And the multiple Brontës, dead.

For arraigning England he
Forgave Heinrich Heine – since
'We echo the blame of her foes.'
How much easier to forgive
Would Arnold find it today
When our 'glory, genius and joy'
Are sunk to a still lower notch!

The sparrow – commonplace, small:
Yes, that is confirmed when a bird
Hops strangely into the house.
And I cup it in my hands
To counter what chilling shock
Brought it to seek the help
Of those impuissant enough
In tragedies of their own.
But beautiful also the bird:
The eye a tiny gem
Found in a bundle of rags.
How quickly one gets to know
A fellow creature – the marks
That make each one unique
(Including such accidents
As a beak with adhering bread)
And even hidden traits
That the character underpin.

Next morning (as one had guessed)
He is dead, and I take him up –
Weightless, unwarm – to inter
Where daffodils all look south.

Moss on the paving, furred
Like caterpillars, gold on green,
May be removed with Jeyes
Fluid, the wiseacres say.
Another way is to run
A Dutch hoe along the cracks –
Labour of many days,
Dead weight of material, doomed
To the socialist compost heap.

What other sproutings, more
Seemly to bourgeois souls,
These winter killings succeed –
Lilies of brown-moled white
Throats and the velvet rose!

Winter one day, the next
Balmily Spring, I throw
The artificial green
Of the first mowings upon
The oddly neutral pile.

Arnold would not have thought
The answer to England's ills,
Whatever it was, to be cold
Verse or hot Ovaltine.
Charm is what makes, he said,
The work of poets divine.
I well can understand
He would think these lines devoid
Of charm, stuck as they are
With the cares of a Philistine world.
Yet no one is more aware
Than I of the Beast-ruled age –
So might be thought lucky to hold
A 'Travel Permit For
Elderly Person' which must
In the end see one safely across
That dark and bitter stream
Beyond encircling hands
– Though in fact I would give it up
For another painful stay,
Cigarettes, corns and all,
On the parlous nearer shore.

A pallid worm drummed up by thunder-rain
In Spring's mere shin-high border
Still writhes like an insomniac although
I sprinkle it with soil;
No easier underground
Than in the rowdy, zig-zagged, yellow air.
Perhaps some bitter season of the soul
Has pitched it against the earth;
But no doubt what will conquer Conqueror Worm.

'Common shrimps are capital skeleton makers,'
Wrote Major Buckland, late
Assistant surgeon in the 2nd Life Guards.
Yes, fish (like birds) are always famished; worms
Also. Or so one might have thought before
Dealing with this neurotic specimen –
Its role changed as was Buckland's in a long
Pacific age when, freed from patching up
His fighting men, he met the Chinese giant
And measured Colonel Ramsay's giant tiger.

As to the race of tigers, the Major said,
Warmly, those preying on the human species
Were 'generally mangy and out of condition'.
Would he have argued that this worm's malaise
Might rise through making buried dry ribs dry?

The rain drives me in at last –
To Poulenc's setting of the strange motet
(For being simple somehow all the stranger)
Telling of that mysterious design
Whereby the animals
See God born in a manger –
Not only horizontally-chewing beasts
But also worms, like serpents charmed from baskets;
And tigers, hiding white saliva'd fangs
With black lips, sheathing their future bourgeois brooches
And even vowing (though
Who'd really trust long puss?)
To be for ever non-carnivorous. . .

Among the moist-eyed kings renouncing war.

MORNING

Through half-drawn curtains distant roses' daub
And a young blackbird, sepia still his prow,
Taking the berries of a berberis,
Each a pythagorean proposition
      Of angle, orb and tangents.

The iteration of the seasons must
Bring to me worsening health and history –
Such thoughts I waken to when noises hidden
In daytime wail far off or overhead
      Creak like John Gabriel Borkman.

And yet how raw one stays. I've never heard
Pronounced the word 'raceme' and look it up.
So much I've never read or heard. Perhaps
Some Spring within my reach will flower my long
      Unflowering wistaria.

As animals stagger up, amelioration
Of human ailments leads to ready tears
Of feeling for art and for the lives of others
And to activity in the noddle one thought
      Had ossified for ever.

This early Summer morning the aperture
Beneath the oriented bedroom door –
And even its keyhole – are incandescent with
The sun in the still somewhat shady room of nights,
      Thrilling as light in childhood.

What a startling notion, really against the whole
Philosophy of what I've always thought of
As pessimistic life, that the end may be
Felicity: ianthine blossoming
      For scions fitter and unfried.

PART TEN

Recent poems
hitherto uncollected

ARION TO THE DOLPHIN

I wonder you were drawn
By songs of human love:
Your eye rose out of the deep
At one end of a grin,
As a bird's at ill-temper's end.

I thought such songs my last
When, from the pirates' plank,
I leapt in my singing robe
Among the crowded waves
Of the listening escort. But
Your curved, fur-coated back
Buoyed my faint thighs and towed
Me straight to Corinth's quay.

You wouldn't leave. I saw
You craved the finenesses,
The stammerings, of air;
And Corinth's luxuries –
From which you died at last,
Like any Corinthian.

My patron, the tyrant king,
Chose the elaborate tomb
I'd raised above your poor
Blubber as setting for
My resurrected self
Proving the sailors false,
The usual human lies.

At his command, they joined
Your nonsensical decay.

Voyages, tyrannies –
Background of song. The fate
Of singers – to be set
By Apollo in the skies,
If lucky. But my love:
As I look down, I see
How marvellous it was –
Amused at your gluttony,
Concerned about the curve,
Not speaking the tongue of clicks
Nor even knowing your sex.
What purity have air,
Water and passion for those
Strange to such elements!

FRAGMENT OF A PLAY

King

Bats should be welcomed in our lofts: their droppings
(Disease-free, dry and crumbly, not unlike
The fuel-saving chemical some spread
At large expense) make excellent insulation.
Moreover, bats themselves are interesting
And pleasant to have around. But if you are
Determined to get rid of them, observe
Their exit points and seal the exits off.
Remember, though, in this the time of year
Is crucial; for if the animals have bred
The young bats will be left behind to starve.
Thus in the commonwealth –

Lord

         O pardon, sire,
Not all our bats, to use your term, are good.
Have you not heard of those that with their teeth
Bore suction vents to gorge themselves with blood?
Some say they're in our lofts to slip with ease

Into the bedrooms of our sleeping daughters.
Seal up their holes, and they will congregate
Elsewhere for mischief, having turned wholly urban,
Wilder homes left for human habitations.
Into the Institute of Terrestrial
Ecology come anxious calls each day,
Enquiring what to do when colonies
Of bats appear on private property.
Conceive them in our thoroughfares at night!

King

Even should this be true, no need to kill.
Plan artificial roosts, including caves;
And make available sufficient funds
For full-time specialists in bats, who'd deal
Precisely with those nervous telephones.
After all, man will always be bats' master.
For many years we must discriminate
In favour of bats – merely pathetic things:
Were it not for their noses and their wings
(So nauseous) I'd let them in the palace roof . . .

Note: Some information and phrases about bats gratefully taken from
an article by Tony Samstag in *The Times*, April 22, 1981.

SIX *STORNELLI*

Bloom of November,
Keeping an agèd fly from winter slumber.
Like ivy, child, you make the old remember.

*

I cut a full rose.
From it a loathed earwig fell, to my surprise.
Was this a true emblem of our love? Who knows?

*

Acacia, pure white:
Although it may blossom late, fades also late.
In verse, dear friend, stands for friendship, as is right.

*

Old England's flower!
I find you near winter – frail, shrunken, fewer.
Will at least our sons see again your hour?

*

O autumn prunus,
Cold winds have stripped your leaves. But still, like Venus
Arriving late, your blossom will be-june us.

*

Wild flowers indoors:
Are they made shabby, or fulfilled – one compares
Them with you! – boxed in by ceilings, walls and floors?

Note: I am indebted to the late Dr Alfred Alexander for my knowledge of the *stornello* and the encouragement to attempt the form in English. Briefly, the rules are:
Line 1. An invocation to a flower. Five syllables, rhyming with line 3, assonance or consonance with line 2.
Line 2. Eleven syllables. In content not necessarily connected with line 1.
Line 3. Also eleven syllables. Relates to the person the *stornello* is meant for, and should constitute some sort of pay-off.
  Assonance and consonance have special meanings in Italian prosody: it seemed to me that in English the assonance/consonance at the end of line 2 should simply be close to the rhyme sound. In the Italian, certain flowers have come to have special meaning, eg acacia = friendship: one of my *stornelli* follows this. In another, I have perhaps broken a strict rule by introducing the person of the poem towards the end of line 2.

YEARS

Islands of girls, ianthine seas
Even in their eyes –
How long ago he sailed from these!

Plucking a crumpled leaf,
He watches a great moon of winter slip
Its cypress cloud.

Night-sensitive sight and finger-tip
Convey a sense of grief
That mimics nature's grief –

[484]

Meaning that arguably insane
Cellular order and disarray
Of sepia girls and ageing men.

This summer, earwig season,
Followed the year of ladybirds.
Now, like the cycles of Cathay,

The years inherit labelling words
From which time steals the reason –
Forgetting how, day after day,

The paleface squaw was burnt as brown
As the half-pips that choppered down,
Turning dry grass to flowerets;

And how in the next year's cool
The differently tender fool
Drew from a bucket in July

A shapeless struggling that
On the same trembling finger-tip
Changed slowly to a fly.

CINQUAINS: CHILDREN, WINTER

Blonde hair
(That underneath
Already shows time's dark
Starting to conquer) flies behind
A girl.

Long life
And gaiety
On two girls' faces: bad
Reflection of concerns behind
My own.

No doubt
I favour girls,
Bestowing my ancient's wink.
Yet some boys respond as though they knew
The joke.

Small girls
Twirling at
The arms' length of mama:
Her worldly cares, mined pulchritude,
How far!

I'm stunned –
Already mastered,
Ellipsis and rhetoric:
A knee-high child halts at a door:
'In here?'

Dark brows,
Chevelure of gold:
Just one of the variants
I catch at school-release time, Dar-
win time.

Sometimes
A strange, bold child
Greets me. I swap hellos –
Mine not as unguarded as if he'd been
A girl.

Lads zipped
In prams, red-faced
And mostly stoical –
But who should not be, pulled like czars
Through snow?

Arms linked
With fathers, tongues
Exchanging fashion lore
With mothers – hates forgotten or
To come.

As though
Reflections: these
Arrows in sprinkled snow;
And those urgent flocks that beat across
The grey.

Snow stays.
All my old verse
Springs up, not current life;
Shaking the bowing periwigged
Green shrub.

Quite still,
The shroud-bedecked
Garden, and empty of life.
Problem of powering frightened wings
Recurs.

She drinks
From the dripping eaves,
The blackbird, late, too late
For me to meddle in her life:
Takes off. . .

Below
The sorbet fluff,
The hard-stuff – ice. Broom finds
This arduous dining: will my heart
Last out?

Always
Cinque-petalled, this
Repeated flower in
The snow; though varying with the breed
Of dog.

Somewhat
Superfluously,
The garden's twigs and boughs
With varied emphasis underline
The snow.

Beneath
The gutter's mash,
Carrots of ice; the bust
With ghostly bulges of age, as though
It lived.

– That bust
For ornament
Placed there, now's like a friend,
Seen seldom, yet known as if gross time
Were glass.

Upon
The virgin snow –
Vivid, but on my path
Unwanted – some dog has left a stain
Like Queeg's.

Night hours:
The sky a shade
Midway between bough's black,
Snow's blanch; a distant ceiling light,
The moon.

I kill
The bedside light.
Beyond the curtain, silence;
Round it, a brightness neither moon
Nor day.

Their slit
Throats drip at first,
And then they're pushed (at times
Varied so as to startle) off
The roof.

I draw
The curtains back:
A vivid baize, twig-strewn –
As one with chalk and ash in some
Low club.

It could
Be thought the snow
Lingering under shrubs
Was peaks and ranges raised above
Brown fog.

Paul Nash
Contrived to escape
The tyranny of green
In nature; a freedom far, this dawn
Of thaw.

Rather
Strange satisfaction,
Treading the white to grey;
Seeing black water furrow at last
Down grids.

How brief,
How winterish,
The glimpse of Venus, through
Bare twigs, she fleeing to the south
At dusk!

It fades,
The western gold –
Flame at the end of a day
That anyway precluded aught
But cold.

I curse
The cold, yet bless
The mercy that allows
Survival in a universe
Far worse.

COPTIC SOCKS

The Victoria and Albert Museum has mounted a special exhibition of knitting. . . The exhibits will include a pair of Coptic socks dating from the fourth–fifth century AD. . .

– News item, 1980

Fancy the Copt
Possessing socks!
– Elastic-topped,
Perhaps, with clocks.

What marvellous wool
From Coptic flocks
To last so well
In Coptic socks!

Some will get shocks
Who cast an optic
On knitted socks –
Then read they're Coptic.

THE NIGHT SKY IN AUGUST 1980

(with acknowledgements to *The Times* Astronomical Correspondent)

Since it was seen in 1862,
Comet Swift-Tuttle will be soon in view.
One hundred and twenty years its period:
Tuttle and Swift by definition dead.

Shall I, by falling down that awkward crack
Of time, miss viewing it? Along its track,
Meanwhile, its scattered 'bits and pieces' give
Their 'annual display'. And I'm alive.

The Perseid meteors, too, are in the air.
Get warm and comfortable in a chair
Facing north-east, and still aspire to sight
Things to astound one in a summer night.

WHALES AND BARNACLES

'A sedentary yet migratory life' – perhaps
That's what I long for in my seventieth year.
But the biography of barnacles,
        Not man's, supplies the phrase.

These 'small, tenacious animals' are found
In grooves, on flippers – even on lips – of whales,
Slowing the plunge from Arctic everydays
        To passionate tropical nights.

Yes, bearing communities of barnacles,
Whales, like Cunarders, may be prone to drag;
Prone to itch, also, for those clinging kraals
        House parasitic whale lice.

The young free-swimming barnacles must collide
With whales in order to survive. Poor thanks
For life they give in age, those crusty voyeurs,
        Bone-idle voyagers.

Note: Quotations and information come from the Nature-Times News
Service (*The Times*, December 19, 1980).

FOUND STANZA

Treated myself, being considerably faggd,
        With a glass of poor Glengary's
Super excellent whisky and a segar.

– Not mine the entry, but Sir Walter Scott's.
        Yet still persist the days
Of private, or semi-private, marques of Scotch.

After a century and a half, I sip
        The 'Special Highland Blend'
Sold by the Wine Society to its ranks.

– Fagged, not through paying off six-figure debts
        By writing fiction, but
In facing squarely lack of genius:

My novels remaindered, never widely read;
        Almost appreciated
More as a lawyer, quite the reverse of Scott.

[491]

The Wine Society is my dead lord:
    No less enduring seems
Its super excellent John Barleycorn.

I gave up smoking in my sixties – daft?
    My consolations else
As in the age when readers purchased books.

More feebly rhythmic than the baronet's,
    My verse; self-pity more
Sleeve-worn, despite the stoical facade.

Not likely to return, my energy
    For making models of
Society, with patiently brick-laid words.

Especially when glasses of *nouveau*
    Glengary simplify
What's to be modelled, in the glistening eye.

ANCIENT SOGDIA

Ancient Sogdia was repeatedly subjugated:
Its products survive only in damaged form.
The Valley of the Thirteen Tombs –
The Spirit Road – is sparsely populated,
Grass-grown ruins haunted by vanished dynasts,
Glimpsed by the visitor across the valley
Through the shimmering summer air
(While gloomily commenting on the dilapidation
Of the funeral-halls and shrines of the emperors).
In winter Hawfinches and Rosefinches abound in the grass,
In the spring Willow Warblers in the trees.

Most Sogdians held to their own traditional faith
Of 'Mazdaism' – a protective screen
To baulk straight-travelling evil spirits
(Linked with the planet Venus).

Quotes the eminent Russian scholar V. A. Livshits:
'The openings of hidden conduits
Were prettily shaped.' Long since obliterated.

Note: The 'poem' is composed of phrases on page 512 of the *TLS*, May 7, 1982. Apologies and thanks to the reviewers and books reviewed.

HOME AND AWAY

1   *The Hospital Garden*

Garden enclosed on three sides by the sick,
I move at last towards your health. As in
The outer sequences of *Caligari*
Some characters already stroll about;
A white-capped Arab notably, in gown
Of green, white-girdled, possibly a sheik.

Centre, a lily-pond. Along its edge
I'm conscious of the risk of falling in –
Though sure of rescue, even resuscitation.
The fish are scrutinized for signs of fungus,
Yet all's pure gold, as in Arabian coffers.
The sprinkler showers a blackbird on the lawn.

Across the garden's open side the jets
Anticipate the airport; but the world
Of sights and tickets seems not worth the sweat –
Though regret chokes me at the sudden thought
Of losing its availability:
Not fearing's different from wishing death.

The longing to see what happens, though we know
Summers will be the mixture as before!
No consolation that catastrophes
Would be evaded by the lesser woe,
Demise. 'In art the beautiful begins
Only when the logical is conquered' –

Dictum that sets these banal thoughts to rights.
Later, I see dusk occupy the grove.
Save for my knock-out drops, day's last pills come.
The tempo changes to *adagio*
As the twin nurses of the night take charge.
My bed-light shines on dotty Nietzsche's page.

Those coming after will consider me
With irony to make my own seem tame:

The 78s long banished to the loft,
Seemingly Hardyesque in embryo,

Found boring as well as nuisances – that set
Of Cohen and the Stratton String Quartet

Playing the Elgar, even – pitiful!
At eighty-six vain Oscar Browning looked

Forward to seeing *William Tell*, and living
Another fourteen years. At sixty-nine

It's almost comforting to think I may
Expire before botherments about decay

In house, car, shares and flesh become by day
As overmastering as in the night.

Already neighbours sail for distant shores:
His hedges neat still, though he's long weeks gone;

Her plum-boughs lower than when she lived last year.
What can I leave that won't degenerate?

On August evenings playing children call
As if the incipient night will never fall.

I listen to the haunting Preludes of
Youthful Scriabin. Windows open, doves

Startle me, losing their footing in the laurel,
Whose berries are already ripening.

Will the pup learn in time to jaw-break home
A can, as did the dog whose place it took?

Will there be always playing in the lane,
In spite of time, of history's decimations?

Almost as long ago as days of play
I dreamt they might crown me with that evergreen –

A hope as vain as OB's century.
Some cheques, a fortnight on my desk, are pale

As if discovered by executors
Instead of simply waiting my return

From the indubitably unrenowned:
Those ruled by stainless girls and stainless basins.

I echo the Tudor preacher, I the uncrowned:
'Because we are in seasons, we speak of seasons.'

– Reasonably happy, giving up
Eternity; and settling for Rossini.

THE TEST

The time of March comes round once more
To satisfy the MOT.
It seems to be a test of me
As well as of the manticore.

The ordeal haunts the previous night,
And afterwards my mouth is dry.
The business makes me wonder why
Life's been a masking of my fright.

When to the hoist I steer the bus,
Then on the rollers for the brakes,
I think: how maladroit – a fake
Suzerain of powerful Pegasus.

The bearded young mechanic's paced
Beneath, with searching lamp. My god,
What has he lighted on that's odd
Or broken or can't be replaced?

At last he reaches Section VI.
The windscreen-washer pisses. Nay,
Even the horn appears OK.
And so he slants the last few ticks.

I vow that I shall never more
Write thus; but should the car survive,
And next year I am still alive,
More apposite the metaphor.

Only postponed the final twist,
From which there can be no escape:
Compression to a lesser shape;
The disappearance from a list.

HOG HAPPINESS

Black chipolatas on the lawn:
    Do hedgehogs in the night
    Emerge to dance and shite?
I wake before the dawn

And look to catch them at their play;
    But all I see are grass
    And striped parabolas
In various tones of grey.

Those empty deckchairs anticipate
    Our voyaging from home;
    The unmoving monochrome
A life of summers' fate.

But back in bed I hear a snuffle
    Outside the window. Not
    Saddened by human lot,
Hogs do a soft-shoe shuffle.

THEY DON'T SHOOT FISH

How did you come to notice it? my dentist asks
About a missing bit of filling. Eating turbot,
Encountered a shred of metal, knew they don't shoot fish
(Unlike horses). And even give the exceptional
Reason for my consuming the expensive game –
Keen to perpetuate the character of one
Worth finest skills yet down for merely modest bills.

Both dentist and Girl Friday seem to be amused.
You say a Woolwich board-day lunch, is that . . .? The one
That you're supposed to be with, still waggish I reply.
Good job you spotted it. Not obvious. It would
Have given trouble in the future. Ah, the future!
– That deeply speculative time for which one hangs
On to the boardroom table and one's scattered fangs.

KITCHEN LIFE

The washing-up water snorts
Away, and in
The umbilicus of

The septuple-apertured
Brass plughole-filter leaves
A pea –

Like a winning turn
On some bright baby
Bagatelle board.

Of fleeting significance
Even for a sessile oldster,
This episode:

How to transfix it, except
Through the imbecile medium
Of free verse?

[497]

NEW YEAR BLUES

For K.S.

The end of my seventieth year
Approacheth fast; and I feel
Guilty at writing verse
Which surely will prove to play
Merely the same old tunes.
Besides, my span nearly up,
I really ought to be at
My devotions or, rather, what
Might serve in that line for one
Irredeemably mundane.

Instead, I worry about
The central-heating device
In this winter of testing cold,
And swallow Trimipramine –
Specific for the blues
You, too, are suffering from,
You say in a letter, friend
Of forty-five years or more.

Writing, I try to take heart
From Hardy's example; his
Still more drawn out – although
(As Harold Nicolson thought)
Along with terrestrial stuff
Hardy contrived to depict
The sense of Earth spinning alone
Through black, inimical space:
Effect a bit out of my scope.

No comfort if I said
(Scout's honour, cross my throat!)
You embody still for me
The stunning girl of our youth;

Since what has intervened
Is not just time, or blows
Struck on ourselves, but loss,
Absolute loss, and that
In the end is the stanchless source
Of our blues – chasms concealed
By simply appearing washed
And dressed, ostensibly sane
(As our turning gaga nears),
Let alone in singing robes
Whose product only in fact
Consoles the voice that sings.

MACKEREL IN THE ATHENAEUM

Lunching alone in the Athenaeum, I choose
To fetch for myself the fillet of mackerel –
Sign of the times, unprosperous times on the whole
For most who habitually patronize this purlieu
(The 'light-luncheon room', so-called, as spartan as school):
Less-senior civil servants, and pensioners,
With more than a dash, I expect, of the merely close-fisted –
All sober-suited, even the shabby retired;
A few more decrepit than I, but none, I suppose,
Harbouring thoughts iconoclastic, ironic,
Yet ever ready to fall into gamy pathos –
　　　Running subconscious of poets.

That long-dead Tory alderman, my mother's
Father, would have approved of my membership
And the premises as a whole – though never himself
Well enough off to eat out as a matter of course,
Even light luncheons, and making it, as I remember,
　　　Once only, Oldham to London.

But how the scaly item twixt me and Pall Mall
Would have upset him. 'Scavenger of the ocean'
His phrase for the mackerel, never allowed to appear
At his modest table, only too plainly nutritious;
Nibbler at the big toes of corpses, or so we
Children, no doubt rightly, used to interpret
　　　The almost proverbial saying.

[499]

Amazing decline in my lifetime of bourgeois standards;
Even my grandparents' household comprised a servant.
How else would my indolent grandpa have risen to Mayor;
Without her friendship, my grandma live on as a widow?
Quite apart from the anti-poetic effect of old age,
I marvel my verse, contending with time-wasting chores,
Continues to flow, and (indulgently treated) in flashes
Seems not impossibly feeble – though, true, its subjects
     Incline very much to the fishy.

AUTUMN 1981

I nearly say: This is a happy time.
– You far from well; myself
With quite a shopping-list of fleshly ills,
And on the verge of seventy, you
Not far behind.

Our diary: dates with the dentist – putting off
Friends who'd put up with us;
Nor seeing even dearer ones enough.
Recluses who have very nearly
Ceased to mind

The world. Could be a mustering of milk
Bottles announces our end –
The sort of commonplace I often make
A jest of, though suspecting your
Grin's merely kind.

And always I refrain from mentioning
Happiness, unsure
Whether at bottom you don't feel a lack;
And also fearful that the word
Itself unbind

Some spell; and worse befall. Hell fire, worse will
Befall! Meantime, verse, discs,
Et cetera, owned, idly listened to, for years,
Suddenly yield their melodies:
Or so I find.

Earlier, undoubtedly I fiercely loved:
Why else would I have lavished
My miser's store, hung on through jealousy?
Yet now appears the most delicate bloom,
On the death-poised rind.

BIRTHDAY PRESENTS

To J.P.S.L.E.

1   From Old Russian Illuminated MSS

One sister got to Moscow!
Brought back this set of cards.
Here's Novgorod, the drought
Of 1162:
Some citizens confer,
Van Goghlike crops are streaked
With bistre, even the sun
Looks down a bit concerned.

Another: Russian soldiers
Crossing a river on rafts.
Dread rubric, peaceful scene.

Eternal Russia! Themes
Played yesterday, today;
And needed by tomorrow.

So to the provinces
The girl returns, her jacket
Weighed by astonished hands;
And with her winter pallor
And tales which could easily
Have been of the market-place
Of Novgorod in the 12th
Century – its discs of cheese,
Suspended scales and pelts;
The beards inclined to the beardless,
Merchants to hunters, west
To east; universal dreams
Of a better destiny.

2 Body-splash

Scented unguent
Sealed in bottle
Shaped so strangely,
Coloured rarely,
Might be almost
Funerary,
Cinerary;
And the liquid
Better fitted
For the lifeless
Not the aged
Splashback surface.

3 Daffodils in Fibre

Since in old age everything seems premature,
These full-length leaves, gold presences (tissue wrapped),
Seem no greater guarantee of Spring than those
Tentatively impudent green tongues outside.

4 10 Symphonien

I have to look up – Mahler so suddenly moved.
Only see glowing dials, twirling disc;
    A ghost in the machine indeed.

Heroic devices: an orchestra offstage;
Voices on; large kitchen-sink department –
    To which one must concede

Artistic admiration, though one's own
Effects achieved with much more slender means,
    Even the stanzas three'd!

Yet the distorted marches and waltzes came
From a time before the two Great Wars had made
    His race and Europe bleed –

Less grave, so one implies, death-dances of
The break-up of tonality, and of
    The psyche's unslakable need.

TWO BOOKS

I see it ushered in a change of style,
The rhyming dictionary at forty-one
I got from you, yourself a mere sixteen.
And now its faded binding falls apart –
Proof of the role of artifice in art,
Proof of the years of labour that have been,
Proof of the early wisdom of the son,
Proof that in puzzling man avoids the vile.

But not a birthday present, that Roget
You gained at Apposition, which I seem,
Despite old Colet, cover-stamped in gold,
To have converted to my use. It, too,
Is now the worse for wear, quite grubby through
The search for saying new what's really old;
For finding some expression of a dream
– Two books I hope to batter while I may.

Note: 'Apposition' – St Paul's School speech-day

ON THE DEMOLITION IN 1980 OF THE ROXY, OLD DOVER ROAD SE3

For John Betjeman on his seventy-fifth birthday

One day from the alley I often walk down,
I look over the car-park and see the roof
Of the cinema has gone, as with the wind:
A scree-littered slope – the Circle *al fresco*.

Seldom we three sat there, liked to be nearer.
Besides, in early days couldn't afford it –
Time now of almost dynastic measurement.
I had forgotten the walls were dirty green;
Perhaps thought them hueless in the encircling gloom
(Eyes on the screen, or even the lit curtain):
No more than I grasped that the pillars rising
On the walls were mock and mauve, and grubby, too;
The fenestration false, and almost
Pathetic today, artily *art nouveau*.

Scrap-men's torches already make livid scars.
What an amount of iron from the ruin!
No need at all to sit beyond the Circle's
Projection, as my nervous nature prompted.
It jibes with the moral background of those days –
Fade-outs discreet; goodies triumphant; naive
Celebration of bourgeois democracy
Exasperating my Marxist bias then.
But did I excuse *Mr Deeds Goes To Town*,
Though arrant sentimentality, I'm sure?
Expect so, being the first film attended
By that future buff, my son; though nothing he
Saw of it, being borne sleeping in our arms.

In the nearby greengrocer's, moved, I touch on
The oft-told family tale. 'Built Thirty-five,'
They say, 'wa'n't it?' 'This was Thirty-eight,' I say,
'I didn't come to Blackheath till Thirty-eight.'
– Days of our youth, atrocious days, joyous days.
'Di'n't half make a row when they knocked that roof in,'
They say. Bad action Hitler failed to bring off.
'Pity,' they say, across the cress and beetroot,
'We could do with some'ink like that round here.'
Yes, but, dear neighbours, just what would it display?
Where is, and how vanished, art's morality?
Instead of my own ancient Lancastrian,
I almost fall into your demotic speech,
Imitable after two and forty years.

Suburban old John of Gaunt, I wheel away
Edwards and carrots. *This land is now leas'd out.*
And all share the blame sound bricks, and sad, come down
– Except, of course, that other time-honoured John.

BRIEF BALLAD IN 1982

For Charles Causley's Sixty-fifth Birthday

At sixty-five or seventy
We heard a young man say:
'O save me from the Navy,
From Biscay and Bombay.
From crab-lice and the Crusher
Preserve my lily-white skin,
And let no Jaunty haunt me
As I lead a life of sin.'

Young man, young man, how little
You know the ways of time!
For the likes of us to be back at Guz
Would be a fate sublime –
A bed booked at Aggie Weston's
The night of the morning of pay,
Slender as guns in bespoke Number Ones,
Neither G nor T, but UA.

Note: G, T, UA – Grog, Temperance, Under Age; categories into which all navel ratings were once assigned.

TH' ANNIVERSARY

For the Fiftieth Birthday of Anthony Thwaite

Thwaite, fifty? A never did!
'E nobbut seems a lad.
A know 'is 'air is turning grey
But t' thickness isn't bad.

'E's kept 'is figure, too, tha knows.
Expect 'e looked much the same
Laiking in 'Uddersfield at tig
Or some such boy'ood game.

'E's done reet well – first wi' them Japs:
Came 'ome to t' BBC;
T' *Listener, New Statesman* – then a prof
At some university.

[505]

And now *Encounter*, joint boss, too.
By gum, 'e's led some dances.
Fancy, we once thowt poetry
Were going to spoil 'is chances.

It 'asn't – in fact, 'e writes it still:
Funny, at 'is ripe age.
'E must make summat from it now
At all that brass a page.

All t' same, 'e ne'er forgets 'is pals,
And 'e keeps up thur pecker
Printing thur prose, and 'awking round
Thur books of verse to Secker.

FOR NORMAN NICHOLSON'S SEVENTIETH BIRTHDAY

It's three score year and ten
Sin' tha wert born   *since*
In th'ouse tha dwells in now –
Some record, Norm!

A envy thee, tha knows:
It mak's mi sad
A left mi own town and folk
When nobbut a lad.   *only*

To me t'owd way of talk
Ull rarely come,   *will*
E'en now at times A feel
A'm far from whom.   *home*

'Appen because thou stuck
To Cumbria's scene
Thy words are reet wick still,   *very lively*
Sharp thy owd een.   *old eyes*

A think it were in that book
Of '43,   *Keith Douglas and*
Wi' Douglas and J.C. 'All,   *J.C. Hall*
A first read thee.

Like 'little nigger fists',
The blackberry
(Tha wrote then), compound like
A buzzer's e'e.   *bluebottle's eye*

Go on years more, owd lad,
To gie's a surprise   *give us*
With what *thy* compound e'e
Round th'ouse espies.

ABBAS

Speculations

I buy the Penguin Sherlock Holmes. What wealth!
– Nearly twelve hundred largish small-print pages.
I wonder what its ownership presages:
A lingering death-bed or fresh years of health?

Why

The felled tree doesn't know it's dead,
And sends out baby fists of leaves.
Even the cruel headsman grieves
For this long illness of the head.

Conjunctions

A fossil urchin on the ledge that hides
Devices playing contrapuntal Brahms.
The captain levelly driving nuclear arms
Under a sea that towers and greenly glides.

[507]

Poets

We hate our countenances as we hate
Our verses, only by fits and starts. What bad
Lines career down the white, yet somehow add
A meaning to annihilating fate!

The Eighteenth Century

Announcer: 'Haydn was about thirty-nine
When he wrote this work.' So much for the 'papa' bit.
Then follows *Sturm und Drang*; at least, as it
Sounded in times of mine and counter-mine.

More From the Radio

Schoenberg: 'Six Little Pieces. Opus 19.'
'Feeble Debussy,' I think, in my armchair –
Writing, or hoping that the ambient air
Inspires me to write, the wholly unforeseen.

Girls

Dangerous theme: bus-boarding schoolgirls. Rapt
The observer, with his agèd person's card.
What follows? Pierced ears – ears! – deplored. Teeth hard
In setting pink as plastic, and more apt.

Granados

The Maiden and the Nightingale kept coming
Into his work. If one is to elude
The pain of unpossessable girlhood,
Beware the tell-tale brown bird's thrumming.

Christmas Eve

We are in bed. The fireplace opposite our station
Emits a bulky figure, and I'm terrified,
And wake myself. Interpretation: can't decide.
Your father? Mine? My infancy? Your defloration?

[508]

Old Man Feeding Birds (1)

The sparrows actually click when eating bread.
Better arrangement to possess a beak,
I think. Though duly thankful I can speak,
I grow more aware of spaces in the head.

Old Man Feeding Birds (2)

I like to single out the crippled kind.
Of sparrows, her I dub the Tailless Wonder;
And him with crumpled claw. Whether a blunder
Of genes, or of luck in life, I do not mind.

Contemporary Music (1)

What if he proved a Wagner, finally!
– It strikes me, reading of a monster work
By the no longer young, perennial Turk.
What if I'd been misled by that mad eye!

Contemporary Music (2)

Forster observed: the vice of a vulgar mind
Is to be thrilled by bigness. Steering clear
Of something for choirs, and tapes, and other gear,
Quite reassuring to think oneself refined.

Simultaneous Games

It seems my grand-daughter made the grandmaster ponder.
Encountering (in the world of stale beginnings,
Analysed endings, and expected winnings)
The face and mind of twelve-years-old, no wonder!

Dreaming

What genius changes in the dream
Overheard coughs to chords of brass?
The waking talent cannot guess
The sound of things that only seem.

Strange Journey

The monstrous fare asked on a New York bus
Is sixty dollars. Through the rotting floor
Comes a great spider a woman kills. Much more. . .
I wake, and can't but admire my genius.

To a Moth

My cupped hands holding you, I awkwardly
With one elbow work the handle of the door –
Though maybe to live and die indoors was your
Proper and even happier destiny.

The Double Vase

I like a vase made like a hand
That holds aloft a flower vase
Much more than other flower jars.
But why, I fail to understand.

Early May

Tree of Spring leaves, and rain!
As though a ghost were there
Descending a rickety stair,
The showers start again.

The Wild Garden

The foxes seem to have been shot or gassed;
No longer at dusk the weighted tail, pared mask.
But am I not thankful that the daily task
Of dining foxes now is in the past?

Grand Hotel, Midnight

I'm wakened by artillery fire –
Guests slamming locks on various floors.
But what can have disturbed, outdoors,
That gull, scaringly human crier?

The Monster

Summer: a moth of ordinary size
Lands on some spouter on the TV screen.
When later I saw it on the prairie green
I knew why he dared not brush it from his eyes.

His Autobiography

I rather hope the memoirs of such a bloke
(Spasmodically attempting to be witty)
May prove that worth is creativeness and pity.
More likely that, wit failing, life's a joke.

Himself in November

A fool wasp lingers on the ivy flowers.
But haven't I written such a line before?
No matter, for the parallel more and more
Applies – death-dealing season, unready hours.

Looking At the Menu After a Dinner

I see what we were drinking was '76;
Novel *château*. I think how I knocked it back
– Life gone entirely thus, though never the lack
Of resolutions to breathe and sip the mix.

The Power of Radio

I speak to my father's secretary on the phone.
He died when I was eight in 1920.
She heard my seventieth birthday broadcast. Plenty
Of shocks in life still, even I must own.

Easter 1982

A single hot-cross bun, twelve pence. I stand
Aghast. In former money, two and four –
The price of seeing Hamlet, early door.
Surely the Second Coming is at hand.

Spring 1982

A fickle sun strikes the terrace. Another year.
Weeds rise, the importunate mother-sparrow calls,
The politicians make their usual balls
– Nothing to stop me being glad I'm here.

Not By Bread Alone

Points out a reviewer in the *Times Lit. Supp.*
Infants delight in their relationships, the more
So when not hungry; and they frequently adore
Those who don't feed them. Now that cheers me up.

Adding To His Oeuvre

I sit down with a notebook, pen and drink.
Not an idea. Still, I can't leave well
Alone. Some nervous fairy cast the spell
Makes me dilute the already dilute ink.

Constricted Palette

Unquestionably, such readers as I have
Are disappointed as they read of birds
And shopping, hoping still for thrilling words –
Ranging from amoret to, say, zouave.

Formal Occasions

Will this be the Dinner where I lose a tooth,
Finish the evening dumb and deeply glum?
That fabled AGM has still to come
At which I drop down dead, for once uncouth.

Annual Reunion

I scarcely dare enquire about the wife
For fear she's halt or blind or gone before.
As in bad mirrors, likenesses of yore.
Yet somehow jollity's the mark of life.

1912–1982

I rather hope my dates (as are a few,
Like Wordworth's) prove easy to recall. Oh dear,
If that's to be I must expire this year:
Unlikely I'll see 1992.

Falklands Islands Crisis, 1982

On the fair image of a girl who plays
Rachmaninov, the TV powers impose
A 'newsflash' of some vulgar act of those
Starting a war. Back come my worst past days.

Shakespearean

Whether or not transported by himself,
I'm pretty sure old Bonamy Dobrée died
The *Comedies* of Shakespeare at his side.
His daughter would return it to the shelf.

Encounter of Teeth

The orthodontized teenager chooses not
To smile, unlike the villain of seventy –
Whose grin, however, is appropriately
Twisted, trying to mask what he hasn't got.

Switching On the Radio

I turn the knob. Pre-Schoenberg . . . European . . .
Of course, *Also Sprach Zarathustra*. Will
My own voice be recognized among the ill
And deafening ones of this ambiguous aeon?

Chilly Season

Hailstones batter the glass: it's May.
Green fans flutter from the once-dead brown.
The rain starts, knocks more blossom down.
Indoors, the evening; outside, day.

In the Small Hours

I doubt if anybody now, even you
Who shared my youth, will summon up at three
The oblong, sticky-papered phantasy
Of Rookcroft's Nougat (French) – 'Pure As the Dew'.

May, 1982

They said I might not live to see
The Arden *Hamlet*. Lo, here it comes!
– While still in-places-ivoried gums
Mumble 'to be or not to be'.

Driving to Oxford, 1982

'The bile-hued fields of May,' I quote,
Driving between cow-parsley. When
I wrote that my son was only ten:
Oxford a marmalade, a boat.

Feeding Sparrows

The sparrow whose feathers' absence at her nape
Makes her look like a half-failed decollation,
Lacks nothing in boldness with bread's transportation –
Appears a perfect mum to those agape.

He Reads a Hardy Biography

I come to 1896 –
The year that Hardy learnt to ride
A bicycle. What can be tried
To teach this ageing bard new tricks?

Tit Box

Blue worried shabby heads, its very size,
Keep on appearing at the box's hub,
About to transport shit, or search for grub.
But would these parents have had it otherwise?

[514]

Mahler and Himself

Three-four and four-four – good formula, too, for verse;
Nor do I take the hint of films amiss.
Whatever lapses one may find in this,
Unrhythmic, strangulated feeling's worse.

Dying Hereafter

That Larsen-Todsen's dead, no shock to know –
I heard her records as a boy, when she
Was great already, and now I'm seventy.
Her dying yesterday's the pleasing blow.

The Weeks

How drastically advancing years abridge
The weeks! Already has come round that day,
Quite notable in life's prevailing way,
To press the button to defrost the fridge.

After the Dining Club Meeting

I glimpsed the label: *Sancerre* 1980.
Time was I little thought to be about
That year – much less, full of its juice, come out
Of the Garrick Club, saluted, grizzled, weighty.

Short Poems

7.30, early June, the blackbird soars
Down, takes the bread, then flies into a tree
And warbles a curtailed melody. Like me,
All day he's been preoccupied with chores.

Unpacking the Shopping

I've known a phrase like 'Have a slice of tongue'
Momentarily turn the inmost soul to jelly;
Just as a guilty horror spears my belly,
Handling this chicken, headless, naked, young.

[515]

Art and Life

Sometimes en route to vain or trifling business,
Passing great galleries, I think of rich
Strangeness unvisited within. The which
Applies to passing faces, more or less.

Sitting Near At a Concert

A second fiddle shares some running jest –
A young and personable blonde. I start
To doubt not just the performance but Mozart
And any feeling he brings to my breast.

Morning After

Booze needed now to reach adventurous lands
In human relations. Struggling with remorse,
Sedatives bring me back. Then strikes with force
How nonchalantly mutual youth holds hands.

Listening to the Youth Orchestra

Waisted less vulgarly than cellos – things
Almost with slighter bellies than violins –
Oddly, enhance the musical response –
Purer attention to divided strings.

A MIRACLE OF ICHTHYOMANCY

In my study's privacy I come across
'The Fortune Teller Miracle Fish' – saved from
A cracker of some Christmas long ago.
The instructions are to place it on the palm –
This sprat-sized film of plastic, made in Japan.
Its movements then will indicate as under:
Moving Head. . . Jealousy; and Moving Tail. . .
Indifference. Moving Head and Tail. . . In Love.
Curling Sides. . . Fickle; and Turns Over. . . False.
Motionless. . . Dead one; and Curls Up Entirely. . .
Passionate. Needless to say, at once I cup
My sixty-eight-years-old right hand to take
Fate's flimsy messenger. Amazing turn!
The Fish is not entirely Motionless.

MOVIES ON TV: 1982

Watching old movies in the afternoon,
The light fades from the western winter sky;
Leaves all as grey and sable as the screen;
Girls prettier even than in memory.

Into the gloaming sometimes comes a shade,
The name remembered though the face forgot.
Today it's Lucille Bremer who has made
Time reappear with chiselled features, not

A scythe. I look her up in Halliwell –
Dancer, for stardom groomed by MGM;
The later Forties was her epoch. Hell!
I think: myself was not yet forty then.

'Retired', says the manual. How can that be?
Still thawing hearts of iced consistency.

[517]

FIRST MOWING

I reassume dominion of the lawn;
After initial hesitation, drive
Straight over several groups of turds which I've
Identified already as the fawn
Visiting-cards of foxes, dropped at dawn.
I skirt the only notionally alive
Apple, its barbs still grey, and so contrive
To save the crocuses, that seem its spawn.

The urban-dark and winter-coarsened grass
Sliced off, a pastoral innocence appears –
Pale green as river nymphs. Guarding the border,
Daffodils, upright still, constrain their ears
In casques of gold. Thus mown and mower pass
From chaos to a brief Marvellian order.

THE FOREIGN OFFICER 190?

I

Already blossom falling, March not done.
The seasons scurry in these latitudes.
I long for the lion outcrop, lion grass,
Of my patria, constant sun between
The rains; like children's summers nostalgic here.
The nests are dark, hatched cones in still-bare trees;
Nubility still concerned with toffee, dolls;
Ice ages underlying rose and verse.

Defaulters marched in by the RPO.
Comes one who skipped his ship: the place, a port
Even more northerly. Who charmed him there
Probably candle-nosed, goose-pimpled, fat
With pelts and cake. He'll never know how light
Diamonds bistre skins, watchsprings of hair.

II

The sun sets in a cirrus haze of March;
Turns orange, dull, discrete, as though the disc
Of sheiks and sandstorms. Then in the pre-dusk sky
A moon emaciated, orange too,
That might come out by the cupolas of home –
A gong, an ear-ring, or an emblem of creeds
That scarcely take mankind into account.
Incongruous bodies for a temperate land!

The spring's already set or soon will set
Humans here searching for their mislaid souls –
These frigid countries where blood's prescribed for sin,
The Fiend defeated by God's agony,
And where sin flourishes and the Fiend. Tonight
Will blanch the grass despite the evening's balm.

III

These weeks of blatant yellow dancing on
Green wicks, or fat and steady nearer earth –
Unlike the quick prisms on the plains at home.
Thence comes an envelope, brought to my cabin
By a young matelot, pimpled by the spring;
Exiguous postage stamps in monochrome:
The one depicting eggs, the other some
White-whiskered fellow at his carpet loom.

Beside the telegraph, the sonar pulse,
The homicidal angling of guns, what shall
I take back with me? Rational supplies
Of eggs, steam-powered shuttles, and a whole
Compelling but inappropriate disguise –
Braid-matching flowers, stillness like squatting gulls?

IV

Eight buttons, like the ark beasts, on my coat,
Who must return to tropical scarcity
Of brass, to folded muslin small-clothes even,
In leisure hours. But I shall not forget
The feel of these dark-blue layers at my breast,
Strangely called doeskin. Though shall I bring the wars
Of Viking seas, killing at distance, to
Miniature fish and coasts of silver sand?

Commonly brave, the past of admirals!
Quite different from our bearded elders, who,
Among their thoughts of other states of being,
Recall the burning dung of villages;
A cheap gem in a little nose's wing;
Revealing shining brown – quite simply rags.

V

Worn on this windy parade-ground by the sea,
Gloves made from animals we milk at home.
Even in coming months we'll carry them –
Udder-shaped artifacts I'll surely find
Always as strange as some will always find
Embattled superstructures towering grey
Above the dhows, and under skies not grey,
Steaming us into an adjacent world.

How to enjoy time's trend, which even Spring
May herald with some wry-necked, shrunken buds?
History records an officer or two
Quitting the Andrew to compose a few
Symphonic works. Amazing that the birds
Of forests howitzered by gales should sing.

VI

The questing pulses penetrate herrings, weeds;
Echo in peacetime merely from harmless wrecks.
Computers of ranges reckoned in giants' boots,
Mahogany-housed, knurl-knobbed. At every lunch,
Among the choice of pudding, rice and prunes.
When some day cruising merely in lagoons,
Or pensioned off, I'm sure I'll boast of waves
And fabulous foes (in fact the latter far
From range of even battle-wagons' guns),
All I consider now as rather good
Forgotten (the anteroom's 'What's yours, old man?';
The creamy rice, the prune juice rich as blood).
It strikes me suddenly those future years
May bring the preposterous fleet I trained to sink.

VII

Aftermath

For those few years, then, strangely I was part
Of foreign history. Though luckily
They never sent me to the polar isles
Where different flags above the frozen veins
Were challenged by identical Marines.
Towards the hatred I was blank. How favour
One garish stripe or cross above another?
I was reminded of going ashore abroad,
When sparrows begged on café tables, beaked
Heavily as Jews, the gunroom antisemites
Did not withhold their cake crumbs and their smiles.
That ancient neutrality of mine returns –
The guilty, almost-pleasure of old age
About the lack or segnity of love.

DREAMING IN OLD AGE

No ideas but in things
– William Carlos Williams

I'm as astonished that I've been asleep
As by the inventive content of my dreams.

I always believe imagination may
Take off: the flesh is harder to transport.

Why can't I parallel in art the things
I dream about? I see why I can't sleep.

True, the deep night protrudes its modicum
In couplets all too consciously composed:

And yet life's far from reasonable dreams –
I mean those falling short of nightmare; though

One must admit to surviving the worst of dreams
Unharmed; life killing with its commonplace.

'Nothing in dreams but things' – a parody
Of William Carlos Williams comes to mind.

'Nothing in verse but things' is verse's best
Preservative; the second-class, at least.

So that I finish doodling such as this
Recording a coined, anachronistic kiss.

For, sleeping, one is ageless: dreaming's thus
Some strange, impossible present of the past –

Running obituary written by oneself:
The wish triumphant, curbed by historic truth.

FOX IN THE GARDEN

I draw the curtains, see a fox
Lying in winter sunlight, still.
My God, I hope it isn't dead:
What load of pity lies ahead,
Disposal problems, feats of will,
From one of human valour's crocks!

Perhaps roused by the runners' hiss,
The cosh-tailed, rusty creature stands.
I make her out as lame, but when
I fetch binoculars she's gone –
Not beyond suffering's scattered lands,
Simply my local cowardice.

PRELUDES, POSTLUDES

Writing, I play some ancient discs I love,
Certainly spun a hundred times or more,
And marvel at poetry coming in old age
And melody's persistent interest,
Like kissing one mouth inexhaustibly
Or the compulsive glancing at a face.

Of course, the Scriabin and Rachmaninov
I listen to are works of youthful ardour.
Will any want to read, reread, this page,
Inspired and filled at secondhand at best?
– The recollections in tranquillity
Of a time-shanghaied, self-drugged tranquil case.

ACCOMPANIMENTS

A dead worm makes a number
As though from the Revelation of St John.
Shapely leaves burn under shapeless smoke.

Already worried, the rising moon is lined
By twigs; rejuvenated later on,
Imparts a whitewash to a whitewashed wall,

Its lofty refulgence interrupting slumber.
No lesser wonder the octogenarian
Dohnányi went on recording, wrong notes and all;

That bird-bath and gutters shallowed still with ice,
A tiny and insecurely-seated bulb
Has suddenly decided to explore

Both earth and air. And yet these are the mere
Accompaniments to existence, as it were;
What could be set down infinitely more

Bizarre, beyond me, secret. Consolation
In what *Maestro* Mehta said the other day:
'Always conduct the counterpoint.'

Rising to turn the disc, I hear
A somewhat unoiled ball-and-socket joint
Complain it is advanced in entropy.

Great stars not always Wormwood, though the Saint
Was apropos about 'the little book';
For poets' words are sweet as honey in
Their mouths, in due time bitter in the gut.

A LAWYER WRITES VERSE, HEARING SCOTT JOPLIN

'Listening to the strains of genuine negro ragtime,
Brokers forget their cares' –
A marking in the *Wall Street Rag*. I'm not so
Enchanted by the airs
(That now come to the ears through twin loudspeakers)
As those other men of affairs.

The cause is not your music, dear old failure,
But nagging foolish rage
(Despite your unlikely posthumous happy ending)
That what goes on the page
Is simply not good enough to be discovered
In some near after-age.

SEASONS

To D.J.M.

The carmine in the floweret of the horse-
Chestnut – a logo of the tree itself!
I should have possessed it in my youth and not
Been blind to it till Tennysonian age.

In Spring the crocus petals opened, hatching
Purple on fainter purple, versatilely
But regularly, like a pendulum against
Earth's turning, the ingenious pattern matching
For chic the Op Art of Bridget Riley.

June breezes pause, allow the acacia blossom
To corkscrew down the air. But what the hell!
The cosmos wasn't started for our pleasure.
And some say now it wasn't ever started;
Always, similitudes and pinks and mauves.

SUMMER HOLIDAY

Stones in the rotten tree-stump in the lane:
Sloppy but slow, inspired arrangement by
A tribal priest; a ciphered intimation
To someone, some thing; by-product of children's play.

Bits twirling down, blossom or leaves cut off
By dryness; yet the time of creviced flowers –
High summer, season difficult to grasp
Despite warm starlight, still extensive day.

In China, fossilized primate teeth suggest
Humans diverged ten million years ago
From apes of Africa, not a mere five
As heretofore believed, says *The Times* today.

Myself can bore now: 'Seventy years ago. . .'
No wonder youth is strange, with memories
Of a mysterious undivided life
In the long mornings and twilights of Cathay.

[525]

EIGHTEENTH CENTURY MUSIC ROOM

It seems obligatory to go
Into the minor when one's patience
Runs out; also to end the show
With a showy set of variations.

What future conventions will dictate
Composers' methodologies?
'Let key be indiscriminate;
Never repeat your melodies.'

One sees such fascinations, just
As sliding off a wig will bring
Excitement; though revulsion must
Prevail for a hairless or hairy thing.

ON THE 160TH ANNIVERSARY OF THE DISCOVERY OF THE FIRST QUARTO OF *HAMLET*

I'm thinking of throwing away my dressing-gown –
The 'summer' dressing-gown, of thinnest wool.
Dark green and black and terracotta stripes,
The colours of some Victorian cricket club;
Repaired by me dim years ago when far
Beyond repair. An alternative would be
To give it to 'wardrobe' at the BBC,
Their slightly period rails. No art could fake
Its thorough tatters at the arse and pap,
Its *exposé* of lining at the cuff,
Its girdle frayed almost as a squirrel's tail.
Though what role would it help an actor chap
To act? Where in contemporary repertoire
Resides a miser formerly quite chic?
It seems rather Ibsenesque than Pinterish.

Nevertheless, as suits the weather still
In mid-September, I put it on again,
Its armholes needing choosing from its holes.
O spider, standing by the bedroom door-jamb,
You look more diffident than menacing.

Is this your milieu or have you come by chance
From shivering mornings, evenings of westing sun,
Nights of the moon's now powerful chandelier?

From nowhere arrives a vague, operatic thought:
Death may appear in a previous century's garb –
A wig, a sword. Just as my dressing-gown
Could serve productions in 'modern dress', and so
The drama back to the Greek antique – a play
(That may exist) about Arachne, who
Her amorous tapestry unfairly bettered
By the cross goddess, prophetically hanged herself –
And including some specialist staging of the Bad
Quarto, the spectre entering 'in his night gowne'
(Threadbare perhaps from sleepless hours of hell).
What curious worlds myself, if not quite yet
The dressing-gown, have lived through, compelling trends
Of art – white-visaged, sharp-nosed boozers, odd
Headgear, French newspapers, deformed guitars.

In Spengler's terms, it was my destiny,
Rather than merely being by birth inserted
Into a certain time and place and race,
To buy my gown from Jaeger in my heyday
And wear it long as Prospero on his isle.

And as to periods of art, I read
The 'night gowne' quickened Goethe's interest,
The unexpected quarto being discovered
As late as 1823. I stalk
Out on the battlements and overhear a ticking
From still-green trees – the orange-breasted bird
Far closer to being immortal than the play.

THE TIMES DEATHS: DECEMBER 15, 1982

At the first casual glance,
Simply a wild coincidence –
'Daughter of James and Nora Joyce.'
Then I see interposed 'the late';
And then 'Lucia'. 'Peacefully' (they say),
From what seems time remote
The echo of a dotty voice
Now dies away.

SKETCHES OF SPRING

The sun breaks out after a rainy day:
Blurred and sharp yellow spoil the general grey.

How soon the daffodil, wind-blown Englishman,
Turns to a kind of paper from Japan.

The apple-tree pinkens by the hour, I see
(And check the strange verb in the OED).

Looked closely at, they almost make me laugh:
Forget-me-nots drawn by a midget Spirograph.

Dead grass high in the chestnut-tree's green hill –
Conveyed by a blackbird's margarine-yellow bill.

Bees at the bird-bath: an African water-hole –
Huge thirsts competing for lees where corpses roll.

Almost more striking in the rain-storm's gloom
Than in the sunlight – blossom of apple, broom.

The daisy, wardrobe of a fay or doll –
A feathered hat or blood-lined parasol.

The blossom falls, comes mourning heliotrope;
And one must remember this is a time of hope.

With soil-crumbed beak a blackbird begs to live:
A greedy child we readily forgive.

[528]

Bluebells: old-fashioned lampshades hung
At random, as though a sucking litter clung.

An apple-blossom petal drops on my Proust –
An anatomical plate of lungs (reduced).

And I recall the *bataille des fleurs* that rages
Between hawthorn and apple in his pages.

The various fallen blossom turns to brown;
The yellow skin of nidicoles to down.

Under the chestnut leaves (low, emerald, still,
Pendant as fruits) one might be in Brazil.

How strange the sunlight at one's boozing hours;
The terrace sprinkled not with snow but flowers.

OLD THEMES

Written for Critical Quarterly,
twenty-five years old

I see in daytime beside the bed my bedside book
and think, with a gush of happiness that astonishes,
of night, the absent middle night of insomnia
that often stretches over dawn, as though full of joy.
When analysed, the promised pleasures are merely that
of reading, near life-long as makes no matter, and that
more recent of old-age, the sense of not being dead.
   The book's Victorian, volume of the *Curiosities
of Natural History* by Francis T. Buckland
(one time assistant surgeon in the Second Life Guards),
my son's gift, doubtless designed to feed my peculiar Muse.
That, a more comprehensible reason for sudden delight.
   Eventually, on my way to bed, occur a few
W. C. Fields routines: to wit, my progress brought
up short as the swinging cord of my dressing-gown drops
through a chair-back's narrowing slats, the massy tassel held;
and then by the garment's cuff engaging (as I switch
out the kitchen light) with the opposed door-handle, in parallel.
   And sure enough, I wake at two, take up the Colonel.

Despite my lust to live, what strike most forcibly
are mortuary passages, also much to Buckland's taste.
'Coffins are generally made of elm, because they last
longer in damp places than any other wood.'
  Of course in the end I have to try to sleep, and fail.
Gone, pleasures of the night; arrived, anticipation
of rotten day – though still a hope or two: that my wife
will waken; wildly premature breakfast send me off;
and, sentinels against utter dottiness, hot milk
plus pills with didactic emollient nomenclature,
emblemed like characters in Jacobean masques.
And somewhat apropos, in Buckland's pages I read
that at the Abbey reinterment of the remains
of surgeon Hunter, between Wilkie and Ben Jonson,
it seems 'the skull of the latter was freely handed about':
grisly, slapstick reward the unfamous nonetheless envy.
  My friend Don Stanford, authority on Robert Bridges,
has pointed out the metre of *The Testament of Beauty*
is primarily iambic. I think myself to try
those 'loose alexandrines', by his pronouncement reassured –
for I'm still governed by the so-called 'model of the language',
scarcely able to verse save through that urgent beat.
But Bridges himself found it hard to scan the *Testament*,
asking friends to tell him of lapses into pentameter
(reminds me of the occasion donkeys years ago,
interviewing Arthur Waley on the wireless, I sometimes
failed to agree the measure of his translated lines).
  Why don't I take the model from my heart? – which like
Bridges has made irregular every foot in the line:
atrial fibrillation through thyrotoxicosis.
Great mystery, prosody; akin to life itself.
I hope not to be cleared up, as peculiar stones
by Buckland's collector father ('this great Geologist')
were proved fossil excrement of extinct monsters.

MIANSERIN SONNETS

Waking, by reason of their continual cares,
fears, sorrows, dry brains, is a symptom
that much crucifies melancholy men, and must
therefore be speedily helped, and sleep by
all means procured . . .

THE ANATOMY OF MELANCHOLY

THE ANTS

Ants at a bus-stop in the Old Kent Road;
Four waltzing round the pavement at my feet;
Typically aimless, late to be abroad
(Clear in the sodium-illumined street),
It being seven on an autumn night.
What I am doing here myself would be
Too boring to tell, though as I wait and wait
I speculate on the ants' activity –
Sad beings, even crevices are few
To find. What do you scavenge for, fag-ends?
Nearest to nourishment on this urban plot.
A few more creatures join us, homeward bound.
Swims into view at last the 53:
We leave the ants to find their way on foot.

NOISES OFF

The place, my grandparents' house in Hollins Road.
In the side lane the cat is crying to be
Let in. So, riding my tricycle, I make
A three-point turn and then proceed outdoors.
Some cars are swishing through the darkening snow:
It's Guy Fawkes Night and in the pointed sky
A rocket bursts. But why do I turn left
And move away from where the cat will be,
And try a strange, barred alley at the back?

I wake to quiet, October, two a.m.,
A grandfather myself of twenty years.
Doubtless sufficient noises off compelled
The dream, some strands of which I now see as
Bizarre; waiting a lifetime to be told.

[531]

What masterly shading to make these look like clouds,
Everywhere still and white and grey on skies
Of Mary's blue, this mid-October day.
And some brown-paper comes clowning over the grass,
By gulls at rest on legs of Euclidean lines.
I feel like a Georgian, certainly simpler, poet,
Seeing in commonplace poetic terms
The everyday. And I think of old friends dead
Who used to walk across this London height –
Rostrevor Hamilton, Day Lewis – through
Whose heads such notes and comparisons would run.
In George's, doubtless, lurking thoughts of God;
In Cecil's, the laurel: but, one must admit,
Neither ill-matching surrounding excellence.

SURVIVING

To John Grigg

Seeing him stamped with recent dates, I wonder
Who on earth borrows Dr Gordon Hake
(Though I myself about to take him out).

Before the time, the poet Hake, no doubt,
Of even older members of the London
Library, in whose Hakean hall I ponder.

Mild readers of Hake, unite! We'll not abandon
Our ancient faith, however much a fake
The notion of peace and progress proved to be.

Returns to mind the theme of public duty,
So often guiltily expressed by me –
No better perhaps than Hake's ideas of beauty.

Why am I not amalgam in the Prussian
Marches; picked bones; heroic or loony Russian?

PERCHANCE TO DREAM

Ten days on Mianserin: amazing dreams
Begin – or perhaps from youthful years come back.
The pills aren't listed in my ancient MIMS,
So what the ills and centres they attack
I have to gather from the specialist's words,
Succinct enough. Will chemicals renew
One's life, and let one slumber through the birds,
And wake and sleep again, and wake and view
A day that fulfils the wishes of the night?
In this fresh power to sleep not everything
Is nice, of course. A period of fright
There must have been that makes the morning bring
A memory of cries against one's death,
Stuck in a throat drug-parched, *à la* Macbeth.

MIMS: Monthly Index of Medical Specialities

WE HAVE BEEN THERE BEFORE

It is the last day of our visit, morning
Already quite advanced, and still I've yet
To get the bill. And won't they want it paid
In local currency, needing a trip to town?
But first the unstarted packing, for the room
Must be vacated by mid-day – the room
I can't locate, the staircases and floors
Grown suddenly ambiguous and strange.
Moreover, I don't know the time the train
Departs for our next destination, planned
To be in an adjacent mountain land.
That journey now must surely take place through
The night – that is, if all those things are done
That make me waken with anxiety.

CURIOUS SHAPES

After the scene where curious shapes of glass
(One used as a monocle) are shown us by
A lady, who says to you aside: 'Be free',
We dine outdoors. The wooden salad bowl
Hides maggots beneath its rim. 'Don't tell her,' pleads
The waiter. However, these and other notes,
Half indecipherable, only hint
At the richness of the dream. So what is life?
Before I slept again, remembered how
My grandfather on Sunday afternoon
Would sometimes bake his cheese and onion dish
For 'tea'. The ichor, crumbled Lancastrian cheese,
Boyhood perceptions, sixty long years on,
I sense as in an impenetrable dream.

SUPERANNUATED

Once more I'm waiting for the 53.
The London plane-trees' droppings' symmetry
Is albumized by countless passing wheels,
And colours Whitehall's dull or shining steels.
The hulking miscellany of stone is dark,
Gone home even the most industrious clerk.
I took at times myself a minor stance
In the tableaux of war and governance;
Tragic the content, usually played as farce.
Often I feel I'd like once more to pass
Before the footlights with a spear, pale green
And brown crushed by my chauffeured limousine
Conveying me to where I might perhaps
Delay some idiotic act or lapse.

[534]

DUOLOGUE

You call: is that the fox, or next-door cat?
I see through the window, before it leaps the wall,
A form that looks round with defiant guilt,
Wild unmistakably. His coat is matt,
His size as ever seems absurdly small
To one whose notions of the fox were built
On fables and fairy tales. Inside the house
Things suddenly seem safer for the two
Septuagenarians who live in times
When missiles, that like hounds can scent us, now
Squat in their kennels, eager to pursue.
And I return to rhymes or lack of rhymes,
The poor fox, in at least this duologue,
Very much, so to speak, the underdog.

HARDYESQUE HOUSEFLY

Probably questioning if I want to be
Inside the house in early autumn when
Conditions aren't too bad outdoors, they have
Unlatched a window so I might go free
Towards a sky the blue of albumen;
Though, like a minor person in some Slav
Drama, I haven't made my own mind up
Whether to soar or stay; in fact my mind
May not accord with my proper destiny.
Last night I intermittently could sup
Upon a poet's lips – perhaps too kind
A fate for days of later history:
More apt, near misses with the folded *Times*,
Incorporation in evanescent rhymes.

FAIRY STORIES

Astonished, I view the full November moon
Shattered by the poplar that by day
Is so comparatively unromantic.
What phantoms may buttonhole me, let alone
Invade the imagination? Some nude fay,
Warmth underlying chill, in my gerontic
Pacings! – Although it strikes home more and more
Stories end usually with the discomfiture
Of the aged or ill-favoured. A vulpine smile
May kid the kids, but very soon a belly
Of stones will wipe it off. In fact, I'm sure
(News of great follies behind me on the telly),
The Grimms were right, confining to days of yore
The truth of the maxim 'wishing is still worthwhile'.

MORNING AFTER

'Didn't you hear it, the hullaballoo outside?
Foxes or cats – do foxes make such noise?'
'It must have come into my dream.' Were, then,
The tiny deer, a bird taking up on high
Some being, and other half-forgotten things
(No more decipherable in my bedside notes
Than in my memory), portion of the real?
Dreaming into the fabulous antique
Transforms the almost-commonplace. But weren't
Bygone happenings somewhat of a fraud?
Horses rather than deer no loftier
Than dogs, and men themselves diminutive
Enough to fly like fishes in a claw
Night-tales portrayed so scaly and immense?

LETTERS AND RUBBISH

A cow-clap clatters through the letter-box;
The refuse vehicle trundles down the lane:
Exemplars of the far too rapid clocks
Of normal life. I remember, still in bed,
That mixture of the banal and the mad,
My dreams. But what of them? I must return
To the usual perils of longevity
In the man of letters. Being out of date
And out of print, and feeling orphaned, I
Can't help a grin at my self-pity. Yet
How dear, as well as more than slightly comic,
The pen-friends, necessarily platonic.
For who else now will start to understand
One's life, spent in a somewhat foreign land?

ANCESTRY

Scenes of a life of Jewish detail seem
Amazingly authentic in my dream.
The simple, generous sentiment, the funny
But clever, imperious concern with money,
I could have made up from a lifetime's fill
Of Jewish art, from Freud to vaudeville.
Nevertheless, I feel my youth's not far –
Manchester merchants in the First World War,
Sixty-five years ago! My goy grandfather,
Moreover, was (my mother told me) rather
Inclined, when my exogamous sire appeared,
To think him Jewish, with putative, black beard.
Perhaps he was; somehow impressed the stamps
Of Shylock, Max Miller, agony at the Camps.

WAKENING

Protean cast, scenes subject to ruthless change –
Even if enigmatic, not obscure:
I wake and think, as ever, that dreams are
More than half way to art; life in its range
And duration available, perhaps the most
Poignant the images from median age;
That is, on wakening. (Last night's personage
Joe Ackerley, not decrepit, nor a ghost).

Chemicals again transport one into day,
Where a high voice sings too outrageously
'The clouds were like an alabaster palace';
Comparing lips to 'a red and ruby chalice.'
I see a leaf, frost falling in the night,
Its skeleton appropriately white.

The quoted words are from 'Midnight Sun' by Johnny Mercer

THE CENTURY

How much they must lament that they are dead,
Those I bring back in sleep so casually,
Despite a tear! I can't myself – among
The living still – be reconciled to not
Possessing earthbound immortality.
Maybe our waking life has lost its turns,
Yet night still staggers the no-longer young.

'Dream when you're feeling blue,' Johnny Mercer said.
Fast comes the ending of the century,
Though nonetheless the odds are sadly wrong
On my experiencing the final rot.
Similarly, its start eluded me –
That strangely-numbered year of strange concerns:
The past of Knossos, and *Die Traumdeutung*.

I wake and read that Norah Blaney's dead –
Stranger than what has just been in my head!
My mother in her twenties liked her, yet
What she sang in the Twenties as Huguette,
I sang, sing still. She acted on into
The age of television. A lucky few
Stretch over seven decades with their art,
Each decade finding beauty in the part –
Just as my mother, widowed in her gold,
Remarried when Blaney had to play the old.

Sleeping, there's mixed up in my aged mind
Decades and characters: the mornings find
Still some confusion as to what has gone,
While ancient melodies still warble on.

Huguette: character in the musical play *The Vagabond King*

ARCHAEOLOGY

Spring never stops: even in winter ground
Persephone's pale gold may be uncovered
Like the material of dreams. What's found
Makes the old excavator feel belovered,
Brushing the soil from long-lost beauteous features
That no one owns. Perhaps there's a touch of pain,
Disinterring tubers, temple dancers, creatures
(As in Freud's dreams the villainous cocaine) –
Youth held such ample guilt. No doubt that's why
The tender yellows are returned to earth
Or lie behind museum crystal. I,
Like all who go on living past their worth
As amorists, treasure the universe of seems;
Nowhere more realistic than in dreams.

CHRISTMAS 1983

The decorations remind me of Allen Tate
So strongly I have to get up and go and look
At his 'Sonnets at Christmas'. What lurks in the book,
Apart from its reminder of poets' fate
To leave behind a pseudo-flesh of youth
Like stars of a film, younger re-run the more?
Early guilt, meditation in time of war –
Like all good verse, near to but far from truth.

I think how strange it was that I knew Allen
(Long-fabulous poet) later than did my son.
The events of life seem an ingenious game:
Strict logic, but scope for clever variation.
Yet poets argue, gassing in pub or salon:
'Dreaming is different, waking much the same.'

POST MORTEM

I.m. John Lindsay ob. January 25, 1984

In dreams I know quite well you're dead, and still
It seems not to require an explanation
That I can take your true, substantial arm,
See your thin patch, and (as it was a good
Few years ago) your hair a lightish brown.
And I account to others plausibly
For your presence here, although beyond the grave.
Yet in one dream it turned out in the end
I had mistaken someone else for you,
That other living; in reality
Merely a surface likeness. But indeed,
Dear friend, it's just your unique shape and soul
Whose absence will sadden what is left of our
Quotidian existence, haunt our dreams.

DREAMS AND ART

Art is to try to impart a narrative
Less boring than dreams. What ought to be removed?
Not all the personally lived and loved,
Nor dotty twists; indeed, the latter give
A deal of art its only excellence.
There are some dreaded dreams that always start
Down a familiar road. Perhaps years apart
Fresh points are reached, with effort and a tense,
Irrational emotion. Who can say,
Until such dreams return, why their feeling-tone
Seems drenched with destiny; the brevity
Yet length of seven decades? Blindly by day
We eat the myriad y's of herring bones;
Sleeping, our stars hang on the garden tree.

INDEX

[544]

[556]